LONDON'S GREEN BELT: CONTAINMENT IN PRACTICE

The London Research Series in Geography

Geography is a wide-ranging field of knowledge, embracing all aspects of the relations between people and environments. This series makes available work of the highest quality by scholars who are, or have been, associated with the various university and polytechnic departments of geography in the London area.

One of geography's most salient characteristics is its close relationships with virtually all the sciences, arts and humanities. Drawing strength from other fields of knowledge, it also adds to their insights. This series highlights these linkages. Besides being a vehicle for advances within geography itself, the series is designed to excite the attention of the wider community of scholars and students. To this end, each volume is chosen, assessed and edited by a committee drawn from all the London colleges and the whole range of the discipline, human and physical.

LONDON'S GREEN BELT: CONTAINMENT IN PRACTICE

Richard Munton

Department of Geography, University College London

London
GEORGE ALLEN & UNWIN
Boston   Sydney

George Allen & Unwin (Publishers) Ltd,
40 Museum Street, London WC1A 1LU, UK

George Allen & Unwin (Publishers) Ltd,
Park Lane, Hemel Hempstead, Herts HP2 4TE, UK

Allen & Unwin Inc.,
9 Winchester Terrace, Winchester, Mass 01890, USA

George Allen & Unwin Australia Pty Ltd,
8 Napier Street, North Sydney, NSW 2060, Australia

First published in 1983

ISSN 0261-0485

British Library Cataloguing in Publication Data   83·08878.

Munton, R.
   London's green belt: containment in practice
1. Greenbelts—London (England)
I. Title
711'.09421   HT395.G7
ISBN 0-04-333020-7

Library of Congress Cataloging in Publication Data

Munton, R. J. C.
   London's green belt: containment in practice
(The London research series in geography, ISSN 0261-0485; 3)
Bibliography: p.
Includes index.
1. Greenbelts—England—London Metropolitan Area. 2. Regional
planning—England—London Metropolitan Area. I. Title. II. Series.
HT395.G73L642 1983   333.77'17'09421   82-22814
ISBN 0-04-333020-7

Set in 10 on 12 point Bembo by Computape Pickering Ltd
and printed in Great Britain
by Mackays of Chatham

Preface and acknowledgements

This is a study of green belt restraint as it is currently practised around London. The study traces the changing perspectives held of green belt by central and local government, and especially the relations between restraint, amenity and land use, and how these perspectives are reinterpreted to suit their own purposes by local residents, councillors and users of green belt land. Green belt was conceived as a strategic planning instrument, and is still regarded as such by central government, but most residents view it as no more than a development control device capable of protecting their interests.

This book extends and develops some parts of a report prepared for the Department of the Environment (DOE) between 1977 and 1979.★ This was a period of rethinking in local authorities brought about by the need to prepare structure and local plans. The process of plan preparation and, in particular, the need to consult the public, and the redistribution of planning powers from counties to districts, have served to emphasise the importance of local views. As far as green belts are concerned, local views seem likely to prevail. This is because few governments will be prepared to accept the political odium that would undoubtedly arise from any critical reassessment of the need for green belts.

The study has evolved significantly since 1977 and its final form owes a great deal to many more people than can be acknowledged here. The original report depended on the willing co-operation of hundreds of interviewees in many walks of life; benefited substantially from the advice of Martin Lubliner, Peter Walls, Bill Solesbury and Gerald Manners; and could not have been conducted without the invaluable assistance of Michael Penny, Basil King and especially Peter Humphreys. Translating a research report into a book is always a demanding exercise and I am very grateful for all the advice received from David Thomas, Liz Sharp and Philip Lowe and, in particular, from my colleague Carolyn Harrison. Finally, no publication sees the light of day without other kinds of specialist departmental assistance and I am heavily indebted to Richard Davidson, Ken Wass and Alick Newman of the Cartography Unit for drawing the maps and to Claudette John for typing numerous versions of the manuscript.

Richard Munton
University College London
May 1982

★ The report is entitled *London's Green Belt: restraint and the management of agricultural land*. It is lodged in the DOE library. Permission has been given by DOE and HMSO for this book to contain material included in the original report. This book, however, has been prepared quited independently by the author.

Contents

List of tables

Introduction

A view of green belt

Green belt is one of our most enduring and widely supported planning instruments. Throughout the first half of this century professional planners and local politicians orchestrated a sustained and successful campaign in favour of a green belt around London, culminating in the 1950s in the first statutory green belt in Britain – the Metropolitan or London Green Belt. Just as this green belt was coming into existence central government published a circular (MHLG 1955) in which it lent its support to the idea of green belts, a support that has not wavered over the past quarter of a century. The circular encouraged local authorities to include green belt proposals in their development plans, and many did so with alacrity. Today, substantial green belts are a key element in the structure plans of all local authorities in and around our major cities and conurbations; and, in defence of this, many authorities refer to the widespread support for green belts elicited during their public participation exercises.

That there is widespread support for green belts cannot be in doubt, despite the objections of those who claim green belts to be negative and blunt planning instruments for shaping regional patterns of urban growth and a quite ineffective means of achieving any desired mix of land uses in the urban fringe. So why is support so widespread? The most plausible explanation arises out of the ambiguity of the concept and as a result the differing interpretations held of its purpose. The views of farmers, residents, district planning officers, county councillors and officials from the Department of the Environment (DOE) vary markedly and to a point where each group employs quite different measures of green belt performance. Yet each group can gain advantages of one kind or another from the effective implementation of green belt restraint and are able to do so because the idea has become diffuse and subject to local interpretation. It can be argued that the ideas in support of green belt have always been imprecise and variable, and this is illustrated in the historical perspective presented in Chapter 1. But the confusion of aims has not been lessened by the failure of central government to undertake at any time a formal review of the purpose of green belt ever since this was sketchily laid out in three circulars a quarter of a century ago (MHLG 1955, 1957; Department of Health for Scotland 1960).

Experience suggests that any central government attempt to alter or to water-down green belt restraint, by reducing the size of statutorily approved green belts or by widening the range of land uses acceptable within them, is met by a howl of protest from local authorities and suburban residents concerned to defend 'their' green belts. Central government might choose to argue that in these circumstances the most it can hope to achieve is to reiterate established principles and practices in an attempt to temper the enthusiasm of local authorities, which would otherwise extend green belts almost indefinitely into the countryside. If this interpretation is broadly correct – and evidence will be produced in support of this position – then we must assume that the notion of green belt restraint has achieved a substantial degree of permanence in the thinking of planners in Britain. With this perspective in mind, it is the *implementation* of restraint, rather than the *principle* of restraint, that forms the focus of this study.

The central themes

In concentrating on this particular focus it is essential to understand what local authorities are seeking to achieve through green belt, for they are largely responsible for putting forward green belt proposals as well as putting green belt restraint into effect. The significance of the latter point to this inquiry is emphasised by the recent devolution of key planning powers to the lowest tier of planning authority – the district or borough* – which, by definition, operates within a local rather than a strategic planning and political context. This point is all the more telling in the case of the Metropolitan Green Belt (MGB)† which forms the basis of this study. The MGB is now approximately 4300 km² in extent and it falls within the jurisdiction of more than 60 local planning authorities.

Three themes are developed in this book. The first concerns the differing interpretations of the purpose of green belt between local planning authorities, and between them and the DOE. The second relates to changes in land use within the MGB during the post-war period and to an examination of how these affect the amenity and land-use objectives of local authorities around the edge of London. The third theme takes the specific case of the maintenance of agricultural land in the Green Belt as an illustration of the problems of ensuring that open land in the urban fringe is purposefully used. The lack of a purposeful use for open land affects the ability of planning authorities to sustain restraint in areas of development pressure. As the Countryside Review Committee says, 'The generally down-at-heel condition of much of the urban fringe must to some extent undermine the credibility of any restraint policies. The poor quality of the environment is bound to lead people to the conclusion that the land would be better used for development and that it is only a matter of time before this is allowed to happen' (CRC 1978, p. 16).

* For the sake of brevity the word district is used to cover both kinds of planning authority where this tier is being discussed collectively.

† The terms London's Green Belt, Green Belt and Metropolitan Green Belt (MGB) are used interchangeably to refer specifically to the area of statutorily approved green belt around London. Where other kinds of non-statutory green belt are in operation this will be made explicit.

These themes also highlight a number of broader policy issues and methodological questions of current concern. They contribute by way of example to the growing interest in the implementation as well as the formulation of public policy, although these two processes are not discrete (Barrett & Fudge 1981), and to relations between local and central government (Young & Mills 1980, Dunsire 1981, McAuslan 1981). They reflect on the increased concern in our society generally, and in outer suburbia in particular, over amenity questions and the 'quality' of land use in both environmental and resource-use terms. Such concerns cannot be addressed solely by a straight-forward analysis of land-use statistics or public documents. They require an interpretive analysis based on a survey of the opinions and experiences of those most closely involved – planners, councillors, mineral extractors, farmers, and so on – as well as an examination of the factual material available in published sources. This book attempts to bring these different sources of information together for the first time, and it does so by drawing upon a number of empirical studies designed specifically to elicit the views of those most closely associated with the implementation of green belt restraint.

The changing context of green belt

Officially, central government policy towards green belt has remained un-changed since its introduction in 1955 (MHLG 1955). As recently as 1980 the Secretary of State for the Environment confirmed this position in a letter written to the Standing Conference on London and South-East Regional Planning★ (DOE 1980a). Green belts continue to be regarded as an instrument of strategic planning policy, and one means of shaping the general pattern of urban growth at regional and subregional scales. This is not to suggest that central government has made no statements on green belt over the past 25 years or that no changes have occurred in the way green belt restraint is implemented. Indeed, DOE officials would doubtless maintain that green belt is continuously under review. There are today, for example, more and larger green belts than in 1955. Ministers have pronounced informally from time to time on green belts, and recently they have been obliged to respond to green belt proposals contained in structure plans – and not always approved them. Occasionally decisions at appeal on individual planning applications have indicated modifications to central government thinking. Nevertheless, the purpose of green belt has not been formally debated and the present affords an excellent opportunity to do so.

The economic recession of the 1980s means that pressures for peripheral urban expansion are weak and the debate can be conducted in the absence of strong demands for building land. No doubt, the current demise of regional

★ Hereafter shortened to Standing Conference. Standing Conference is an advisory body consisting of representatives of all the local planning authorities in south-east England.

planning contributes to an unwillingness to raise the matter, and the general tone of self-congratulation over the perceived success of London's Green Belt in the statements of local (e.g. Standing Conference 1981a) and central government (DOE 1978a) further reduces any apparent need for public discussion. However, such blandishments conceal the disagreements that have always existed as to the purpose and effectiveness of the MGB. Advocates claim it to be one of the few successful post-war planning concepts when seen in conjunction with the new towns programme and other planned overspill schemes. They maintain that the outward growth of London would not have been curtailed near to its present limit were it not for the MGB. Yet critics would say that this achievement has been accomplished at a high, even unacceptable, cost. They would point to development leap-frogging the MGB, leading to longer and more costly journeys to work, and would argue that the Green Belt has led to higher housing densities in London and higher development land prices in the region than would otherwise have obtained (Hall *et al.* 1973).

The strategic context has also changed markedly. The South East region's economic fortunes have altered along with those of the rest of the economy, and since 1970 the industrial decline of Docklands and other parts of the East End of London has been dramatic. It requires considerable imagination to argue that a concept expounded under wartime conditions (Abercrombie 1945) can have retained its purpose throughout a period of population expansion, affluence and mobility (1955–70) and then one of economic stagnation and inner-city decline (1975 to the present). And these observations exclude those effects on the region that stem from the improvements made to London's radial road and rail communications, now being augmented by the M25 motorway which is to encircle the capital almost wholly within the Green Belt.

The implementation of restraint

Notwithstanding these important matters, the main purpose of this book is to address those issues that relate to the implementation of green belt restraint in south-east England in the post-war period, namely the changing size of the MGB, the redistribution of planning powers among local authorities and the growing concern over environmental matters.

In response to the results of public participation exercises associated with the preparation of structure plans, many local authorities have sought to create new green belts or to extend the area of existing ones. The Secretary of State for the Environment has agreed to many but not to all of these requests, leaving the responsibility for local implementation in many hands (see Gault 1981). As previously noted, the problem of consistent execution is especially apparent in the case of the MGB. The MGB is different from other green belts in Britain because of its longer history, greater size and the strength of urban development pressures acting upon it. Under the development plan proposals of the home counties,* and the amendments to these agreed during the 1960s and early 1970s, central government had ratified a Green Belt of approximately 307 000 ha by 1975. Since that time, county planning authorities have sought major extensions to its area, amounting to almost a doubling of its 1975 size (see Chs 1 & 2). In the event the secretary of state has stuck firmly to the view that the MGB should be only 20–25 km wide and today's Green Belt only covers about 430 000 ha. Nevertheless, its sheer size means that restraint is being applied to widely differing local planning situations, in terms of both their resource endowments – quality of agricultural land, mineral deposits, landscape quality, and so on – and the pressures for urban and industrial development operating on them.

Just as green belts have been getting larger, so central government has been reallocating planning powers down the hierarchy of planning authorities. Central government believes that devolution will speed up the taking of planning decisions and make decision makers more responsive to local wishes, thereby creating a more efficient planning system (see DOE 1980b,c (s. 15A), DOE 1981a). Clearly, what this change is also intended to do is to undermine the authority of structure plans and county planning authorities. Despite the requirement for districts to consult counties over their proposed decisions –(DOE 1981a, para. 8), by no means does this requirement compare with the fact that county planning authorities are 'no longer [to] have the power to direct district planning authorities to refuse a planning application for development on the grounds that it would substantially and adversely affect their interests as a local planning authority' (ibid. para. 3).

The importance of this change for the Green Belt, as some of the empirical evidence will show (see Ch. 2), is that district authorities do not see themselves as being concerned with strategic planning matters, whereas at least in part county planning authorities do. To the districts, green belt is an additional development control device with which to prohibit unwanted development and to protect local amenities. Moreover, through the process of reallocation not only has the district acquired greater development control powers but it has also obtained the right to determine in detail green belt boundaries. Whether consultation with the counties in the latter regard will prove effective – in other words whether any strategic notion of the purpose of green belt will filter through to local decision making – depends very much on whether there are ideological or political incompatibilities between the respective counties and districts and how each has come to terms with the redistribution of planning powers (Brazier & Harris 1975, Leach & Moore 1979). Personal relations between planning officials may prove to be crucial. In practice, of course, local authorities in different tiers of local government have to collaborate to some extent, but the relations between them will undoubtedly change as the districts become more experienced and more confident in their new roles. Indeed, the

* Kent, Surrey, Berkshire, Buckinghamshire, Hertfordshire, Essex and Middlesex (incorporated into the GLC in 1965).

need to collaborate over planning matters 'does not alter the crucial fact that local authorities are not only corporate entities providing a wide range of services and performing duties other than planning, but are also political organizations fulfilling political objectives' (Lewis & Flynn 1979, p. 128).

The growing environmental awareness of residents, planners and local politicians living within or close to green belts has increasingly affected local planning policies in green belt areas. The argument sometimes put forward by central government that green belt restraint is being successfully implemented, if land is simply being kept open and undeveloped, has been regularly criticised over a long period (MHLG 1964, DOE 1973a, Skinner 1976). This debate is traced in Chapter 1 and is yet to be resolved. Local authorities are still confused about what the relations should be between local environmental or countryside policies on the one hand and green belt restraint on the other (see Ch. 2). They have not been helped by central government which has persisted in disassociating environmental from urban restraint considerations (DOE 1979a), preferring simply to talk in terms of approved and non-approved land uses in green belts (MHLG 1955). To this extent at least central government has failed to give a lead and failed to appreciate the strength of local feelings over amenity questions. It has also incorrectly assumed that the list of approved and non-approved land uses contained in Circular 42/55 (see p. 19) can easily be linked to the land-use classes contained in the General Development Order (DOE 1977a) and is sufficient to determine which land uses are acceptable and which are not. In practice, it is no longer possible to assume, for example, that land nominally in agricultural or recreational use is either well managed or productive.

These three themes – the changing size of the MGB, the implications for green belt of the redistribution of local authority planning powers and the growing importance of amenity considerations to the implementation of green belt – are to a degree related. The requests for extensions to the Green Belt from the late 1950s onwards arose from local initiatives and not from central government, although some encouragement to apply for extensions was given to local authorities early on (MHLG 1957). Indeed, after the mid-1960s central government declined to take a firm or even remotely consistent stand on extensions to the MGB, delaying most of its decisions until after the submission of structure plans in the 1970s (see Ch. 2). Inevitably, the request for extensions reflected local vested interests, and especially the wish to control the growth of urban areas that had sprung up beyond the Green Belt but outside planned overspill schemes. The influence of these interests has been reinforced by local government reorganisation with the result that local green belt policies now strongly emphasise amenity considerations and the minimal release of green belt land. These interests express ambivalent if not hostile attitudes towards the use of 'local' money in the positive management of public open space in any way that might be construed as serving a wider need than that of the local district (see Ch. 4).

It can be argued, perhaps, that this 'shire' view has always dominated green belt planning *decisions*, and those regional planners concerned to improve the living conditions of Londoners have merely held the *ideals* (Dix 1981, Sharp in preparation). Such explanations of the pattern of suburban growth are widely acknowledged in the United States where the suburbs are normally administratively separate from the city (Teaford 1979, Johnston 1981). It took two Americans to see through the 'neutrality' of the post-war planning system in Britain as it affects green belt (Foley 1963, Mandelker 1962), and more recent studies of the West European urban system continue to demonstrate that suburbanisation encourages social segregation (Hall & Hay 1980). Mandelker emphasises the *cordon sanitaire* role of the Metropolitan Green Belt, a role that preserves the amenities of outer suburbia from the ravages of the city (for an historical account, see Young & Garside 1982). He might also have gone on to explain rather more fully the extent of the financial interests held by private home-owners in their attempts to preserve green belt. Empirical research has established that open-space amenities raise house prices, substantially in the case of those properties overlooking the countryside, and at virtually no cost to the owners (Bowen 1974, Correll *et al.* 1978).

Previous studies of green belt

These three themes are not addressed directly in most of the literature on green belt. Partly this is because they have assumed an importance recently and post-date, for example, the major study of London's Green Belt by Thomas (1970). Partly, and more surprisingly given the widespread use of green belt restraint, it also reflects the general lack of empirical research into the effectiveness of green belt as a planning instrument. There is, however, a great deal of writing that examines land-use or amenity problems in the urban fringe and in which reference to green belt is made (e.g. see MAFF 1973, Coleman 1976, 1977, 1978; Lowe *et al.* 1977, Ferguson & Munton 1979, Fitton 1979, Elson 1979a, Best 1981, Blair 1981, Countryside Commission 1981, Harrison 1981a, Thomson 1981). There is also an extensive literature that describes the historical evolution of green belt as an instrument of policy in particular regional or local situations (see Mandelker 1962, Foley 1963, Thomas 1963, SEJPT 1971, Hall *et al.* 1973, Clark 1974, Skinner 1976). But again, with the partial exception of Hall *et al.* who were involved in a much broader analysis of post-war planning in Britain, these particular publications do not introduce much new empirical material on green belts.

Of more direct relevance to this study is the work being undertaken on restraint-area policy at Oxford Polytechnic (Hebbert & Gault 1978, Elson 1979b, Healey *et al.* 1980, Gault 1981). This investigation includes a comprehensive review of green belt policies as reported in structure plans and a discussion of how green belt policy is formulated at local, regional and national levels, based on interviews and seminar discussions with planning officers. The research demonstrates the confusion that has arisen over various aspects of green belt among both local authority planning officers and DOE officials alike. One example of this is the uncertainty about who is responsible for the drawing of green belt boundaries (see Ch. 2). A few analyses have also been made of land-use changes within green belts, paying particular attention to the growth of 'non-conforming' land uses (GLC 1969, Thomas 1970, Standing Conference 1976, Rettig 1976, Rural Planning Services 1979). The authors of these studies employ a variety of data sources ranging from aerial photographs to parish summaries of the June Agricultural Census (see Ch. 3). These investigations are largely descriptive in character and make only limited attempts to explain why the implementation of restraint is more effective in some locations than in others. In none of these studies are the two key processes that underlie urban development, namely the operation of the urban-fringe land market and the development control system, examined at any length.

An analysis of development control decisions is, however, included in a study of green belt carried out by the London Borough of Hillingdon (Hillingdon LB 1973) and in two important investigations into the operation of the development control system in the West Midlands (Gregory 1970, 1977; JURUE 1974, 1977). In the West Midlands, only the work of Gregory is specifically concerned with green belt but all four papers contain an analysis of development control decisions in the West Midlands Green Belt to the west and south of Birmingham. Gregory's (1970) study in Seisdon Rural District between 1955 and 1966 showed that applications for development totalling an area of nearly 3000 ha of green belt land (some applications were resubmissions following refusals) were made. Applications covering 86.5% of this area were refused by Seisdon RD although a further 85 ha were released on appeal. The refusal rate was especially high for residential development (in excess of 97%) and Gregory felt able to conclude that green belt restraint was being effectively maintained in Seisdon RD by both local and central government at that time. Nevertheless, it was noticeable that applicants did not seem unduly deterred from seeking planning permission in the green belt and this point also emerged from two subsequent studies (JURUE 1974, 1977). These studies were based on planning applications for the period 1968–9 to 1972–3 to the south-west of Birmingham in the general direction of Bromsgrove. When the planning applications were weighted by the areas they represented, only 28.4% of residential planning applications were for land zoned for housing whereas 46.6% were for land in the green belt. However, the success rate at 6.2% was eight times lower in the green belt than on land zoned for residential development, although this level of success was quite sufficient to ensure a regular flow of planning applications for green belt sites. There is also evidence from other research of a similar degree of pressure and success rate on land with amenity designations (Areas of Outstanding Natural Beauty, national parks, etc.) and on which there is a presumption against development (Cornwall County Council 1976, Anderson 1981, Blacksell & Gilg 1981).

Other research is concerned with the changing use of open land in green belts and with two matters in particular. The first relates to the perceived 'under-use' or even dereliction of farmland, and the general concern that more land goes out of food production than goes into a clearly defined urban use (Low 1973, Rettig 1976, ACAH 1978,* Coleman 1978, CRC 1978†). This is seen by Coleman and the ACAH in particular as evidence of inefficiency in the planning system and as an indictment of green belt. Low, working in Hillingdon LB, uses data from the June Agricultural Census (cf. Best 1981) to measure the loss and changes in use of farmland, whereas Coleman and Rettig employ the field sheets of the Second Land Utilisation Survey, against which they compare data derived from a later resurvey and aerial photographs respectively, in order to measure change. None of these authors, however, delves very deeply into the precise causes of the changes they observe, what roles they feel farming *should* play in the urban fringe or how in practice the 'under-use' of farmland could be minimised.

The second and related question concerns the link between land use and amenity in green belts and the problems that arise from landscape deterioration in the urban fringe. Deterioration is often the result of the poor maintenance of farmland, the inadequate reclamation of mineral land and the secondary effects of various existing, non-conforming land uses that predate the introduction of development control (Standing Conference 1976, 1977a). A study of these issues by Standing Conference entitled '*The improvement of London's Green Belt*' broke new ground. In its commentary, Standing Conference emphasised the need to approach landscape questions positively, not only to satisfy the amenity aspirations of those living in the Green Belt but also to avoid deterioration in the landscape being used as a reason to justify development of the land (see Ch. 1). Important and constructive though they are, Standing Conference's reports lack detail and consistency and depend almost wholly on the local planner's point of view.

The need for a new approach

Together, these studies make an important contribution to our understanding of various aspects of green belt. But on the whole they neither address themselves directly to the themes to be discussed in this book nor do they embody a methodology that is likely to be more than partially successful in evaluating the performance of green belt. There are two main reasons for this.

First, many of these accounts rely too heavily on the official written view as

* ACAH stands for Advisory Council for Agriculture and Horticulture, a standing council of agricultural interests that advises the Ministry of Agriculture, Fisheries and Food.

† CRC stands for Countryside Review Committee, an *ad hoc* interdepartmental committee of civil and public servants set up in 1974 to review the future of the countryside and disbanded in 1979.

contained in public documents – government circulars, structure plans and the like – and fail to pay sufficient attention to what the relevant officials think or do. As a result much of the discussion is focused on the purpose of green belt rather than on its detailed implementation. In addition, these analyses tend to imply, or even to presume, a formal, consistent and mechanistic relationship between statements of intent (policy) and outcome (practice). This is sometimes termed a 'top down' view of implementation in which those putting the policy into effect are seen as no more than the agents of those who draw up the policy. Such a view does not allow for the implementation of policy to be a process in its own right, a process subject to its own *internal* conflicts among its own actors as well as one that displays value systems and priorities that do not necessarily accord with those who formulated the policy in the first place (Hood 1976, Dunsire 1978).

The process of implementation obviously does not operate outside a general framework laid down by policy, but there is nearly always room for manoeuvre, negotiation, renegotiation and discretion among the parties involved (Bardach 1977, Dunsire 1978, Lewis & Flynn 1979, Rhodes 1980). Indeed, discretion may be deliberately built into the policy to allow for local circumstances, and this in itself may lead to misunderstandings. All these practices certainly apply in the case of green belt, the purposes of which were laid down by central government, but the implementation of which on a day-by-day basis is the responsibility of numerous local planning committees. Thus within the context of a single planning instrument – green belt – different perspectives derived from different scales, interests and responsibilities are being promoted at one and the same time.* The view from DOE is clear-cut, principled and highly generalised. At the other extreme, the views of those whose livelihoods (farmers, developers, mineral extractors) and living environments (residents and recreationalists) are directly affected by green belt planning decisions are quite different. Their views are sharp, specific and self-interested; and the broad tenets of government policy encroach on them only if they can be brought to bear in support of the particular case. Somewhere in between stand local authority planning committees. Their officials, especially in county halls, comprehend the strategic purpose of green belt – a comprehension that is less obvious at district level (see Ch. 2) – but are constantly being bombarded with planning applications that relate to the particular and are being pressured by residents who are primarily concerned with the amenity aspects of green belt. This means that without talking to people at all these levels the problems of implementing and assessing the 'success' of green belt are unlikely to be understood. There has, to date, been no such study.

Secondly, most studies of land-use changes in green belts have been seeking statistical generalisations from sources that are one or even two steps removed from the causes of the changes. A good example is the analysis by Thomson (1981). He examines agricultural change based on parish summaries of data

* Underwood (1981) discusses this particular point in the general context of development control.

returned by farmers in the June Agricultural Census. The farmers themselves are not consulted and the process of aggregation further detaches his analysis from what is actually happening on the ground. At best such analyses can only be a partial reflection of the processes operating within the urban fringe. Furthermore, if, for example, the main concern is with the appearance or standard of maintenance of open land in green belts, then analysis by conventional land-use classes – as contained in the General Development Order, the Agricultural Census or the Second Land Utilisation Survey – may not be very helpful. Such analyses may provide important clues but they are no substitute for detailed information on the operations and views of individual mineral companies, developers and farmers; nor are they a substitute for purposefully designed surveys aimed specifically, in this case, at the key issues of amenity and the maintenance of farmland.

A study of the Metropolitan Green Belt

The study seeks to elucidate the differences of view that exist among local planning officers and between them and their planning committee chairmen with regard to the general purpose of green belt, and to contrast these views with the positions held by officials from the DOE.* These differences are discussed in Chapters 1 and 2. The book then goes on to examine the available evidence on land-use change in the MGB, especially the growth of 'non-conforming' land uses (Ch. 3), and the attitudes of local and central government officials towards changes in the *form* and extent of approved land uses (Ch. 4). The nature of these approved land uses and what is now expected of them have changed dramatically since 1955 when they were listed in MHLG Circular 42/55. For example, over the past quarter of a century agriculture in the MGB has either become much more intensive in its use of land or simply run-down, in neither case meeting the expectations of amenity-conscious local residents and politicians. What they want is something quite different – farming systems that retain the habitats and landscapes of a former period. They also seek less mineral extraction and higher standards of reclamation of former workings and these demands present difficulties for planners who claim to be inadequately equipped in terms of powers and resources to deal with them. This issue is examined in Chapter 5. Finally, the inadequate maintenance of farmland is used to illustrate this theme more fully (Ch. 6). It is a particularly apposite illustration as farming in some form or another is still easily the largest user of green belt land.

Most of these themes have required the collection of original data and this has been very largely achieved through a number of semi-structured interview surveys conducted with key groups of people (see below). However, essential

* Differences of position are also often held among DOE officials even if their public statements on behalf of the Department reflect a common position. Over the strategic purpose of green belt there are few differences.

though this experiential perspective is, a framework is needed for it and this is provided by an historical and legislative review of London's Green Belt based on published documents. Much of this review falls into Chapter 1, being brought right up-to-date in Chapter 2 through a careful analysis of the correspondence between successive secretaries of state and county planning authorities when DOE was seeking changes to structure plans. The analysis of land-use change in Chapter 3 is dependent largely on other published and unpublished sources, although original material on the nature of planning applications and land market trends is also used (for details see Appendix). It would have been an enormous task to analyse planning application data for more than a very small proportion of the MGB, and this has not been attempted. Instead, details pertaining to a very small but representative sample, as planning officers see it, of applications that raise matters of green belt principle have been examined. Detailed information on land market trends, and especially land price changes in a variety of property markets within the MGB between 1969 and 1977, has been obtained with the assistance of the Chief Valuer's Office from nine district valuers whose districts contained a substantial amount of green belt land. This procedure was necessitated by the lack of spatially disaggregated data in the published statistics. 'Representative' properties were defined and independently valued (see Appendix) to produce a unique source of data.★ Parish summaries from the June Agricultural Census for 1976 for the whole of the MGB (243 parishes) have also been analysed extensively but the findings of these statistical analyses have done little more than confirm what was already known (see Ch. 4).

The interview surveys

The data collected specifically for this study were derived largely from interview surveys (for further details see the Appendix). A semi-structured interview technique was adopted. A schedule of questions was prepared in advance, some requiring factual answers and others opinions. This procedure ensured that the same issues were raised at each interview without making any attempt to control either the duration of the interview or the amount of time a respondent wished to spend in answering a particular question. A detailed letter explaining the purpose of the study was sent to interviewees, informing them of the main issues to be raised. This provided them with an opportunity to collate factual material and to consider their positions carefully. It also served to increase trust by being as open as possible about the nature of the interview, something that was especially important in the interviews with farmers. The questionnaires themselves were agreed with members of DOE, MAFF and Standing Conference, were piloted wherever possible, and then checked with

★ Much of the detailed information from this survey is not included in this book (see Munton 1979).

other relevant organisations such as the National Farmers' Union and the Country Landowners' Association.

Not all the groups with an interest in the MGB could be included in the surveys. Those that were can be divided into three – planners, local politicians and users of green belt land (mineral companies, developers and farmers). The first group, that of local planners and central government officials, included five officials from DOE and four from MAFF. The aim of these discussions was to establish current government policies, views on these policies and whether changes in them were expected in the near future. At local government level, approaches were made to the chief planner or planning officer in the 7 counties and 49 districts and London boroughs with significant areas of land which either had been granted statutory green belt status or were being planned on green belt principles with DOE agreement (see Ch. 1 & Fig. 1.1). Only one interview was refused.

The second group consisted of the chairmen of planning committees in the same authorities. The interviews were oriented towards the local political aspects of green belt, rather than the technical questions covered by the discussions with planning officers. These interviews threw light on officer–member relations, revealing the different perspectives that each group held of green belt. Some chairmen felt it was not worth their being interviewed as 'their planning officers would have said all that needed to be said'; others wanted their planning officers present but this was not agreed to, and in some cases officers doubted the value of interviewing their chairmen. This suggestion was also ignored, but these opinions help to explain why only 38 out of the 55 chairmen approached were eventually interviewed. Residents in the MGB could not be included in the interviewing programme and discussions with elected representatives was the closest the study came to eliciting their views. There is no reason to believe that councillors represent, except in a very general way, the views of their electorates (Lowe & Goyder 1983) but at least some insights were obtained from their observations. Residents' opinions necessitate and indeed warrant a complete study of their own.

The third group constituted users of green belt land. Again, not all groups of users could be included but contact was made with mineral companies, developers and farmers. Eleven mineral companies were approached but only three consented to an interview. The exploitation of sand and gravel in the MGB is a politically sensitive issue (see Ch. 4) and this, combined with the ongoing discussions between the companies and Standing Conference (see Standing Conference 1979a,b), and the amount of effort put in by the mineral companies to prepare evidence for the Stevens committee (1976) and the Verney committee (1976), led to the poor response. Developers, on the other hand, were much more prepared to co-operate and were more open about the details of their activities. Many of those known to own land in the MGB were approached. Thirteen agreed to an interview and eight refused or failed to reply.

The survey of farmers was of a totally different order. It involved interviews with 185 occupiers whose farms covered 14 810 ha or approximately 7.5% of the farmland in the MGB in 1975. The 185 farmers, both tenants and owner-occupiers, farm in three separate areas in the inner half of the Green Belt, one area being to the west of London near Beaconsfield, one to the south in Croydon LB and north Surrey, and one to the north-east in Havering LB and south-west Essex (see Fig. 6.1). The reasons for choosing these areas and how the farms were selected from within them are discussed in the Appendix. The information collected is much more detailed than that obtained from other farm surveys conducted around London (e.g. see Gasson 1966, MAFF 1973). It provides a much improved understanding of the tenure and business structure of farms in London's urban fringe, and of farmers' attitudes to farming in the Green Belt. To complete the agricultural study a survey was made of land maintenance standards on the land occupied by the 185 farmers interviewed. The details of how this was done and how the findings have been related to the specific circumstances of the occupiers are described in Chapter 6. All that needs to be said here is that this survey was specifically designed for the purpose of establishing the extent of and reasons for the poor maintenance of farmland in the urban fringe. The achievement of these objectives was greatly facilitated by the study being conducted on farms for which other kinds of information were available but which could not be found in any published source.

The interviewing programme began in August 1977 and was completed by the autumn of 1978. Interviews in local authorities came early, being completed by March 1978, and those with farmers were carried out between January and June 1978. This was a crucial period for many planning authorities as most counties were in the final throes of completing their structure plans (see Table 2.1) while districts and boroughs were still trying to sort out their local plan priorities.

To put all this information in context and to establish the changing currents of opinion over what matters in London's Green Belt it is necessary to provide a brief history of the MGB and it is to this that the book turns first.

1 *London's Green Belt: an historical perspective*

In the history of the green belt idea, and in particular in its changing
justification and changing form, we can find perhaps the most
accurate idea of planning objectives as they were seen by the founders
of the British planning system during the 1930s and 1940s (Hall *et al.*
1973, vol. II, p. 52).

Introduction

The importance of green belt concepts to the early development of planning
ideas in Britain contrasts sharply with the fixity of central government thinking
about green belts during the past 25 years. Perhaps this is only to be expected.
Debates over matters of principle are frequently dissipated by the practical
realisation of policies, with the effect that attention becomes increasingly
focused on the bureaucratic problems of how to maintain them rather than on
why they were instituted in the first place. Moreover, defence of the status quo
is the easiest response to criticism, and ever since it made its first and last major
statement of principle on green belt (MHLG 1955), central government has
clung to the view that the pre-eminent purpose of green belt restraint is to
contain the growth of particular urban areas. In south-east England this has
meant restricting the outward expansion of London while endeavouring to
accommodate the capital's surplus population and the rest of the region's urban
growth in planned overspill schemes and other preferred locations.

From time to time local planners, politicians and academics have assigned
other objectives to green belts. These have included the provision of open space
for countryside recreation, the protection of agricultural land, the maintenance
of amenity in the urban fringe and the creation of a *cordon sanitaire* between the
residents of the shire counties and those of the conurbations (Mandelker 1962).
The vigour with which these separate objectives have been promoted has varied
over the years. In the case of the MGB improved access to recreational
opportunities for the urban population was a widely canvassed objective in the
1930s and again in the 1970s (see GLRPC 1929, 1933; DOE 1975a; CRC 1977).
Urban containment was uppermost among the aims of outer metropolitan
authorities during the 1960s, and the maintenance of local amenity has received
considerable public support in the 1970s. One consequence of changing the
relative importance of these objectives is that they imply green belts of differing
size and shape, and this not only serves to confuse but also to make any
assessment of the effectiveness of green belt as a planning instrument almost

impossible to achieve. Even defining a green belt presents its own difficulties. It has been described, for example, as 'an area of land near to or sometimes surrounding a town which is kept open by permanent and severe restriction on building' (MHLG 1962, p. 3), even though experience shows that some land in green belts is neither open nor green.

As pointed out in the Introduction to this book, arguments continue over what the size and shape of green belts should be, whether they are effective in prohibiting urban development and whether the land within them is being maintained in an acceptable rural use. It was suggested that answers to these questions depend largely on whether a local or regional perspective is adopted and on the particular interest held in the future of green belt by those being questioned. These inconsistencies call for a brief historical review of the flux of green belt ideas as they have affected the evolution of the MGB. The review is divided into three historical periods. These broadly conform to those of fluidity in official views (up to 1955), the problems of ensuring urban containment through the use of green belt restraint during the post-war period of economic growth (1955–74), and that of increasing local confusion as to the purpose of green belt in an era of economic stagnation and entrenched, protectionist views among those living in or around the Green Belt (1974 onwards). The details of recent changes in the size of the MGB following the approval of structure plans in the late 1970s are described in Chapter 2.

A variety of views: the period up to 1955

Much of the basic thinking about the form and purpose of green belts occurred during the first half of this century, stimulated largely by the rapid growth of London and its attendant problems. The views of Ebenezer Howard, Raymond Unwin and Patrick Abercrombie were by far the most influential and Howard's writings are known to have had a major impact on Unwin and Abercrombie (Meller 1981, Sutcliffe 1981). However, each made substantially different proposals, reflecting the different professional tasks they were set, or in Howard's case set for himself, and the changes in the planning powers that became available to local authorities over the period during which they were writing.

Howard does not concern himself directly with London but with developing the more general concept of the cellular 'social city' (Howard 1898). The urban cells were to be evenly spaced and surrounded by narrow belts of countryside which would prevent the cells from growing beyond the maximum desired size while ensuring the preservation of farmland and the provision of open space for outdoor recreational activities. The countryside would blend in with the towns creating a mixed environment that would stand in contrast to the growing separation of town and country represented by the large late-Victorian conurbation.

Howard was not alone in expressing concern over urban conditions around the turn of the century (e.g. see Geddes 1904, Unwin 1912) or even in suggesting solutions (Pepler 1911, Webb 1918, Purdom 1921), but legislative response was meagre and largely ineffective. By the 1920s concern over urban growth had become much more widespread and much of the concern was directed at the rate of suburban development of London (Unwin 1921). This alarm contributed to the passage of new legislation, such as the Town and Country Planning Act 1932, which widened the scope of local plans even if it failed to give sufficient powers to local authorities to implement their plans in such a way as to control the general pace of urban growth. At the same time advisory panels of counties and other groupings of local authorities were established. These drew up regional and subregional plans and the Greater London Regional Planning Committee, which was in existence from 1927 to 1936, was of particular importance to the Green Belt. Its enormous committee, consisting of representatives from 138 separate local authorities and responsible for an area of 4780 km^2 within a 40 km radius of central London, appointed Unwin as its technical advisor (Gibbon & Bell 1939). His ideas had a major impact on the committee's two main reports of 1929 and 1933. In the latter report in particular, Unwin argued that there was an urgent need to compensate for the lack of playing fields and open space within the capital by acquiring a chain or girdle of sites around the edge of London. This land could then be turned over to playing fields and other forms of recreational use.

The girdle of land identified by Unwin consisted of a comparatively narrow strip, often no more than 2 km wide and in some places incomplete, but it still amounted to 200 km^2. Unwin did not expect it to provide an obvious break in the residential sprawl of outer London and he never assumed it would contain the growth of the conurbation. Thus in this respect and with its emphasis on recreation this particular green belt proposal differed from those of Howard and Abercrombie (see below). But Unwin always regarded the girdle as but one part of his more general approach to green belts (see GLRPC 1929), an approach that was developed by Abercrombie in preparing his *Greater London plan 1944* (Abercrombie 1945). The girdle was merely an attempt to find a feasible means of reducing the lack of recreational facilities within London given the limited planning powers then available. Nevertheless it demanded public land acquisition on a hitherto unknown scale, and of land that had development potential that would have to be bought at its full market value. By this time local authorities around London had already begun to purchase land to stop its development as one means of implementing the town planning schemes drawn up in the 1920s (Young & Garside 1982, Ch. 7; Sharp, in preparation). Unwin's proposal did not, therefore, mean a break with established practice but its sheer scale and potential cost did. Financial assistance for this venture was not forthcoming from central government and so, to further the process the London County Council (most of whose land was already built upon) set up a green belt scheme in 1935 (for the role of George Pepler in this scheme see Cherry 1981).

Subsequently this was codified in the Green Belt (London and Home Counties) Act 1938, under the terms of which the LCC would contribute to the cost of land purchased by adjacent authorities. The amount of grant aid contributed to each purchase depended on whether the land in question would be opened up for recreational use and whether it was readily accessible to Londoners (Dalton 1939). By 1939 approximately 110 km² had been either purchased outright, covenanted or was in the process of being acquired under the LCC scheme, with a further 90 km² acquired by local authorities on their own account. A substantial area of land, much of which is not in recreational use to this day, thus passed into public ownership (see Ch. 5).

In 1942 Abercrombie was commissioned to prepare a plan for the Greater London region (Abercrombie 1945). In this he treated green belt as only one element in a strategy aimed at reducing congestion within London and providing the best opportunity for the post-war rehabilitation of the capital. In a region that was expected to decline rather than to increase in population, one million Londoners were to be dispersed largely to eight new towns and other overspill centres located beyond a green belt of 8–15 km width encircling London. Abercrombie had returned to the notion of the all–purpose green belt advocated by Howard and endorsed in the Scott committee report of 1942 on *Land utilisation in rural areas* (Ministry of Works and Planning 1942). The belt would include most of the fragmented collection of holdings acquired under the green belt schemes, but the cost of purchasing the remaining land in the proposed belt, over 2000 km², was prohibitive. Instead, the green belt was to be maintained by the eagerly anticipated land–use planning system which Abercrombie assumed would largely but not completely stop all further urban development within it.

Abercrombie's objectives for the belt were to restrict the growth of London, to maintain the character and identity of settlements by preventing their coalescence, and to safeguard land for agriculture and recreation. In drawing on the Scott committee report, Abercrombie assumed that within the green belt itself comparatively little would change. As Thomas explains, in paraphrasing the report, green belt was 'conceived as an ordinary tract of country . . . where the normal occupations of farming and forestry could be continued so that, as elsewhere in rural areas, the farmer was the custodian of the land. But . . . it [the green belt] would normally include golf courses and other recreational land for the townsman's use' (Thomas 1970, p. 84). Along with most of his contemporaries what Abercrombie failed to foresee were the pressures that the MGB would experience in the post-war period. As a result he did not question the stewardship role of landowners and farmers in maintaining the character of the countryside, nor did he envisage the possibility of conflict between agricultural and recreational interests.

In 1946 the Ministry of Town and Country Planning gave its formal approval to Abercrombie's green belt proposals and the Town and Country Planning Act 1947 provided much of the institutional framework that Abercrombie was relying upon. In particular, the Act laid a requirement on local planning authorities to prepare development plans, it established a development control system to regulate changes in land use and it instituted compensation and betterment provisions – effectively 'nationalising' development rights (for a discussion of the 1947 Act see among others Hall *et al.* 1973, vol II; Leung 1979, McKay & Cox 1979, Lichfield & Darin-Drabkin 1980). It also drastically reduced the number of planning authorities, leaving only the London County Council and seven other county authorities with an interest in Abercrombie's green belt proposal. But there was to be no regional authority to co-ordinate county policies. Co-ordination was left in the hands of the ministry which in 1950 produced a green belt map based on Abercrombie's plan. Between 1954 and 1958 all the relevant county development plans were approved by the MHLG, creating a Green Belt that was similar in size and shape to that proposed by Abercrombie.

Coping with growth: 1955–74

In the period up to 1955 the need for a green belt around London had been regularly debated and some progress made. Central government, however, had remained largely on the side-lines and even in early 1955 had yet to endorse the idea of green belts or even to announce a set of principles upon which it would act in support of green belt proposals if they were submitted to it by local authorities. These principles were only made public later in 1955 and 1957 after most of the MGB had been statutorily approved. The first statement, a circular entitled *Green belts* (MHLG 1955), indicated that central government would only endorse green belt proposals where they were intended to check the growth of an urban area, to prevent the coalescence of neighbouring towns or to preserve the special character of a town. To assist local authorities maintain green belts through the use of their development control powers the circular listed those land uses that were acceptable in green belts. The circular stated that 'inside a green belt approval should not be given, except in very special circumstances, for the construction of new buildings or for the change of use of existing buildings for purposes other than for agriculture, sport, cemeteries, institutions standing in extensive grounds, and other uses appropriate to a rural area' (para. 5). This list fails to indicate what roles these particular uses were expected to play and omits specific reference to the provision of informal recreation facilities, one of the major arguments traditionally employed in support of green belts. Indeed the circular was immediately criticised for its emphasis on urban restraint and its lack of concern for the positive use of open land within green belts (Collins 1957).

In response to this criticism there followed a period of uncertainty in government thinking. At one moment central government appeared to endorse an amenity function for green belts, at least as a secondary objective, and at the next to backtrack. Thus, for example, in 1957 a further circular stated that the amenity value of land could be taken into account in defining the local extent of green belts (MHLG 1957). But this view was then contradicted by the minister, Henry Brooke, who in 1961 claimed that 'the very essence of a green belt is that it is a stopper. It may not all be very beautiful and it may not all be very green, but without it the town would never stop, and that is the case for preserving the circles of land around the town' (quoted in Heap 1961, p. 18). This statement was followed by a more carefully worded one in the MHLG's booklet *The green belts* (1962). This hinted that one reason why central government wished to exclude amenity as a green belt objective was the weakness of the development control system in ensuring that standards of amenity could be maintained. This was a realistic assessment of the situation, and it was also prophetic in the sense that environmental issues were to come to dominate so much of the discussion over the implementation of restraint, as well as the objectives of green belt, in later years.

It has been argued that a plethora of post-war environmental legislation had been passed and this could have been invoked to aid a more positive approach to amenity questions. Designations such as AONB (Area of Outstanding Natural Beauty) or SSSI (Site of Special Scientific Interest) could have been used more widely to return the green belt to the multiplicity of aims espoused for it by Howard and Abercrombie (Thomas 1963). The dangers inherent in this approach are that, if the criteria for these designations are adjusted to meet the requirements of green belt, then the standing of the designations might themselves be reduced when put into effect elsewhere. Moreover, there is also the risk of creating two classes of green belt with one being undermined as of lesser worth. In Scotland, on the other hand, and later on in Yorkshire and Humberside (Yorkshire and Humberside Regional Economic Planning Council 1974), no such inhibitions existed. There, the Department of Health for Scotland (1960) made it clear that land protected from development must have a distinct agricultural, recreational or amenity use. These points were also picked up in successive regional plans for south-east England (MHLG 1964, South-East Economic Planning Council 1967, SEJPT 1971) and in the report of the panel of inquiry, the Layfield report (DOE 1973a), into the draft Greater London Development Plan (GLC 1976, as finally approved). In the *South East study 1961–1981* (MHLG 1964) it was argued that in return for the imposition of restraint, green belt land must be put to the best possible use. Use and amenity considerations should be seen as fully fledged objectives and not minor issues. In a key passage the study claimed that 'All land in the green belt should have a positive purpose, whether it be its quality as farm land, its mineral resources, its scenic value, its suitability for public open space or playing fields for Londoners, or those land uses generated by the main built-up areas, which cannot be suitably located within it – such as reservoirs and institutions needing large areas of open land around them' (Ch. 16, para. 24). And in the context of releasing land for housing, the Layfield committee said 'Scepticism should also be the response to the argument that, even if land in the London sector of the Metropolitan Green Belt is not used for any purpose and has no access, it serves a valuable green belt purpose simply in not being developed and in being different from the City' (DOE 1973a, para. 19.21).

The committee went on to criticise the draft Greater London Development Plan for its inadequate treatment of the recreational and amenity functions of the MGB within the GLC boundary. It was especially critical of the amount of semi-derelict land and of the council's tendency to place the recreational potential of green belt second to its scope for agricultural use. The plan, as eventually approved, committed the GLC and the relevant boroughs actively to promote the recreational use of green belt land and to have a programme of land reclamation. They were also required to examine the long-term economic viability of agriculture, but rather less was said as to *how* this might be achieved.

These discussions on the amenity value of green belt were related indirectly to the widespread demand from local authorities to extend green belt further into the countryside in order to control the burgeoning urban growth that was developing just beyond the MGB. But if all this land were to be sterilised from development, what guarantee was there that it would be used to its full potential in some acceptable rural use? And secondly, would not such poorly used land become a natural target for central government that from time to time was seeking to make selective releases of green belt land to meet the region's housing needs? The population of south-east England rose from 15.2 million in 1951 to 17.0 million in 1971 (SEJPT 1976) and throughout this period, but especially in the 1960s, there was decentralisation of the metropolitan population from the urban core of London (Hall *et al.* 1973, DOE 1976a). This was accompanied by a substantial increase in real standards of living and a high demand for new housing. A furious but still unresolved debate on whether enough land was being made available for residential development in the region ensued (e.g. see Warren-Evans 1974, DOE 1975b, 1978b, 1980d).

MHLG Circulars 42/55 and 50/57 spelled out the procedures under the old development plan process by which local authorities might establish or amend the area of a green belt. First, after consulting neighbouring authorities, the local authority submitted to the ministry a sketch plan indicating the approximate boundaries desired and a Written Statement in support of the need for a green belt. Secondly, central government then discussed the matter with the local authority and in consultation with it defined the green belt's inner and outer boundaries. The alignment of green belt boundaries could be reconsidered each time the plan was reviewed. This meant that in principle the boundaries were less permanent than, say, those for national parks or AsONB – designations determined outside the local plan-making process and by reference to their own national legislation. In practice, making changes to green belt boundaries proved to be an extremely protracted business especially where one authority's proposals affected the planning policies of its neighbours. This led to delay and uncertainty and to numerous compromises by governments that were un-willing to commit themselves firmly to extending the area of green belts in situations of high housing demand. This can be demonstrated by examining the situation around London as it stood in 1975 (Fig. 1.1). By then four categories of green belt were in operation. Two of these represented green belt statutorily approved by central government, one being land originally approved under the development plan submissions of the 1950s and the other

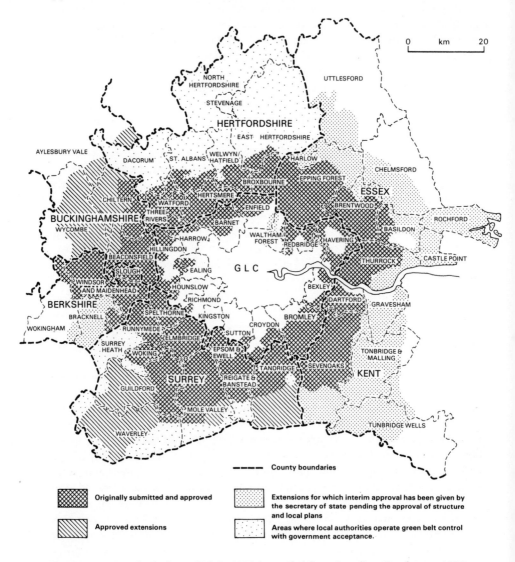

Figure 1.1 London's Green Belt in 1975 (amended from Standing Conference 1976, p. 7).

extensions to this in Surrey and Buckinghamshire. Two consisted of interim green belt where central government had yet to make up its mind and was deliberately delaying its decisions until structure plans were prepared. This meant that interim arrangements were in operation for 15 years in some areas, and local authorities could never be certain that central government would uphold green belt restraint on appeal with the same vigour in those areas as in those that had been statutorily approved. A similarly confused situation existed in the rest of England. In 1974 only 35.5% of the area subject to green belt policies had been statutorily approved (Gault 1981).

The unwillingness of central government to approve extensions to the MGB resulted from its concern over development pressures in the region, and especially the wish to avoid encapsulating economically buoyant towns within the Green Belt. Encapsulation would lead either to the green belt boundary around the town having to be drawn away from the town's edge to allow for its continuing growth, leading to land speculation, or drawn close to the urban edge in the sure knowledge that consent for development would have to be given on green belt land sooner or later (SEJPT 1971). Central government's unwillingness also stemmed from the more relaxed approach it adopted than most local authorities towards the release of green belt land for development. In this it was supported by the *South East study 1961–1981* and by the Layfield committee report but not by Standing Conference, which complained that central government was releasing land on appeal for housing against the wishes of local authorities (Standing Conference 1976). In two separate white papers central government argued that land had to be released from the MGB if the region's housing construction targets were to be met (MHLG 1963, DOE 1973b). On both occasions the responsibility for finding the land was placed by central government on the shoulders of the local authorities. In 1963, a 160 ha site consisting of disused glasshouses was eventually found in the Lea Valley. Second time round considerable opposition was experienced from the local authorities when they were asked to bring forward 800 ha of green belt land. They objected on the grounds that these land releases would undermine public confidence in the Green Belt, lead to further requests from developers for green belt sites and would compromise other local planning policies. To central government the loss of 800 ha out of a green belt of over 300 000 ha could not possibly affect the strategic objectives of green belt restraint. But this was not how the local authorities saw it, and the whole incident led to a cooling of local–central government planning relations in south-east England for a couple of years (see Ch. 3).

The recent past: changing economic fortunes and environmental concerns

In 1970 the South East Joint Planning Team published its *Strategic Plan for the South East* (SEJPT 1970). The study was commissioned by central government,

Standing Conference and the South East Economic Planning Council and was prepared jointly by their respective staffs. The plan developed strategies for the region up to 1981 and 1991 that were designed to act as frameworks within which central government could take decisions about the scale, nature and location of public investment in the region and local authorities could prepare their structure plans (see Ch. 2). The strategic plan anticipated a buoyant economy and further growth in the region's population, largely from natural increase, with a substantial gain outside the capital offsetting a decline in numbers in London. Urban growth was to be concentrated in five major growth areas (south Essex, south Hampshire, mid-Berkshire, Milton Keynes and Crawley) and seven medium growth locations. Outside these, development was to be restrained in order to protect extensive areas of open country, fine landscapes and good quality farmland. The MGB was to be retained around London to assist in this task.

Only as the 1970s progressed was it appreciated that the region's economic and population growth was faltering. Nevertheless, the persistent decentralisation of jobs and people from London continued to put pressure, first, on the Outer Metropolitan Area (OMA), or the counties immediately around London, and subsequently on the Outer South East (OSE) or the area beyond the OMA (DOE 1976a). This changing pattern led to a re-examination of policies for the South East and this was contained in the *Strategy for the South East; 1976 review* (SEJPT 1976). The review confirmed the broad outlines of the strategic plan but placed greater emphasis on the need to regenerate central London. It also accepted that the amount of growth to be accommodated in the region was significantly less than had been anticipated six years earlier. It was hoped that by concentrating growth in the same five main centres identified in 1970 it would prove economical of government investment in services, and provide some protection for central London by restricting the choice of those wishing to leave the capital. To this end the review endorsed even more strongly than the strategic plan the need for areas of restraint and the requirement that these should be strictly adhered to. But the achievement of this objective has raised many difficulties. Partly this is because regional plans have no statutory force and partly because planning at this scale is by its very nature coarse (see Ch. 2). More particularly, the restraint areas identified were made up of an amalgam of zones covered by a wide range of planning (green belt), environmental (heritage coasts, areas of great landscape value) and resource (Grades 1 and 2 agricultural land) designations culled from a wide variety of legislative backgrounds and introduced to serve quite other purposes. Were they all to be enforced equally strictly? And what of development pressures in those centres surrounded by restraint areas but not identified for growth? Were they all to be prevented from expanding?

With the delay in structure plan preparation caused by local government reorganisation in 1974, the *Review* became the main strategic policy document upon which the counties could draw in the preparation of their plans. This was followed in 1978 by a statement of the government's position (DOE 1978a). This rather limited publication reaffirmed the broad strategy presented in the *Review*. In its statement central government indicated its concern over the decline of London and the growing level of unemployment in the region. It also questioned whether there was much economic growth or mobile industry to divert to growth centres and hinted whether it might not be more realistic to relax the severity of restraint in some areas to meet local needs and to permit the creation of jobs wherever these might occur. Standing Conference (1979c) reported continuing pressure for residential development in the MGB in the later 1970s, reflecting primarily a fall in average family size and an increase in population in the outer districts. The populations of all the districts immediately adjacent to the western edge of London, from Tandridge in the south to Welwyn–Hatfield in the north, fell between 1971 and 1981 by 3.6% on average in line with all the outer London boroughs. Modest gains were recorded to the east of London (OPCS, 1982).

In his statement the Secretary of State for the Environment indicated his continuing support for London's Green Belt on the basis of the principles laid down in Circular 42/55 (DOE 1978a). In particular, he argued that the MGB need not be more than 20–25 km wide, or rather larger than the approved Green Belt of 1974 but less than the area covered by interim green belt (Fig. 1.1); and this position was reaffirmed in a letter he sent to Standing Conference in August 1980 (DOE 1980a). This zone could, he claimed, be firmly maintained and was of sufficient width to restrain the outward growth of London. He would also consider cases made out in support of local green belts designed to prevent the merging of towns but, in general, countryside policies were to be used to limit development in rural areas. Green belt restraint was not to be widely employed in case it restricted the growth of too many economically buoyant towns. The South East region had to contribute fully to the revival of national economic fortunes. In support of this position he referred to the government's policy outlined in *Local government and the industrial strategy* (DOE 1977b). This circular was designed to promote industrial development and was ambiguous about the potential conflict between job creation and areas of restraint. This conflict had also not escaped the attention of Standing Conference (1977b). Standing Conference accepted that in the present economic climate some flexibility might have to be accorded to districts with limited quantities of housing and industrial land available for development. But it went on to warn that 'If flexibility means incremental land allocation for development in the Green Belt then the Green Belt cannot really remain a long-term instrument of strategic regional policy' (para. 8).

Following the strong comments made by the Layfield committee of inquiry into what it regarded as the rather bland approach of the GLC towards the use and appearance of green belt land within the council's boundaries (DOE 1973a), Standing Conference undertook a thorough review of the state of the MGB, publishing its findings in a report entitled *The improvement of London's Green Belt*

(1976). The report included a description of the nature and extent of unsightly and poorly used land and discussed how the appearance of landscapes in the urban fringe might be improved. Standing Conference assessed frankly the limited scope of development control powers and other planning instruments to resolve landscape problems, but does make a valuable contribution to the debate on the environmental aims of green belt (see also Standing Conference 1977a, 1978). The main impact of the report stemmed from its claim that large areas of land in the MGB were visually unattractive and in need of remedial treatment, and that further areas of land would also deteriorate unless remedial measures were taken to prevent it happening.

In presenting evidence in support of its case, Standing Conference identified two kinds of unwanted landscape. These were termed 'damaged' and 'threatened'. Neither was rigorously defined, their definitions containing both descriptive and functional elements. 'Damaged' landscape was defined as 'General zones within which individual sites, of more than one square kilometre, exhibit serious landscape deterioration requiring urgent improvement either because they suggest deletion from green belt notation or are liable to cause deterioration in adjoining areas' (Standing Conference 1976, p. 20). Such landscape was observed to be frequently associated with unreclaimed gravel workings, industrial land uses and waste tips. 'Threatened' landscape was described as 'General zones of deteriorating agricultural and woodland management mainly in the urban fringe, characterised for example by the incidence of neglected hedgerows, pony paddocks, piggeries and scrap yards and public utility installations' (p. 20).

The extents of these two landscape types were not determined in detail by ground survey, and their mapping was conducted on a broad brush basis. The data were compiled with the assistance of various planning officers who inevitably held different interpretations of what the terms 'damaged' and 'threatened' meant. Despite attempts by Standing Conference to standardise the various returns, it is almost certain that bias became built into the study (see pp. 89 & 110). This is not to suggest that Standing Conference was seeking to demonstrate a particular state of affairs but it can be argued that the inadequacies of its research methods undermine the validity of its findings. Its findings impart a clear message as they suggest that much of the open land in the MGB is in a state that leaves much to be desired (Fig. 1.2). Substantial areas of land fall into one or other of its categories, especially within the inner half of the MGB. Both types of landscape are widespread around Heathrow Airport, 'threatened' landscape is widely distributed close to the GLC/Surrey boundary and 'damaged' landscape dominates the Lea and Darent valleys and land to the east of London. Standing Conference at least avoided the trap of trying to define the 'best' Green Belt landscapes and tackled the slightly more straightforward task of identifying visually unacceptable areas where remedial action was felt to be called for. By mapping 'threatened' landscapes Standing Conference also sought to delimit areas that required attention now if they were not to become

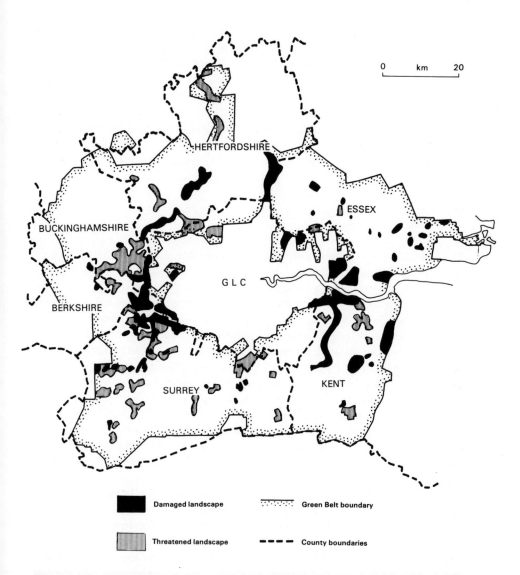

Figure 1.2 Damaged and threatened landscapes in the Metropolitan Green Belt (amended from Standing Conference 1976, pp. 16, 17). (Green Belt boundary as approved in 1982 – see Fig. 2.2.)

'damaged'. Stopping deterioration in these zones was seen as important as treating 'damaged' landscapes.

Following the publication of its report, Standing Conference attempted to raise the issues of appearance and use of land in the MGB with DOE. No substantive discussion took place. DOE opted to stick to its traditional position that green belt was a strategic urban restraint policy and that the appearance of urban-fringe areas, even if designated as green belt, was a local environmental matter. Nevertheless, the secretary of state in his statement on the region did observe that 'restraint aspects of planning policies in the approved green belt have been dominant in the past and that it is important that positive policies are adopted and implemented to secure the improvement of despoiled and degraded areas as well as the restoration of activity in "underused" areas' (DOE 1978a, p. 14). But he did not go on to spell out what he meant by positive policies, how they should relate to restraint, or what he regarded as despoiled, degraded or 'underused' areas. Were these categories to be equated with Standing Conference's 'damaged' and 'threatened' landscapes? No guidance has been forthcoming.

Summary

This brief historical review illustrates the continuing debate on the purpose of green belt. Central government continues to emphasise the overriding importance of the urban restraint function of green belt as one element of a more general population distribution strategy being effected at a regional scale. This role for the Green Belt is also accepted by Standing Conference but it commented in its response to the 1976 review that 'The strengthening of Green Belt controls against development may not on its own be an adequate way of ensuring the success of restraint policies and in particular maintenance of the urban edges of the Green Belt. Unfortunately the 1976 Review report failed to propose how development pressures could effectively be diverted away from restraint areas' (Standing Conference 1977b, para. 7). Both local and central government concur that development pressures will continue to affect the MGB almost irrespective of the state of the regional economy and may even be increased by the continuing poor performance of the national economy and the desperate search for new jobs.

This current review also suggests that it is easier for central than local government to maintain a detached and consistent outlook on green belt in its role as creator of broad-scale policies. Matters are often less clear to local planning authorities where decisions have to be made on numerous planning applications, each of which has to be assessed on its individual merits. It also means that, when viewed at the regional scale, small-scale releases of green belt land are a matter of lesser concern to DOE than to those local authorities in which the releases are to occur. But is DOE sensitive to the implications for green belt of this different perspective? How aware is it that environmental issues are of considerable importance locally and that the credibility of restraint is judged partly by the appearance of green belt land? The recent revision of the development plan-making system and the devolution of development control powers to district and borough planning authorities only serve to emphasise the importance of this point and it is to this issue that this book now turns.

2 Local planning and the Metropolitan Green Belt

Introduction

Differences of view over the purpose of green belt have clouded central–local government relations from time to time (see Ch. 1). These differences are examined further in this chapter in the context of the new development plans system and especially with regard to the preparation, submission and approval of the structure plans of the home counties. The significance of these differences to the implementation of restraint has been increased not only by the devolution of planning powers from the counties to the districts but also by the general downgrading of regional planning. The regional economic planning councils, the obvious bodies to advise over the strategic role of green belt, were disbanded by central government in 1979, and the strategic perspective now has to be promoted by the weakened county planning departments or by the DOE itself dealing increasingly directly with the districts. In this respect it can be argued that central government is, by negotiating with districts and boroughs, which have relatively small and inexperienced planning departments, extending its centralised control over planning matters (see McAuslan 1981).

It is too early to try to anticipate all the consequences for green belt of these changes in the administration of planning, especially as the preparation of many local plans is far from complete. Nonetheless, it is possible to examine recent structure planning experience and to review the attitudes of local planners and councillors towards green belt at the time at which they were preparing their plans. Three matters are selected for discussion.

The first relates to important procedural questions over the division of responsibilities between districts and counties. For example, which tier of planning authority should determine green belt boundaries and how 'permanent' should these boundaries be? Changes in boundary alignment may have minor strategic implications but be of major local significance. Discussion of this issue draws on what is now a wide range of structure planning experience. Secondly, what are the objectives of green belt restraint as seen by local planning officers and the chairmen of their planning committees? Do objectives vary substantially among the numerous local authorities around London when those with land of interim as well as statutory green belt status are taken into account? (see Fig. 1.1). To what extent do local views correspond with those of DOE officials? To answer these questions interviews were held in late 1977 and 1978 with local planners and politicians and DOE officials (see Introduction & Appendix). In this chapter, discussion of their replies is restricted to broad matters of principle – the respondents' attitudes towards specific land-use changes in the MGB being examined in Chapters 3 and 4. Finally, how are these views reflected in the structure plans of the home counties? How consistent are these proposals and has the secretary of state reacted equitably to them? Evidence on these matters is drawn from the counties' structure plans and the later correspondence between the county planning departments and the secretary of state in which proposed modifications to the plans were discussed.

The new development plans system and green belt

The development plans system instituted under the Town and Country Planning Act 1947 remained largely intact until the early 1970s. But throughout the 1960s criticisms of the system were widespread. These were of two main kinds, one lamenting the lack of public participation in the plan-making process and the other complaining of the slowness with which plans were being revised. The plans were regarded as inflexible, too dependent upon a land-use base and the physical aspects of planning, and overly influenced in their detailed policies by central government (Hall *et al.* 1973, McLoughlin 1973, Roberts 1976). To meet these charges central government set up the Planning Advisory Group (PAG) in 1964 to review the existing system and to propose remedies. PAG did this in its report *The future of development plans* (MHLG 1965).

PAG argued that local authorities should produce two kinds of plan. One would be a strategic plan (structure plan) covering the whole of its area and examining only major issues (see DOE 1977c). It should consist largely of policy statements and diagrams illustrative of the authority's general intent (see MHLG 1970). It would not provide a detailed land-use plan upon which development control decisions could be based as this would be supplied by a second tier of local plans. Central government would need to approve only structure plans as these would contain the matters of broad principle of concern to it, and not local plans provided these conformed with their relevant structure plans and had been subjected to public scrutiny. Most of these recommendations were subsequently incorporated in the 1968, 1971 and 1972 (Amendment) Town and Country Planning Acts.

PAG assumed that the existing local planning authorities, the counties and the county boroughs, would prepare both kinds of plan, but this expectation was ended by the reorganisation of local government in England and Wales under the Local Government Act 1972. Under this Act planning powers were divided. The counties were to draw up structure plans while their constituent districts or boroughs were to prepare local plans. The powers to implement the plans through development control were also split between the two tiers, requiring considerable amounts of discussion between separate authorities, and this inevitably led to delays. In an effort to ensure consistency each county had to certify that each local plan within its jurisdiction conformed with the structure plan. But this has proved a fragile arrangement. For the scheme to work effectively both tiers of local authority needed to have similar planning objectives in social terms, and both sets of plans needed to be produced speedily so that local plans were not prepared under radically differing economic conditions or in response to different policy guidance from central government. These requirements have not been met. The preparation of structure plans has been slow (see p. 39) and this has not only undermined their value but also called the whole plan-making process into question (House of Commons 1977). The delays have been partly the fault of DOE becoming too involved in local issues (Healey 1979) and being constantly concerned to strike out much of the social content of structure plans (Jowell & Noble 1981), neither aspect of which PAG intended, but both of which have contributed to central government's arguments for further devolving development control decisions to the district level. It has been assumed that this devolution would lead to greater flexibility and the faster processing of planning applications, so reducing delay, and thus expense, for the development industry (DOE 1979b, 1980b,e, 1981a).

These changes in planning responsibilities and the uncertainties they have created are of special relevance to green belt. As a strategic policy, central government retains an interest in it, counties regard it as a key structure planning issue and the districts now find themselves responsible for much of its day-to-day implementation. In principle, as a strategic planning policy, green belt is primarily a structure planning matter. But to be implemented green belts have to be clearly and precisely defined. Boundaries have to be drawn on maps, and yet structure plans are only meant to be schematic documents. The precise definition of boundaries on them is *ultra vires*, and boundaries on structure plans have been struck out by the secretary of state (see Hebbert & Gault 1978). They may only be inserted on local plans by the relevant district planning authorities and the districts may not be in agreement with their counties over the scale of their local development needs. This leads to two further questions – by what method should green belt boundaries be determined? And how permanent should they be?

Under the new system there are two main ways of determining green belt boundaries. They can either be drawn on comprehensive local plans by district authorities or be drawn by counties in consultation with their districts on green belt subject plans. There are a number of arguments in favour of the subject plan approach. These include the speed with which the exercise can be completed by a single set of criteria. Many counties, including Shropshire, Berkshire, and Tyne and Wear, for example, have taken this approach and DOE originally advised in favour of it. DOE, however, has changed its mind and now questions whether green belt is a suitable topic for a subject plan. Topics for subject plans have to have 'Such limited interactions with other planning matters that neither these matters nor the subject itself will suffer if the subject is planned in isolation' (DOE 1977c, p. 4); and it is doubtful whether green belt qualifies on this basis. Indeed, if interpreted literally, it is difficult to think of any policy worth a separate subject plan that does qualify. Moreover, counselling in favour of the drawing of boundaries on local plans, as DOE now does, accords with the wish of central government to devolve more responsibility to district authorities. This is especially so in cases where districts, such as Basildon and Salford, have objected to green belt subject plans produced by their county planning authorities that in their view reduce their scope for expansion (Hebbert & Gault 1978).

The alternative approach, that of defining green belt boundaries on local plans, is also subject to a number of criticisms (Gault 1981). It can lead to delay, uncertainty and inconsistency, and not all districts are proposing to produce comprehensive plans (see p. 46). The matter is, then, still to be satisfactorily resolved, and so is the question of the permanence of green belt boundaries. As a strategic policy in structure plans, a planning period of 15 years (allowing for revisions) can be assumed, whereas boundaries in local plans will be reviewed every five years. Will this lead to green belt boundaries being realigned every five years, thereby encouraging land speculation? It also raises the question (see p. 45) of whether boundaries should be drawn tightly around settlements and withdrawn step by step as development needs dictate or drawn loosely in the first instance to allow for medium-term needs. The DOE (1979c) favours the latter approach but confusion in the minds of planners remains. The inspector, commenting on the Sutton Coldfield District Plan, said that 'Although green belt policies should normally be of a relatively long-term duration they cannot be immutable and should be subject to the same review processes as other policies. However, they should be as reasonably permanent as possible' (DOE 1977d, p. 4; quoted in Healey 1979, p. 20).

Attitudes towards green belt in the MGB area

The second issue to be examined is the responses of local planning officers and planning committee chairmen around London (for details see Appendix) to questions put to them concerning green belt principles. They were asked to comment on what they regarded as the basic principles of green belt, whether they felt these were applicable to them in their particular authorities, and on the relationship between local environmental objectives and the goal of urban restraint. Similar questions were put to five officials from DOE.

General objectives   In their responses the officials from the Department of the Environment made it quite clear that they still regarded the principles contained in Circular 42/55 (MHLG 1955) as the corner-stone of green belt policy (cf. DOE 1978a). In the context of the South East region this meant limiting the spread of London. To the officials, land-use and environmental problems in the Green Belt were secondary considerations and, although deserving attention, decisions concerning them could not be allowed to conflict with the imposition of restraint. Furthermore, the MGB should be of limited width. 'Blanket' green belt over whole counties led to inflexibility and weakened the policy by encompassing too wide a range of planning situations. A broad green belt would also leave the impression that *any* growth within a reasonable distance of London was unacceptable as this would conflict with the industrial strategy of central government (DOE 1977b).

A much more diffuse picture of restraint emerged from the discussions with local planning officers. When asked about the strategic objectives of restraint in general, all seven county planning officers, bar the officer for Surrey, prefaced their replies with the view that green belt should be regarded as a planning tool. It should not be seen as an end in itself. To this extent they were in agreement with the position expressed by DOE officials. In marked contrast, only one out of 44 district and borough planning officers volunteered the same view. A local rather than a strategic perspective immediately sprang to mind, foreshadowing differences of approach between the counties and districts. All 51 officers, that is those from both county and district authorities, agreed that urban restraint was a key function of green belt, but as many as 41 insisted that the recreational needs of the conurbation should be treated as a strategic green belt planning matter too. A further five argued that the protection of high quality farmland should also be a strategic goal. These were the officers for Barnet, Elmbridge, Enfield, Rochford and Surrey (see Fig. 1.1). With the partial exception of Rochford, farmland in these authorities is not of especially high quality, although much of it has been lost to other uses in Elmbridge. When questioned specifically about environmental goals within green belt only six officers maintained, as the officials from DOE had done, that such objectives must be seen as secondary to that of urban restraint. Seven, a completely different group to that above, raised the inadequate treatment of agriculture, and about half raised the need to ensure the openness of land, improvement in the conservation of landscape and the encouragement of countryside land uses as complementary green belt goals.

Local planning officers were then asked to list the objectives of green belt as they saw them *in their own authorities*. The frequency with which particular objectives were mentioned is shown in Table 2.1, some officers recording several and some only one. Answers differed to those given to the general question, being both more varied and more specific. No single objective as categorised in the table was mentioned by half the respondents and a significant number placed considerable emphasis on environmental aims. Eight put the highest priority on using green belt to avoid any change at all. Thus although there might be broad agreement in principle over the purpose of green belt this was not extended to policy decisions at local level. This divergence between principle and practice was replicated in the discussions held with the chairmen of local authority planning committees. Again, broad acceptance of the principle of restraint was expressed, *provided* it helped to ensure the 'effective use' of green belt land and did not conflict with their assessments of local housing needs. About one-quarter of the chairmen claimed that they would only endorse

Table 2.1 Local green belt objectives.

Objectives	No. of mentions (51 interviews)
containment of urban sprawl	25
improvement and protection of rural landscape	21
maintenance of 'openness'	21
prohibit coalescence of urban centres	15
promotion of recreation	13
protection of agricultural land and commercial farming	11
preservation of the *status quo*	8

restraint while these other local objectives were also being met. What was meant by 'effective use' varied. Five chairmen emphasised the importance of recreation and three emphasised the commercial viability of agriculture; a further eight stressed the maintenance of rural character which, broadly translated, meant rejecting all planning applications.

Two patterns could be identified in the responses but there were exceptions to each. Officers in London boroughs and districts with more than 20% of their areas covered by urban uses were most concerned to maintain 'openness', whereas those in less urbanised authorities immediately adjacent to the GLC placed particular emphasis on restricting urban sprawl and avoiding any kind of land-use change. Respondents further away from London, whose green belt was only of interim status and whose authorities were only experiencing limited pressure from urban expansion, placed higher priority on the protection of valued resources such as high quality farmland and pleasant landscapes. Those in the inner half of the MGB, sometimes equally concerned over the loss of farmland, were more positive in their attitudes to public access to the countryside, the enhancement of degraded landscapes and the use of high quality farmland for food production. These differences are only to be expected. The fact that they were not more clear-cut owed as much to the lack of attention being given to countryside policies in some authorities (see Ch. 4, Davidson & Wibberley 1977) as to dissimilarity of views over the purpose of green belt.

The officials from DOE concluded that, in terms of the principles laid down in Circular 42/55, green belt restraint had been highly successful. Restraint, it was argued, had been consistently and vigorously applied and urban sprawl curtailed. Planners, developers and the public accepted it and behaved accordingly. Support for this contention was forthcoming from some planners and some chairmen, but many were critical saying that land had been released on appeal from time to time when it suited the political purpose of central government. Further discussion of development pressures, which certainly remain whatever impression DOE officials sought to convey, is contained in Chapter 3. When asked to assess the performance of restraint at local level, planning officers and committee chairmen gave ambivalent and variable replies. This was most noticeable among planning committee chairmen. Only 12 of the

38 interviewed expressed unqualified approval of the way in which restraint was being applied in their authorities, even though they were implicated in these judgements as chairmen of their respective planning committees. Their main reservation was over the inflexibility of green belt as a negative instrument of policy. This was especially apparent when it was seen as contributing to the widespread practice among local planning committees of seeking to avoid setting precedents, even if particular planning applications were not unreasonable when viewed on their own merits. This situation had led committees to go to inordinate lengths to maintain 'silly boundaries'. The general effect was to fossilise existing situations, although this was an outcome that a significant minority wholeheartedly endorsed, and one of the adverse effects of this was that local inhabitants were often priced out of the private housing market. A further complaint surrounded what was seen as the limitations placed on local autonomy. It was claimed that green belt land was regularly lost to various forms of development stemming from other government policies, such as those for aggregates, transport and employment. Some of these developments lay beyond the statutory control of the local authority and some occurred as a result of decisions on appeal. In particular, chairmen commented adversely on the lack of advanced notice and the insufficient specifications they received as to the scale, location and duration of developments associated with government departments. This led to considerable annoyance. They were unhappy that having reluctantly refused local initiatives in order to maintain restraint, often over a number of years, decisions outside their control then undermined their efforts and their local credibility.

It is certainly the case that in most local authorities all significant planning applications were forwarded to parish councils and major amenity societies for comment. The MGB harbours numerous amenity societies and in only four authorities did they fail to take an active interest in green belt matters. In some places they had come together under umbrella organisations, such as the Surrey Amenities Association and the Standing Conference on the Buckinghamshire Countryside, acquiring formal representation on advisory committees set up by their county councils and charged with the management of the countryside. Many of the more substantial societies provided sensible and authoritative advice to planning committees and some committees had come to depend on their local knowledge and expertise (see Lowe & Goyder 1983). But just as the quality of advice varied so did the reactions of the committee chairmen to such consultations. Some felt that their independence of action was threatened and as elected representatives attempted to distance themselves from these 'undemocratic bodies'. Others welcomed the advice, but whatever their personal views all the chairmen agreed about one thing. The advice they received almost always counselled against change whether the change was being proposed by a body from outside the local authority (developer, gravel company, DOE, etc.) or by a local resident, and largely irrespective of either the local situation or the wider planning context in which the decision needed to be evaluated.

Urban restraint and green belt land-use objectives   With the growing concern over land-use and amenity in the MGB, confusion has crept into many statements by local authorities over the relationship between the urban restraint function of green belt and their other environmental objectives in the urban fringe. This confusion was confirmed by the range of replies received at interview. No consistent pattern of any kind emerged except to endorse once again the importance of amenity issues to the thinking of local authorities. The clearest position is that of separate but complementary objectives. This was best expressed by Kent CC Planning Department in its green belt study. This states that

> There is no logic in treating land of, for instance, good agricultural value or landscape importance differently inside the green belt than outside it and the green belt should not be used to bolster protective policies for such areas. Although it can thus be argued that the green belt and countryside policies should be distinct, because they are separately derived, it is not to say that they have no relationship; they are both concerned with open land and this complementary (rather than supplementary) purpose needs to be clearly stated in framing such policies (1976, pp. 19–20).

Kent CC Planning Department thus treats green belt restraint as a means of maintaining an area of open country in the west of the county for which other planning policies are then required. These tackle urban-fringe countryside management problems as they arise, and any zoning of the open country is based on these considerations and *not* by the limits of the MGB. Countryside policies can then be used to determine priorities between acceptable green belt land uses within the MGB where there is a conflict of interest. This approach avoids the need to defend the boundaries of the Green Belt on the basis of whether the land is, or is not, serving a green belt function in land-use or amenity terms. It also conforms to the view of DOE but is much more positive in its approach to the countryside.

  Linked to this approach is the further question of the extent to which the attainment of countryside policies in the urban fringe is dependent upon the additional protection from development afforded by green belt restraint. Many authorities believe green belt restraint to be essential in this regard and have little faith in the view of DOE that other rural restraint policies based on such designations as Area of Great Landscape Value, SSSI and Grades 1 and 2 agricultural land are sufficient to prevent development (e.g. see Surrey CC 1978). This may prove to be a false concern as it is only recently that positive steps have been taken to manage the countryside in areas of restraint. A realistic response to this question was received from Buckinghamshire CC Planning Department which noted that

> Policies to divert pressure from urban growth away from certain areas (e.g. the Green Belt) cannot prevent those elements of change which either

cannot be diverted because no suitable alternative site exists outside the restraint area (as in the case of the M25 Motorway around London) or result from the cessation of a use (such as the abandonment of farming and forestry). The designation of green belt and the current planning legislation will therefore influence only some of the changes occurring in an area but cannot freeze the status quo. There is a need for *complementary* policies of urban restraint and countryside management in the Green Belt. Unfortunately this conception is not widely recognised and the role of countryside management policy is only just beginning to be accepted (letter dated 15 November 1978).

Two objections can be raised to this approach. First, some authorities might try to use the principle of complementarity as one of supplementation in order to effect a no change policy. Secondly, how will conflicts be resolved where urban restraint and countryside policies, in the context of acceptable green belt land uses, do not coincide? (Elson 1979c). For example, should industrialised farm buildings or sports facilities be permitted in agricultural or recreational zones – the outcome of countryside policies – that happen to lie within the Green Belt? Would such developments not conflict with the requirements of 'openness' and 'rural character' laid down in Circular 42/55? Even if they do, it is suggested that in the light of the preceding argument countryside policies should prevail, permitting the local authority to act positively in both its plan-making and implementation roles. The notions of 'openness' and 'rural character' are vague, judgemental and relative over time; and they are usually employed negatively as an additional means of avoiding any further consideration of land-use change.

In its favour, the approach of complementarity minimises confusion. It retains a single objective for green belt (urban restraint) but recognises that the credibility of green belt will be reduced by the limited use and unattractive appearance of green belt land. It follows that local authorities should introduce urban-fringe environmental policies, and that DOE should insist that they do so through a clear statement of what local authorities are to include in local and structure plans in areas of green belt (see Standing Conference 1977a, para. 91).

The MGB: structure plan proposals and modifications

In the light of the views expressed, what proposals have county councils included in their structure plans for the future of the MGB? Before commenting on these and how the secretary of state responded to them, it is important to recognise that the whole of the 1970s and more was required for the preparation, examination in public and ministerial approval of the structure plans for Greater London and its surrounding counties. Following the reorganisation of the GLC in 1965, the Greater London Development Plan preceded the other structure

Table 2.2 Timing of the submission and approval of the OMA structure plans.

Structure plan	Submission to DOE	Examination in public	Final approval	Total period (months)
east Berkshire	June 1978	Feb.1979	April 1980	23
central Berkshire	June 1978	Feb. 1979	April 1980	23
Buckinghamshire	Nov. 1976	Sept. 1977	Dec. 1979	38
Essex	July 1979	March 1980	March 1982	33
Hertfordshire	April 1976	Dec. 1976	Sept. 1979	42
Kent	Sept. 1977	May 1978	April 1980	32
Surrey	April 1978	Nov. 1978	April 1980	25
mean	Nov. 1977	Aug. 1978	July 1980	31

plans, being finally approved in 1976 – having taken 10 years to prepare and agree (GLC 1976). A period of three years covers the submission dates of the plans for the OMA authorities, ranging from April 1976 for Hertfordshire CC to July 1979 for Essex CC. Three and a half years elapsed from the submission to DOE by Hertfordshire of its plan and its eventual approval, and the seven OMA county plans took an average of 31 months to complete their passage from submission to approval (see Table 2.2). This delay occurred during, and may have partly resulted from, a period of rapidly changing economic fortunes in the South East. Local government was also faced with reorganisation and a new plan-making system; and central government was forced to clarify its own policies for the region, including those for the MGB (see Ch. 1). In this respect it is unfortunate, to say the least, that central government did not make its own views known (DOE 1978a) until all the OMA counties were well advanced in their structure planning exercises and a full year after the panel of inquiry had completed its report on the *Hertfordshire Structure Plan* (Hertfordshire CC 1976).

All the OMA counties have argued for an increase in the size of the statutorily approved green belts within their authorities (see Fig. 2.1). In doing so they referred to the widespread support for the MGB elicited during their public participation exercises. The proposals of those counties producing their plans early affected the policies of neighbouring authorities and almost always with the effect of seeking an ever larger Green Belt. For example, the proposals of Surrey CC and Hertfordshire CC to extend the Green Belt to the whole of their counties led Cambridgeshire CC, Bedfordshire CC and West Sussex CC to seek approval for their own green belts. A local green belt around Luton in south Bedfordshire was eventually confirmed by the secretary of state (DOE 1980f) but a northward extension of the MGB to include Cambridge and a southward extension around Gatwick Airport have not been approved – an inevitable consequence of the modifications made by the secretary of state to the Hertfordshire CC and Surrey CC structure plans (see below, DOE 1979c, DOE 1980d).

The first observation on the county councils' proposals must be that they do not always adhere to the purpose of green belt as described in Circular 42/55. Justifications reflect local concerns as much as regional planning objectives, except where the latter can be used in support of local demands. For example, both Surrey CC and Hertfordshire CC note that the current plans for the region (SEJPT 1971, 1976) treat their counties largely as areas of restraint. To them it was logical to argue for the extension of the MGB to the whole of their areas as they continue to experience severe development pressures throughout their

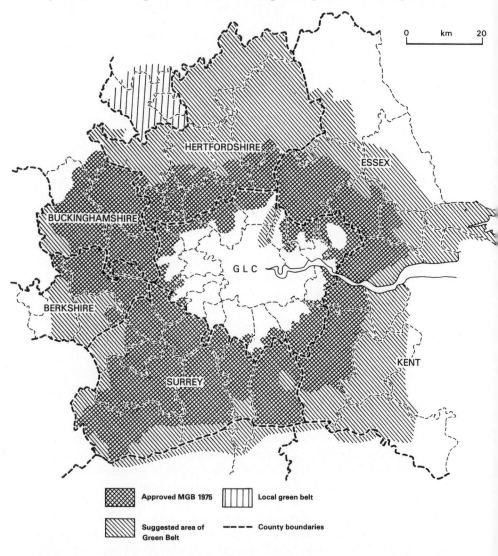

Figure 2.1 Area of the Metropolitan Green Belt as proposed in structure plans.

counties as a result of improved road and rail communications (Hertfordshire CC 1976, Surrey CC 1978). Berkshire CC made out a similar case for the whole of the eastern end of its county which was treated separately for structure planning purposes (Berkshire CC 1978a).

In the other counties it was more a matter of determining in general terms where to draw the outer boundary of the Green Belt, thereby establishing its width. The arguments made in support of particular proposals varied. For example, Buckinghamshire CC proposed to extend the MGB westwards in the south of the county to its border with Oxfordshire so as to provide additional protection to this part of the Chilterns AONB (Buckinghamshire CC 1976). Berkshire CC, on the other hand, was more concerned to stop the coalescence of free-standing towns, one possible result of development leap-frogging the MGB (Berkshire CC 1978b), and Kent CC argued along similar lines (Kent CC 1977). In the latter case the council argued that the MGB was a key element in regional strategy and as such should include almost all the area of green belt with interim status in the county (see Fig. 1.1). This would provide a broad band of firmly imposed restraint between London and the medium-scale growth area of Maidstone and the Medway towns. Hertfordshire's proposals prompted Essex CC to consider extending the Green Belt to their border with Cambridgeshire as well (Essex CC 1978). Essex CC eventually compromised on a boundary further south so as to include only the area of interim green belt in the expectation that Hertfordshire's proposal would not be approved. Moreover, extension to the Cambridgeshire border would have firmly embedded Stanstead Airport within the MGB, a proposal that the secretary of state was unlikely to endorse just prior to the public inquiry, commenced in September 1981, into its suitability as London's third international airport.

Central Berkshire posed other problems (Berkshire CC 1978b). The county council not only wished to confirm the area of interim green belt around Bracknell but also wished to move the boundary west to the edge of Reading, encompassing most of the district of Wokingham. The intention was to stop the development of a 'growth corridor' between London and Reading. The difficulty with this proposal was that the area between Reading, Wokingham and Farnham, including a part of north-east Hampshire and a strip of western Surrey as well as part of mid-Berkshire, had been identified in the regional strategy as one of substantial growth (SEJPT 1971). In anticipation of the objections that DOE was bound to raise, the county council argued that the region's housing needs had declined during the 1970s, maintaining that it would be premature to leave the area unprotected from urban growth until such time as the region's needs clearly warranted major development in the area. The county council recognised, however, that some development in the near future was inevitable and so four areas of white land (two on the edge of Bracknell, one at Owlsmoor and one near Wokingham) were omitted from the Green Belt. The county council undertook to review the green belt boundary quinquennially in the light of evolving needs and, in so doing, raised the issue of permanence of green belt boundaries in relation to both regional and local development needs. It also drew attention to the matter of which authority should define the boundary. Essex CC, Berkshire CC and Surrey CC originally proposed to draw up green belt subject plans (e.g. see Berkshire Planning Department 1979). Surrey CC and Hertfordshire CC as well as Berkshire CC (1978a) also indicated a preference for the idea of tight boundaries around towns which, if necessary, could be relaxed later in the light of evolving local needs.

Local needs policies have arisen in many areas of restraint. They represent an attempt to satisfy local demands for growth stemming from the natural increase of the existing population and its employment base while endeavouring to fend off metropolitan intrusion. It is an attractive concept to councillors trying to balance the conflicting claims of local businessmen with those of amenity groups (Healey *et al.* 1980, Gault 1981, pp. 114–23). Within the OMA this issue has been aired most fully in a green belt context in· the Buckinghamshire Structure Plan. The county council was concerned that its southern districts of Wycombe, Chiltern and Beaconsfield would not have enough land to meet local housing needs – never mind the needs of those who wished to move into the Chilterns but commute to the Heathrow, Hillingdon and Slough labour markets – without making incursions into the Green Belt. The seriousness of this issue is open to question given the very small rise in the populations of the Beaconsfield and Chiltern districts during the 1970s (OPCS 1982). Nevertheless, the planners were immediately confronted by a number of problems of how to effect a local needs policy.

There are three main areas of difficulty: how should local needs be defined? Who should define them and then allocate the necessary land for development? And can such a policy be implemented with the present planning powers? The problems of defining 'local' and, more especially, 'needs' are self-evident. Furthermore, definitions may well differ between counties and their constituent districts, and some counties, including Surrey, have sought to dictate the answers by requiring their districts to agree their figures with them. Elsewhere, as in Hertfordshire and Buckinghamshire, county development totals have been fixed centrally, although the districts have been allowed some latitude over determining their individual figures. This has left the districts with effective control over the drawing of green belt boundaries, and this is as central government intends. There have been several cases of disagreement between counties and districts such as those between Wycombe and Buckinghamshire CC, Basildon and Essex CC, and Tunbridge Wells and Kent CC. It has been agreed in each case that the district will define its boundary largely as it thinks fit. Finally, even where local needs totals are agreed, can the intent behind the policy be realised? With the repeal of the Community Land Act (DOE 1980c) local planning authorities have been left with few positive planning powers. How can the authority ensure that local people occupy those houses it gives permission to be built? Or even that houses of the right size and price are built to meet the needs and pockets of the local population? In practice, the local authority's powers are limited, but they can exert some influence. They can, for example, control housing density and can try to impose appropriate planning conditions on developers; but developers are not attracted by restrictive occupancy conditions and their legal status remains in doubt (DOE 1977e, 1978c; Elson et al. 1979).

Central government's response

A careful examination of the OMA structure plans reveals the central importance of green belt restraint, even if the Green Belt is not accorded much attention in some of the plans (e.g. Hertfordshire). Several counties, including Kent, Buckinghamshire and Hertfordshire, argue that green belt should only be regarded as a means to an end and therefore does not require much discussion in itself. Nevertheless they also maintain that other bases of restraint, such as amenity designations, will prove ineffective in controlling development in the countryside, and thus success in meeting many of their open space and resource policies, such as those relating to amenity corridors and agricultural priority areas (Hertfordshire CC 1976), are dependent on green belt. This implication that green belt is essential to the achievement of environmental aims has not been accepted by the secretary of state. He still argues that countryside policies should be implemented by other means. This is illustrated by his reasoning in refusing to accede to Buckinghamshire CC's wish to extend the MGB to its Oxfordshire border in the Chilterns AONB. He refuses to approve this proposal in full, saying that 'The very severe restrictions on development implicit in a Green Belt notation can only be justified over a limited area and to attempt to apply such a restriction over too wide an area, and where other policies would provide a more appropriate form of control, will inevitably weaken the value of any Green Belt as a special measure for restraining the outward spread of large built-up areas' (DOE 1979a, p. 13).

Throughout, successive secretaries of state have argued consistently that to restrain the outward growth of London there is no need for a green belt of more than 20–25 km width, except in special cases where it should be extended to prevent the coalescence of free-standing towns. The only exception is south-west Surrey where they have not been prepared to de-register green belt that has already been statutorily approved. The overall effect on the size and shape of the MGB is shown in Figure 2.2. The new MGB is significantly broader in Hertfordshire, Essex and Kent than it was in 1975 but little changed elsewhere. Hertfordshire and Surrey have not been permitted to extend restraint over the whole of their respective counties although the panel of inquiry had supported Hertfordshire CC in its report to the minister (DOE 1977c). The minister has, however, permitted green belt extensions along the A1 road to Stevenage and Hitchin and the A11 towards Bishop's Stortford, both in Hertfordshire, and to

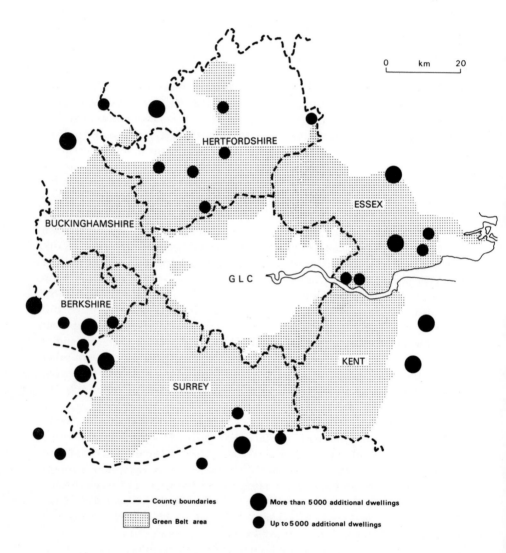

Figure 2.2 Area of the Metropolitan Green Belt in 1982 (as approved by the secretary of state) and closely located housing growth nodes (amended from Standing Conference 1981a, pp. 12, 15). (NB: the precise boundaries of the MGB are to be established in local plans.)

the north of Southend-on-Sea in Essex, where development pressures could result in urban sprawl along major lines of communication. The net effect is for the MGB to be extended by approximately 45% of its 1975 area to about 4300 km^2 instead of the 5800 km^2 requested by the counties.* The secretary of state has also (in areas of foreseeable local and regional needs) ruled against tight boundaries being drawn around settlements which are then progressively relaxed (see Elson 1980). He is not persuaded that 'loose' boundaries will lead to land speculation on the edges of expanding towns. Instead, he argues that

It is important for the future preservation of the Green Belt that prospective developers should be made aware of the precise boundaries beyond which further development to cater for the accepted needs of a settlement will not be available. Where current development needs and the growth levels now in the Plan (for Buckinghamshire) are less than the levels of development implicit in the acceptable long-term size of a settlement, the gap should be the subject of other restraint policies which can take account of shorter term considerations than are implicit in Green Belt policies. The detailed Green Belt boundaries to be determined in local plans should be established as a long-term planning feature and should not be subject to frequent review (DOE 1979a, p. 10).

As a result he did not approve the extension of green belt restraint to much of mid-Berkshire (DOE 1980g) or the far west of Surrey (DOE 1980d), which are designated as part of a growth area in the regional strategy, to the very south of Surrey and the area around Gatwick Airport (DOE 1980d, 1980h), and in the immediate vicinity of Stanstead Airport in Essex (DOE 1981b). In south Essex he has also insisted upon a more flexible use of restraint to accommodate growth in the districts of Thurrock and Basildon (ibid.). At the same time he has argued for more local independence for districts and the use of local rather than subject plans to define the inner boundary of the MGB. His basic position is clear from the reply he made to Hertfordshire's proposals. He says that the boundaries of the green belt around settlements contained within it should be 'Defined in local plans by reference to the limits of developments of those settlements which are acceptable to the authorities preparing the particular plans and not solely by reference to current development needs' (DOE 1979c, p. 4). The minister is thus putting much of the effective power over the implementation of green belt in the hands of districts and placing considerable faith in various other urban-fringe policies to ensure the orderly transfer of land from rural to urban uses in the 'gap' between the present edge of development and the new 'permanent' green belt boundaries.

The county councils have expressed their concern to DOE over this

---

* This latter figure does not take account of the extensions proposed by West Sussex CC, Cambridgeshire CC and Bedfordshire CC.

approach, especially as subject plans, following more recent advice from DOE, are no longer to be used as *statutory* tools to establish green belt boundaries. Even allowing for the fact that the counties are unhappy at a reduction in their planning powers *vis-à-vis* the districts, their worries can also be traced to two other sources. First, they are aware of the wide range of attitudes towards green belt among their district authorities, as reported here, and the difficulties this will create in maintaining a consistent approach to the implementation of restraint. Some districts take green belt issues seriously, developing local policies and plans (e.g. see Hillingdon LB 1973, 1977; Bexley LB nd, Countryside Commission 1981), but others have barely considered them at all. Secondly, they are also aware that only a proportion of local districts are preparing district-wide plans that will permit the complete definition of the green belt boundary. The new, extended MGB would require 62 districts and London boroughs to consider the boundary question, if coverage were to be comprehensive. But only 33 are producing, by one means or another, plans that would cover the whole of their areas, and not all of these will necessarily include the definition of the boundary as one of their main aims. Some additional *guidance* may be provided by subject plans in Berkshire and Essex, but only Hertfordshire and the GLC seem likely to achieve county-wide coverage. Furthermore, although most districts are now preparing plans for at least some parts of their areas – usually the major settlements – only one-third will have completed their plans by the end of 1981 and at current rates of progress perhaps as many as one-third will not be in operation until some time in 1983.

These trends suggest that the pattern of development proposed by the South East Joint Planning Team in their reports in 1971 and 1976 – a pattern based largely on an attempt to concentrate development in a few key locations – will in practice be watered down. Development is likely to be more dispersed and in much smaller individual quantities than anticipated in 1971 (Healey 1980). It remains to be seen what effect this may have on the MGB, as opposed to other areas of restraint in the region covered by amenity designations, but it can be seen from Figure 2.2 that in some places a significant amount of growth can be expected in and around the Green Belt over the next ten years. Following its joint study with the House-Builders Federation, Standing Conference antici-pates that over the period 1981–6 land sufficient for 53 000 houses will be made available in the green belt ring (districts predominantly in the MGB) or 22% of the total for the South East region (Standing Conference 1981b).

Summary

The new plan-making system may prove to have profound effects for green belts. The emphasis on policy formulation in structure plans has required structure-planning authorities to think carefully about the purpose of green belts from their own points of view, and they have not all come up with the same answers. It also means that many more local planning authorities are now involved. All three main tiers in planning, district or borough, county and DOE, with the notable absentee of the regional economic planning councils, have an interest in green belt restraint. But their perspectives, powers and responsibilities are different. These differences have been aggravated by the slow preparation and approval of structure plans, and districts are now preparing local plans in the light of changed economic circumstances and central government advice. They have also been encouraged to think independently by the devolution of planning powers to them, including primary responsibility for development control, the assessment of local development needs and the determination of green belt boundaries. This devolution will not lead to a reduction in the size of the MGB, far from it, but almost certainly to its amendment in the face of local wishes. Inconsistency in outlook and wide differences in practice from the views expressed in principle have emerged from the interviews in local authorities; and although few districts have yet to sort out what the relationship between local environmental and urban restraint objectives should be, considerable emphasis is clearly going to be placed on local amenity issues. These issues are picked up again in Chapter 4.

More generally, DOE officials maintain that central government can ensure a consistency of local authority approach through its approval of structure plans and the decisions it gives on planning applications at appeal. In support of this view it would point to the consistent outlook of successive secretaries of state over the width of the MGB and the continued emphasis placed on the pre-eminent importance of the urban restraint function of green belt. This ability to ensure consistency may well be impaired, however, by the failure of many districts to prepare district-wide plans within which green belt boundaries will be determined and the policies for green belt will be laid down, unless central government invokes its increased powers under Section 15A of the Local Government, Planning and Land Act 1980 to call in local plans with which it disagrees. Indeed, the whole prospect of a clearly defined regional strategy has been watered down in favour of accommodating local needs (see Fig. 2.2). Incursions into the Green Belt will undoubtedly be made around some towns as the economic recession passes but the pattern of incursions will more likely reflect a combination of local views and the secondary effects of other government programmes, such as the construction of the M25 motorway, than any preconceived plan.

With a few notable exceptions the clear resolve of most local authorities is to restrict development in and around the MGB to an absolute minimum and to demand that development over and above local needs be directed elsewhere. Their ability to date to achieve this, as recorded by the rate of growth of non-conforming land uses and the state of the land market in the MGB, forms the subject of Chapter 3.

3 The growth of non-conforming land uses in the MGB

Introduction

In Chapter 1 it was argued that development pressures could be expected to continue in and around the MGB during the present economic recession as central government is keen to create as many new jobs as possible, even if on occasion this may mean sacrificing broader planning and environmental objectives. The OMA contains one of the more buoyant regional economies in the UK and this particular economy can be expected to grow rapidly with any general improvement in national economic fortunes; and its growth will be encouraged by the building of the M25 motorway. Furthermore, at the end of Chapter 2, attention was drawn to the residential development pressures that the Green Belt might experience following the watering-down of the *Strategy for the South East* and its review (SEJPT 1970, 1976).

It is too early to say what the precise land-use effects of these developments will be but it is possible to gain some insights by examining the past performance of local authorities in implementing restraint. One measure of performance is the growth of non-conforming land uses, as defined in Circular 42/55, and this formed a key element in the earlier study of London's Green Belt by Thomas (Thomas 1970). The growth of non-conforming land uses and the processes that lie behind it thus form the focus of this chapter, with questions relating to the nature of conforming or acceptable land uses being examined in Chapter 4.

This chapter has three objectives. The first is to review the available evidence on the growth, and the spatial pattern of that growth, of non-conforming land uses. It is important to try to identify which non-conforming uses have grown most rapidly and to establish whether this is primarily the result of public or private initiative. To do this, the account employs a variety of sources and in particular the work of the GLC (1969), Thomas (1970), Standing Conference (1976) and DOE (1978d). The second, arguing that land-use change is only one indicator of the pressures leading to non-conforming uses, aims to examine the two key processes that underlie the implementation of restraint, namely the operation of the urban-fringe land market and the development control system. Evidence on these processes was collected as part of this study, calling on the experiences of local planning officers over development control decisions, district valuers over land market trends during the 1970s, and farmers of the loss, willing or otherwise, of some of their land to other uses. Drawing on some of the lessons gleaned earlier in the chapter, the third objective is to try to anticipate some of the local land-use and strategic implications for the MGB of the building of the M25 motorway which, when complete, will represent easily the largest single development in the Green Belt.

Green belt land use

Central government has always assumed that some development would occur in green belts. Green belt is a strategic planning instrument that must allow for local circumstances, and some development can always be justified as being in the national interest, some as essential in meeting local needs and some as unacceptable in the urban area. The debate between local authorities and central government has thus focused on what amount of change is acceptable to the local community (often very little) and yet lies within that deemed as eligible on strategic grounds by central government. Dispute between local and central government also arises as to what land uses are acceptable. Circular 42/55 defines just two categories. These are non-conforming uses, such as housing and industry, which in the normal run of events should be prohibited, and conforming uses including farmland, woodland and public open space which are often acceptable to all concerned. But other uses raise difficulties. Mineral extraction, for example, is a conforming use but is hardly of a rural character. Public utilities and major roads are non-conforming uses but essential to the functioning of modern urban societies. Their siting often lies beyond local planning control and they may become concentrated within green belts because of the impracticality of locating them in the urban area.

With these points in mind it is possible to examine a number of land-use studies conducted in the MGB. As will become apparent, the data sources employed vary from air photographs, to field surveys, to the annual census of the Ministry of Agriculture, Fisheries and Food, and comparing findings is hazardous. The best known study is that by Thomas (Thomas 1964, 1970). Working from air photographs taken in 1959 and checked by field survey in 1960, he defined 11 main land-use classes. Using a systematic sampling method based on line traverses, he established the proportions of the total area covered by each class. His study included a very large proportion of the MGB as well as an area he termed the 'green belt zone', or all land extending for 16 km beyond the inner boundary of the Green Belt whether it was designated as green belt or not. Comparative analysis of this zone with the MGB was felt to be important as it gave a better impression of the urban-fringe environment as a whole. As Thomas pointed out (1970, p. 123) the boundary of the Green Belt had not been drawn in a consistent fashion by local authorities in their original development plans. Some counties had included small, scattered developments within the MGB whereas others had excluded them and this meant that in land-use terms the Green Belt was something of an arbitrary zone.

Thomas' findings are summarised in Table 3.1. Land-use classes 1–5 were

Table 3.1 Land use in the Metropolitan Green Belt and green belt zone, 1960 (per cent of development plan green belt, as approved).

Land use	MGB	Green belt zone
1 residential and commercial	6.2	14.3
2 manufacturing	0.2	0.7
3 extractive	1.8	1.6
4 transport	1.5	2.1
5 public services	0.9	1.2
6 institutions standing in extensive grounds	1.1	1.4
7 woodland	11.8	10.3
8 water	0.6	0.5
9 recreational	6.2	5.4
10 agricultural	69.5	62.3
11 unused	0.2	0.2

Source: Thomas (1970, Tables II & III, pp. 130–3).

categorised by him as non-conforming, 6–11 as conforming. Conforming land uses accounted for 89.5% (after rounding) of the area of the MGB and 80.1% of the green belt zone. Agriculture was easily the most important single land use, covering 69.5% of the MGB. The residential and commercial category was significantly larger in the green belt zone than in the MGB (14.3% as opposed to 6.2%) as it included within it many substantial urban centres embedded within the Green Belt. Thomas also broke down his results by quadrant (NW, NE, SE, SW) for both the Green Belt and the green belt zone. These revealed some interesting differences but did not contradict the basic pattern, and his analysis was too coarse to disclose local variations that might affect day-to-day policy formulation at district level.

At a strategic scale it was possible to draw some comfort from these findings as most green belt land supported a conforming use, and this seemed to be confirmed by Thomas' analysis of change in the area of housing and industrial land in the MGB between 1955 and 1960. This revealed an increase of only 700 ha, or 0.3% of the MGB, in the area of these uses over the five-year period and much of this development had taken place on the edges of existing settlements. These uses had, however, expanded rather more rapidly in the green belt zone and this expansion was regarded as an inevitable consequence of green belt restraint increasing the demand for development on land adjacent to the MGB. It also fuelled the concern that the Green Belt itself would come under increasing pressure unless growth was diverted to other parts of the region.

In response to growing demands from central government for the release of more housing land in the region (MHLG 1963), Standing Conference undertook a survey of land use in the MGB in 1963 – a survey that was repeated in 1974 (Standing Conference 1976). Unlike Thomas' study it was not based on evidence derived from air photographs but from data compiled by county planning authorities. Comparisons between the findings of Standing Confer-

Table 3.2 Land use in the Metropolitan Green Belt: a comparison of Thomas' and Standing Conference's findings.

Land-use category	Thomas (1959) ha	Thomas (1959) %	Standing Conference data					
			Standing Conference (1963) ha	Standing Conference (1963) %	Standing Conference (1974) ha	Standing Conference (1974) %	net change 1963–74 (ha)	% change 1963–74	change as % of total area
(i) Villages, groups of houses and land where other surface development predominates	—	7.9	8 000	3.5	9 050	3.9	+1 050	+13.1	+0.5
(ii) airfields, War Department land, reservoirs and waterworks, mineral workings, tips and other land uses of a predominantly open character	—	3.2	11 100	4.8	10 850	4.7	−250	−2.3	−0.1
(iii) institutions in extensive grounds, cemeteries, playing fields and other land uses appropriate to the Green Belt	—	3.5	16 950	7.4	17 750	7.7	+800	+4.7	+0.3
(iv) public open space	—	3.9	17 300	7.5	18 400	8.0	+1 100	+6.4	+0.5
(v) remainder, mainly agricultural land and woodland	—	81.5	176 250	76.8	173 500	75.6	−2 750	−1.6	−1.2
Total	—	100.0	229 550	100.0	229 550	100.0	—	—	—

Sources: Thomas (1970, Table IV, p. 139), Standing Conference (1976, Tables 2 & 3, pp. 9 & 13). Decimals correct to the first place. The original imperial measures have been metricated and rounded to the nearest 50 ha.

ence and those of Thomas need to be treated with caution, especially as there were other important differences in approach. For example, Standing Conference did not use the same land-use classification as Thomas although Thomas has attempted to recast his classes to meet those of Standing Conference (Thomas 1970, pp. 137–42). Standing Conference also covered the *whole* of the Green Belt, and used a slightly different definition of the inner boundary to Thomas. Most importantly it ignored land-use blocks of less than 2 ha in extent. Direct comparisons can be made between Standing Conference's two surveys as the same procedures were employed on both occasions. The results are shown in Table 3.2.

The land-use categories used by Standing Conference relate, wherever possible, to those outlined in Circular 42/55. As a result, their lack of specificity must have presented problems of interpretation to the seven county councils which drew up their figures separately. Overall, the results were broadly in line with those of Thomas, but there were important differences. In particular, the area in categories (iii) and (iv) were double those of Thomas, whereas 'settlement' (category (i)) covered only half the area reported by him. The latter difference is almost certainly explained by Standing Conference's failure to record land-use blocks of less than 2 ha. This would have had the effect of excluding much of the scattered rural settlement that predated the creation of the Green Belt. Thomas' figure must be preferred in this case. Again, viewed in its totality, the amount of land-use change recorded by Standing Conference between 1963 and 1974 was quite modest. There was some increase in the amount of settlement and the number of institutions in extensive grounds, as well as an encouraging gain in the amount of public open space, and these uses appear to have gained ground at the expense of farmland. The area under settlement has risen by 13.1% but remained at less that 4% of the MGB area. At face value, these figures indicated that green belt restraint had been largely successful in minimising urban growth, but Standing Conference cautioned

Table 3.3   Developed Areas in 1969 within the 1975 approved MGB.

County	Approved MGB (1975) (ha)	1969 Developed Areas in 1975 MGB (ha)	1969 Developed Areas as % of 1975 MGB
Kent	25 184.5	2 610.9	10.37
Surrey	108 162.3	18 151.1	16.78
Berkshire	20 069.9	3 449.1	17.19
Buckinghamshire	46 841.0	4 676.3	9.98
Hertfordshire	35 749.7	5 990.5	16.76
Essex	41 481.6	6 582.9	15.87
GLC	33 762.0	13 098.5	38.80
MGB	311 251.0	54 559.4	17.53

Source: DOE (1978d, Table E 1, App. E).

that its use of a 2 ha cut-off point could have led to an underestimate of the rate of growth of non-conforming uses, perhaps by as much as 50% (Standing Conference 1976, p. 15).

Green belt Developed Areas

What neither of these surveys do is to give a detailed spatial picture of how the land-use pattern is changing. Some relevant evidence is provided by DOE as part of its survey of Developed Areas in England and Wales (DOE 1978d). Using air photographs for 1969, all continuous Developed Areas of more than 5 ha in extent were recorded and their areas measured. Included in the Developed Area category were five land uses – residential, industrial and commercial, public utilities and services, transport, and 'urban' open space. The extent of these Developed Areas in 1969 was matched against the area of the MGB of 1975, and the results are shown in Table 3.3. The percentage of Green Belt so classified ranges from less than 10% in Buckinghamshire to nearly 40% in the GLC around a mean value of 17.5%.

Two general points need to be made about these figures. First, as only discrete Developed Areas of 5 ha or more are included, then the figures understate the true extent of Developed Areas. Secondly, Developed Areas *cannot* be equated with non-conforming green belt land uses as they include open space, reservoirs and hospitals, as well as well recognised non-conforming uses. These figures therefore overstate the amount of land in non-conforming uses and there is no way of knowing whether this overstatement cancels out the understatement referred to previously. Nevertheless, the distribution of Developed Areas can be regarded as a useful indicator of the general appearance and urbanisation of the MGB. The distribution of such areas is shown in Figure 3.1. The London boroughs in particular have a high proportion of Developed Areas and in some

Table 3.4 Net increase in Developed Areas between 1947 and 1969 in the approved MGB.

County	Increase in Developed Areas 1947–69 in 1975 MGB (ha)	Increase as % of 1975 MGB
Kent	701.1	2.78
Surrey	1932.7	1.79
Berkshire	616.2	3.07
Buckinghamshire	1006.9	2.15
Hertfordshire	1101.0	3.08
Essex	914.1	2.20
GLC	1540.3	4.56
MGB	7812.2	2.51

Source: DOE (1978d, Table E 2, App. E).

it reaches 100%, whereas in the outer Green Belt the proportion is usually less than 10%. The pattern emphasises the great differences that exist in the nature of the Green Belt between its inner and outer halves.

The same study went on to describe change in the extent of Developed Areas between 1947 and 1969 (see Table 3.4), but for the reasons listed above the change cannot be equated directly with effectiveness in maintaining green belt

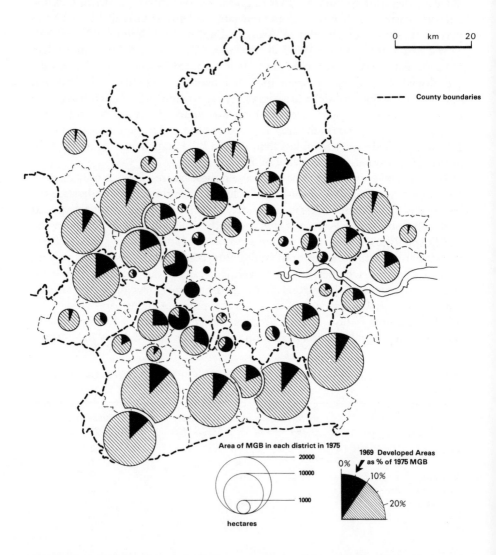

Figure 3.1   Developed Areas in 1969 as a percentage of the 1975 Green Belt. (Statistical source: DOE 1978d.)

restraint, especially as the Green Belt's boundaries were also altered during this period. Nevertheless a valuable, if general, picture of the rate of 'urbanisation' of the MGB is discernible from these figures. Overall, as with the surveys of Thomas and Standing Conference, a slow rate of change is indicated. Although no local authority recorded a net decrease in the extent of its Developed Area, the total net increase (7812 ha) is only equivalent to 2.5% of the MGB area

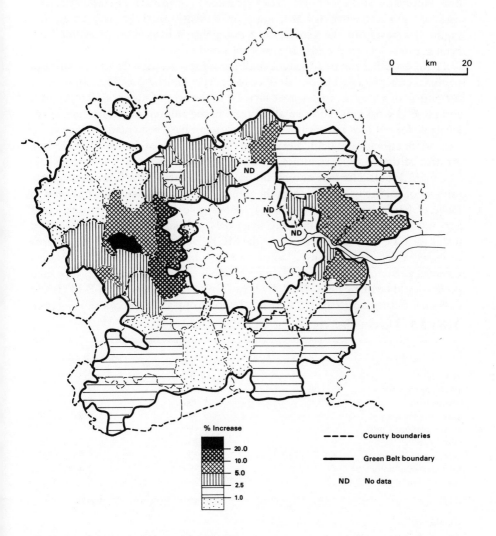

Figure 3.2 Net increase in Developed Areas between 1947 and 1969 in the 1975 Green Belt. (Statistical source: DOE 1978d.)

in 1975. Again, two observations need to be made. First, the inclusion in the figures of discrete Developed Areas only when they exceeded 5 ha in extent can either exaggerate or underestimate the true amount of change. On the one hand, all discrete areas of less than 5 ha were not recorded but on the other any addition sufficient to bring an area in existence in 1947 up to 5 ha by 1969 led to its inclusion in full in the 1969 figures. Secondly, despite the small increase overall, some local authorities recorded sizeable gains, most notably Slough, Hillingdon, Hounslow and Spelthorne. The expansion of residential and industrial land uses and mineral workings all feature prominently in these authorities, and Figure 3.2 bears out the general contention that urbanisation pressures have been greatest just to the east and west of London.

To these studies can be added the findings of more restricted surveys, surveys confined either to a part of the MGB or to a particular land use. They all support the notion of a slow but persistent increase in the area of non-conforming uses and mineral workings, and a small increase in the amount of public open space available for outdoor recreational use. These gains have been made largely at the expense of agricultural land. Yet even in the inner parts of the MGB, including the area of the GLC, agriculture remains the predominant land use (see Table 3.5, GLC 1969). The loss of agricultural land has also been documented in a number of studies using data from the annual Agricultural Census. The *Report of studies of the Greater London Plan* (ibid.), for example, included an examination of agricultural change within the GLC *as a whole*, although over 93% of farmland inside the GLC boundary was also in the MGB. Between 1955 and 1966 the area of *improved* farmland fell by 2450 ha to 19850 ha, a decline of 11% that also reflected an increase in the area of rough grazings (see Thomson 1981). One final point should be made here. Work by Low (Low 1973, Hillingdon LB 1973) and Coleman (Coleman 1976, 1978; SEJPT Land Group 1976, pp. 45–60) suggests

Table 3.5 Uses of open land in the GLC Green Belt[1], 1966.

Land use	Area (ha)	% total area
farming	19 100	62.3
public open space	4 550	14.8
vacant land	1 900	6.2
private open space	2 800	9.1
school playing fields	450	1.5
allotments	200	0.7
cemeteries/crematoria	200	0.7
nurseries/smallholdings	750	2.4
mineral workings	700	2.3
total	30 650	100.0
all other uses	6 150	—

Source: GLC land use survey – GLC (1969, Table 5.1, p. 120). Original imperial measures metricated and rounded to nearest 50 ha. Decimals correct to the first place.

[1]As approved in the initial development plan.

that farmland losses have been greater than the increase in the area of urban land. Land, they argue, has been allowed to go to waste, scrub or other unproductive uses following mineral working or while awaiting planning permission for urban development (see Ch. 6).

Some aspects of the development process in the MGB

The growth of non-conforming land uses as measured by land-use statistics is only one indicator of urban development pressures and a fuller understanding of the situation can only be acquired by taking a closer look at the process of development itself. Two matters are examined here. These are the behaviour of landowners on the urban edge in the MGB and the responses of local and central government planners to planning applications for the development of green belt land.

Landowners and the urban-fringe land market Very little is known about the role of landowners in the development process in Britain despite the efforts of researchers (e.g. see Drewett 1973, Bather 1976, Goodchild 1978). Our ignorance stems largely from the absence of a publicly available land register recording beneficial interests in land and a general reluctance on the part of either landowners or developers to discuss specific cases. But before some of the evidence collected for this study is examined it is necessary to explain why landowners in the MGB are regularly tempted to seek planning permission in an area where restraint generally has been firmly imposed.

Ever since the return to office of the Conservative party in 1951, the positive planning and land market powers placed in the hands of local authorities by the Town and Country Planning Act 1947 have been steadily weakened, even allowing for short-term reversals of policy by subsequent Labour administrations. The reversion to a free market in development land in the 1950s, in which the owner was able to retain a significant capital gain from obtaining planning permission and for bringing his land forward for development, strengthened the hands of private developers and landowners (for discussion see McKay & Cox 1979, Lichfield & Darin-Drabkin 1980). Indeed local authorities became largely dependent upon landowners and developers for the execution of their development plans even during the period of faltering operation of the Community Land Act between 1975 and 1979 (Barrett *et al*. 1978, Barrett & Whitting 1980). For the landowner the incentive to bring land forward lay in the size of the capital gain, net of tax, that he realised from selling his land with, or with the clear prospect of obtaining, planning permission. Likewise for many private developers the primary stimuli have been the profit made from building and selling homes *and* the capital gain they could also expect to derive, perhaps in conjunction with the landowner, from the speculative purchase of an option in, or even the freehold to, undeveloped land for which they then sought

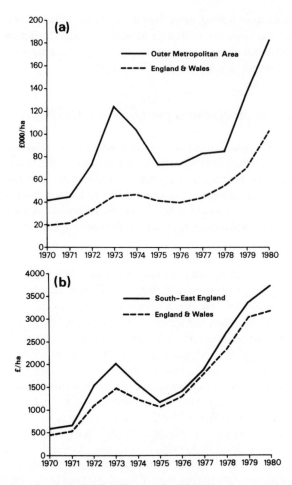

Figure 3.3 Development land and agricultural land prices, 1970–80: (a) residential development land; (b) agricultural land. (Statistical sources: Housing and Construction Statistics, DOE; MAFF–Inland Revenue Agricultural Land Price Series.)

planning permission. Public sector purchasers have been in a different position. They have been required to pay the full market price for the land, including any element of 'hope' value, and this has on occasion restricted their ability to buy on the open market. Nevertheless, in anticipation of future needs some public utilities have acquired quite substantial areas of urban-fringe land although under Section 10 of the Local Government, Planning and Land Act 1980 they are now required to disclose for the purposes of sale those areas of land that are under-used and surplus to their foreseeable requirements (DOE 1980c).

The land market in the urban fringe is complicated. There are numerous competitors for land and there is a complex and fragmented pattern of land ownership and occupation. Owners have widely varying motives and ways of assessing the current value of their properties. They have a wide range of opportunities not only to develop new kinds of enterprise on their own account but also to relinquish all or some of their interests in land to others with very different objectives. However tightly restraint is imposed in the urban fringe, some land will always be released for development and owners will always harbour the 'hope' that planning permission can be obtained for their land. The effect of green belt restraint is to reduce the chance of their being successful, but not to eliminate it. 'Hope' becomes highly concentrated in space, falling largely upon those serviced properties adjacent to the urban edge. The current use of land, therefore, is not always indicative of either its market value or the intentions of its owner. Some owners make their intentions clear, speculating against the planning system by deliberately running-down the use of the land, and although this does not guarantee by any means the success of their planning applications, applications relating to well kept land are even less likely to be successful.

One way of demonstrating the existence of 'hope' value and the scale of capital gain that can accrue to owners is to compare land prices in the agricultural and development land markets (see Fig. 3.3, Neuburger & Nicol 1976). These show that residential development land prices in the OMA were much higher than in the country as a whole during the 1970s and that agricultural land prices in south-east England were also higher than the national average. Regional price movements in both markets paralleled national trends. Most striking of all, however, was the very substantial difference in price of agricultural and residential development land. Development land prices in the OMA regularly exceeded £70000 per hectare whereas those for farmland were closer to £2000 per hectare until the end of the decade. To obtain even more precise information for the MGB than was available in published statistics, valuations for typical farmland and residential development land transactions were provided by district valuers responsible for areas around London. The results are in Table 3.6 (see Appendix for details of procedure). These show that an even larger gain could be realised by owners of land in the MGB than in the OMA generally and reveal the immense fluctuations in value that occurred during the decade.

By national standards these figures are extreme but the sheer size of the capital gain generally had become a political embarrassment to central government by the mid-1960s. Attempts to tax the gain away began in 1965 with the

Table 3.6 Agricultural and residential development land values in the MGB, 1969–77 (£/ha).

	1969	1971	1973	1975	1977
agricultural land	703	742	2 169	1 574	2 256
residential development land	56 680	70 650	171 200	83 170	115 530

Source: District valuers' survey. Table based on valuations of 'standard' properties (see App.) and not actual sales information. The figures should be treated as *illustrative* of general price levels at the dates shown.

introduction of a Capital Gains Tax (CGT). Since then changes in capital taxation have been frequent (see Turner 1977) and only their key features are outlined here. Broadly, between 1965 and the end of 1973, CGT was charged at 30% on gains in capital values since 1965, although this could be 'rolled-over' by owners of land provided they repurchased similar property, that is they replaced their 'business assets', within a specified period of the sale. By this means payment of CGT was deferred until the assets were sold and not replaced. To counteract this push effect on land prices a Development Gains Tax (DGT) was introduced in December 1973 to operate alongside CGT. The rules applying to DGT were complicated but overall the tax rate was not necessarily a great deal higher than under CGT alone. So in 1976 a Development Land Tax (DLT) was introduced to replace DGT with a marginal rate of 66.6% on the first £150 000 of gain and 80% thereafter. These rates were reduced to a standard 60% in 1979. It had been the Labour government's intention steadily to raise the rate of DLT to 100% under the terms of the Community Land Act 1975 (see DOE 1974), leaving the vendor with only the existing use value of the land, but this legislation was repealed in 1980 with DLT standing at 60% (DOE 1980c). Given the enormous gain if planning permission is granted, a tax rate of 60% leaves the vendor with a handsome post-tax profit and sufficient incentive to seek planning permission. He risks nothing unless he decides to run down his existing rural business.

Contacts between owners and developers Acquiring planning permission for residential development in the MGB is difficult. Developers often work in concert with landowners over planning applications as they have the necessary resources and planning expertise to fight public inquiries, which is where most major applications end up. Some developers act independently and buy the freehold to land, but purchase is risky. It requires the outlay of considerable monies in advance, and it has become a less favoured means of bringing land forward in green belts since the collapse of the property boom in 1974. The time taken to process controversial planning applications has lengthened and interest rates have risen, and together these factors have significantly increased the costs of holding land. At the same time landowners have become better informed about the development process and are less willing to sell their land in advance to developers. The main outcome of these separate trends is that many developers now take out options on sites or draw up conditional contracts with their owners. This establishes a common interest between the parties and one that only requires the developer to part with significant sums of money once planning permission has been obtained – even if the owner then captures a significant part of the speculative, capital gain.

These circumstances would suggest that in the urban fringe developers and private landowners are in frequent contact with each other, and in order to ascertain whether this was so a series of questions concerning the development of their land was put to the 185 farmers who were interviewed in three separate

Table 3.7 Sales of farmland for non-agricultural uses, 1970–77.

	No. of sales	Area (ha)
total	27	370
Purchaser		
Public	22	276
Private	5	94
New use		
reservoirs	3	94
roads	14	137
housing	3	12
recreation	4	56
mineral extraction	3	71

Source: survey of green belt farmers.

areas of the MGB (see Appendix). Of these, 37 *admitted* to having lost land to other uses between 1970 and 1977 but only 27 were prepared to give details (see Table 3.7).★ These 27 had lost a total of 370 ha or about 5% of the total area of their farms. Although the sample is small, and therefore too much should not be read into the figures, it is interesting to note that little land was sold for housing, much less than went for mineral extraction, recreational use, reservoirs or roads. Public bodies acquired 75% of the land and these regularly served, or threatened to serve, Compulsory Purchase Orders (see Blair 1980).

Occupiers were asked how frequently they were approached by developers to sell their property, or to enter into an agreement with them to develop their land. Many occupiers received numerous, informal approaches by letter each year. These kinds of approach are omitted here and only those discussions which led to specific proposals from the developer are included. Even so, 78 received proposals between 1970 and 1977. Only 31 of these were prepared to disclose details and for them the total area under consideration amounted to 629 ha. If they are representative of the 78, then an area of 1500–1600 ha must have been subject to various firm proposals in this eight-year period. This is equivalent to about 10% of the *total* area of all 185 farms and to about 75% of the land in fields immediately adjacent to existing residential development (see p. 123). Furthermore, 49 (out of 122★) owners of land had sought planning permission on their own account. Most of their applications were for smaller, less complicated permissions than those prepared by developers. Most were for housing only and can be regarded as naïve in a green belt context where an

★ Almost all the farmers were prepared to indicate whether sales had taken place but some refused to give details. Some tenants pointed out that they were not well informed as it was their landlords who were approached by developers. Only 122 out of the 185 farmers owned any part of their land and only 66 owned all of it (see Ch. 6) and the figures must be seen as *minimum* estimates. Not all the farmers occupied land on the urban edge.

offer of some form of planning gain by the applicant has become accepted practice.

Many of the deals discussed between landowners and developers were substantial, involving complex, multiple-use proposals primarily for housing, sport and recreation, and mineral extraction. But as with so much speculative activity, much was discussed and proposed but little came to fruition. In many cases one or other party withdrew after the initial negotiations and on other occasions proposals failed to get planning permission. Nevertheless it would seem that most, if not all, owner-occupiers with land on the immediate urban edge have *seriously* considered its development potential and a significant proportion have submitted planning applications. Yet few have been successful and development by public sector agencies has been much more extensive than that initiated privately. These data support those who say that green belt restraint has been firmly imposed, at least for private sector developments, but does not support those, including DOE officials, who maintain that restraint is now accepted and that owners and developers 'behave accordingly'.

Development control decisions   Development control decisions are one indicator of the success planners have in maintaining restraint policies, and success has not always been apparent (Gregory 1970, JURUE 1977, Blacksell & Gilg 1981). The effectiveness of development control is discussed further in Chapter 5, but some idea of the kinds of difficult decision that regularly confront local planning commitees can be gained from the information returned by local planning officers as part of this study. It was impossible to monitor development control decisions for the whole MGB and so officers were asked to send, with their comments, details on a small number of decisions that had raised matters of *principle*. Details of 86 decisions, taken in 24 separate authorities between 1974 and 1977, were returned.

Some of the basic characteristics of the applications are shown in Tables 3.8

Table 3.8   Planning applications: number and area by size of site.

Size (ha)	No.	Total area (ha)
Extension/single dwelling	30	—
< 1.0	9	3.6
1.0– 1.9	3	4.6
2.0– 3.9	5	12.9
4.0– 7.9	8	51.3
8.0–19.9	6	82.6
> 19.9	9	356.4[1]
inadequate data	16	—
total	86	511.4

Source: survey of planning officers.

[1] Only 119.9 ha out of 356.4 ha were to be developed under the planning applications submitted.

Table 3.9 Planning applications: existing and proposed uses.

Existing uses	Proposed uses							Total
	residential	recrea-tional[4]	commercial	industrial	woodland	agricultural	mineral extraction	
residential[1]	18	1	2	—	—	—	—	21
agricultural[2]	28	5	2	1	—	2	1	39
woodland	4	1	—	—	1	—	—	6
mineral land[3]	3	2	—	3	—	—	—	8
recreational	1	2	—	1	—	—	—	4
industrial	—	—	1	—	—	—	—	1
commercial	—	—	1	—	—	—	—	1
vacant	14	—	—	—	—	—	—	15
total	69	11	6	5	1	2	1	95[5]

Source: survey of planning officers.
1   Includes gardens.
2   Includes grazing and nursery land.
3   Extraction completed in all cases.
4   Includes public open space.
5   Sums to 95 as some of the applications refer to more than one existing and/or proposed use.

and 3.9. The information contained in Table 3.8 reveals that a significant number were for large sites, or precisely those applications that raise strategic as well as local issues. The fact that only one-third of the area of the largest category of sites was to be developed indicates the complex nature of most large proposals and the perceived need on the part of the applicant to include in them some element of planning gain, usually in the form of recreational open space. The large number of decisions concerning *single* buildings, yet raising such matters of principle as agricultural occupancy conditions, reflects the rigorous approach adopted by local authorities towards them. Decisions concerning residential development predominate (Table 3.9) both in terms of the development of vacant agricultural land and in the redevelopment of land already in residential use. In the 84 cases where permission was refused, or not given by the local authority within the statutory time period, 82 went to appeal. Of these 23 were successful including one case where the DOE's inspector was overruled by the secretary of state in favour of the applicant.

DOE's role in land releases   The high percentage of applications that went to appeal and the fact that one-quarter of these were successful at this stage is not indicative of development control in general in the MGB. These were hand-picked decisions relating to matters of principle. Nevertheless, the issue of the release of green belt land on appeal by the secretary of state, or at his behest following amendments to central government policy towards green belt, and against the wishes of local authorities, is one of long standing. The period of greatest tension occurred in the early- and mid-1970s and followed the publication of two circulars (102/72 & 122/73), both entitled *Land availability for housing* (DOE 1972a, 1973c). These emphasised the need to bring forward more land to meet London's housing needs and were succeeded by a white paper, *Widening the choice: the next steps in housing*, in which central government requested the release of 800 ha of green belt land (DOE 1973b), otherwise known as the '2000 acres exercise'.

These central government initiatives happened to coincide with a particularly frantic period in the development land market (see Fig. 3.3) and, in the opinions of many local planning officers, contributed to the release of several sizeable blocks of green belt land, which seriously undermined restraint at a local level. DOE officials do not accept this argument and maintain that the effects of these initiatives have been exaggerated. It is difficult to obtain reliable data to support either of these claims and again it seems to be a matter of interpretation. Nevertheless, Standing Conference felt sufficiently aggrieved about land releases in the Green Belt to collate the records of its member authorities for the period 1971–4 (see Table 3.10). These show that only a small amount of land in the MGB itself (386 ha) was released for housing, but infilling in and around the MGB was continuing (1506 ha) and rather more house building (2205 ha) occurred in areas of green belt with only interim status.* The figures endorse

* These figures relate to *site* area and not to the area of *houses* requested.

Table 3.10 Residential planning permissions, 1971–4.

	Within the origin- ally approved green belt ring (ha)	Withing the extended or proposed extended green belt ring (ha)
on land covered by green belt notation	386	1086
on land without green belt notation	1506	1119

Source: based on Standing Conference (1976, Table 1, p.5).
Total area approved for housing in the South East outside Greater London during the period was approximately 16 200 ha.

Thomas' experience that the 'green belt zone' was becoming urbanised much faster than the approved MGB (Thomas 1970).

Subsequently, Standing Conference turned its attention to land released on appeal by the secretary of state (Standing Conference 1977a). This followed the assurance given to Standing Conference by the minister that he would in future support local authorities in their efforts to resist encroachment into the Green Belt once the 800 ha had been released for housing under the terms of the white paper (DOE 1973b). Standing Conference continued its monitoring until December 1976 to ensure the minister kept to his word (Table 3.11). On this evidence, at no time could applicants expect to be given permission on appeal. Percentage success rates did fall, however, in 1975 and 1976. In the case of number of appeals it fell from 15.9% to 8.3% and, as a proportion of the area requested, it declined from 22.9% to 3.2%.

It was, however, the specific direction that 800 ha of green belt land be released for housing that caused the greatest stir. Local authorities were asked by central government to find the land and this allowed local discretion and preference to guide the decisions as to which land to release. Although this kept DOE's hands clean from the politically sensitive task of actually identifying the land and made the whole exercise marginally more acceptable to the local authorities, it can be asked where, if DOE insists on seeing green belt as a strategic planning tool, was central government's strategic guidance on which

Table 3.11 Housing appeal decisions in the Green Belt, 1973–6[1].

	April 1973–December 1974		January 1975–December 1976	
	no.	area(ha)	no.	area(ha)
appeals allowed	54	346	15	49
appeals dismissed	286	1163	165	1466

Source: Standing Conference (1977a, p.28).
[1] Included are sites in the MGB and in other areas of interim green belt.
Figures exclude single dwellings and sites of less than 0.4 ha.

Table 3.12   State of development of land identified under the '2000 acres exercise'.

Land identified	Area (ha)	State of development (ha)			
		fully developed	in progress	PP granted (inc. appeal)	no progress (PP lapsed etc.)
released on appeal during search period	299	134	121	—	44
put at risk by appeal decisions	207	8	—	49	150
further identified by local authorities	386	72	28	83	203
total	892	214	149	132	397

Source: based on Standing Conference (1979d).

parts of the MGB were best suited to contribute to the 800 ha? Moreover, in these circumstances could DOE ensure that the land identified was actually brought forward by this exercise? DOE has not chosen to monitor the outcome and it was Standing Conference (1979d) which produced evidence on the progress of the exercise in response to a question in the House of Commons. Standing Conference claimed that nearly 900 ha of building land had been identified (Table 3.12). Of this, 299 ha had been released on *appeal* during the search period, that is, it did not contribute to a *net* gain in the amount of housing land. On most of this land, development was either completed or being executed by 1979. Much less progress had been made on the remaining area and, indeed, none at all on 45% of it. This general state of affairs was endorsed by developers who maintained when interviewed, no doubt correctly, that many local authorities never intended to meet the spirit of the white paper. Rather more important, however, is the fact that by the time the land was identified (after 1974) the property boom had collapsed and most developers were more interested in selling than buying land. More recent evidence culled from the structure plan monitoring reports of various counties suggests that DOE has returned to a position of firm support for green belt restraint (Surrey CC 1981, Hertfordshire CC 1981).

The effects of the white paper seem to have been a few additional releases of land on appeal, contributing minimally to the housing land needs of Londoners, and to a legacy of mistrust among local authorities towards central government and its long-term intentions for the Green Belt. Central government has sought to allay this mistrust by reducing the amount of green belt land it has released on appeal in recent years and in the event the concern expressed by local authorities over this issue seems in retrospect to have been exaggerated. On the other hand, local authorities could argue that the limited outcome of the exercise was the result of their vocal objections, their ability to drag their feet over identifying land for release and the sheer financial inability of the construction industry to take advantage of the situation at the time. In other words, this might not have been the result under other more favourable economic circumstances. The whole exercise is an intriguing example of central–local government relations and an illustration of the powers held by each party. The ability of local authorities to play for time and wait for central government's attention to be diverted elsewhere (or for the state of the economy to worsen in this case) is especially illuminating. In other situations where central government actually carries out the development process itself, as in the case of the construction of the M25 motorway, the long-term outcome may prove to be very different and it is to this matter that the chapter now turns.

Construction of the M25 motorway

Evidence has already been provided from a variety of sources – from interviews with local planning officers, local councillors and farmers for example – which suggests that with a few exceptions local authorities will continue, if they can, to release as little green belt land as possible, usually just enough to meet local housing needs if these cannot be accommodated elsewhere. The result is that most of the successful initiatives that have led to non–conforming land uses have occurred on the edges of towns, or in Thomas' 'green belt zone', most of which has now been incorporated into the statutory Green Belt following the approval of structure plans, and most of these initiatives have stemmed directly or indirectly from central government. Central government agencies have built reservoirs and roads and provided new public utilities; central government has from time to time demanded the release of green belt land for housing; and the DOE's inspectorate, working to guidelines contained in the department's white papers and circulars, have recommended the release of green belt land on appeal.

The M25 motorway introduces a different but not wholly novel element. Motorways have been built in the Green Belt before (see Fig. 3.4) but not on this scale; for obvious reasons the M25 will be sited away from existing settlements; and as a major development it will have strategic as well as local implications for the Green Belt.

It is difficult, therefore, on the basis of past experience to anticipate the motorway's full range of effects. It will undoubtedly fuel land speculation but this may become more evident in local towns than in the MGB itself. The motorway will almost certainly undermine restraint because of the amount of land it will require, because of the secondary development it will attract and because of the impact it will have on conforming land uses, such as through the severance of farms (Frost *et al.* 1976, Hearne *et al.* 1977; see Ch. 4). The really significant question, however, is whether in the absence of strategic guidance from DOE, the motorway's economic benefits will be dissipated by each local authority seeking to minimise the motorway's impact on itself.

Completion of the M25 motorway is given high priority in the nation's road-building programme (DOE–DTp 1980), and it should be finished by 1986. Throughout its length of approximately 190 km it will run through the Green Belt approximately 30 km from central London, linking existing radial trunk roads and motorways (Fig. 3.4). Its purposes have been variously described as a bypass for London, reducing heavy traffic in the centre of the capital, as a distributor road for those travelling to London and as a bypass for towns on the edge of London, some of which experience heavy commuter

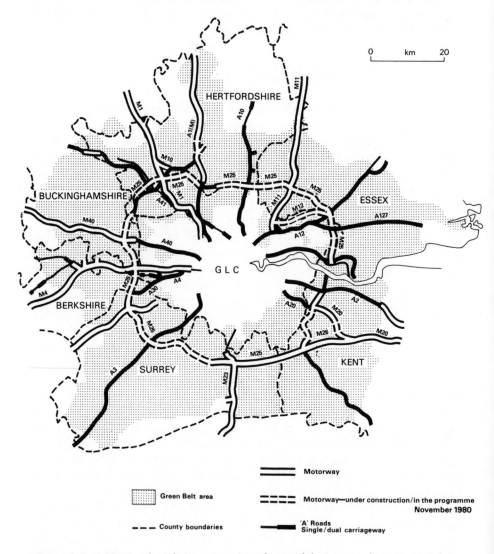

Figure 3.4 Major roads and motorways in and around the Metropolitan Green Belt (as at November 1980).

traffic. Up to 45 minutes will be saved on diagonal journeys across London.

Exactly how much land will be affected by the motorway's construction is unknown. Studies by Bell *et al.* indicate that the amount of land needed for motorways varies substantially depending on the number of intersections and local topography (Bell *et al.* 1978). However, taking a figure of 10 ha/km, a figure marginally above the mean established by Bell *et al.* in their study of three-lane motorways in the area of the MGB, then approximately 1900 ha will be needed for the motorway itself. At least a further 200 ha will be affected by wayleaves, easements and drainage schemes, while remaining in private hands, and much more land will need to be redistributed following severance. The motorway will inevitably be a major source of aural and visual intrusion in some parts of the Green Belt, as admitted in the recent decision on the route of the Swanley–Sevenoaks section of the motorway (DOE–DTp 1981). It will also lead to secondary, and hopefully temporary, land-use problems, such as borrow pits for fill, and will undoubtedly create new planning situations in the MGB where pieces of land become detached from the main body of the Green Belt. Pressure to develop land for industrial uses will occur on strips of land left between the motorway and areas of housing. It remains to be seen what the pattern of response by local and central government will be, for example, to applications for transport depots and warehousing close to motorway inter-sections. The official position of central government is that the building of the motorway will not affect the general presumption of restraint (Hansard, 10 June 1981, p. 162), but the need to treat individual applications on their merits may make this bland statement of intent untenable in practice. The motorway *will* create new local situations but there is precious little evidence to date of any constructive thinking by either local authorities, in their structure plans, or central government on how they might contain or take advantage of the motorway's presence.

Beyond the immediate impact created by the motorway's construction lie the more unpredictable medium-term effects of its existence. Government clearly wishes to encourage new industrial development and expects the region to play a full and leading part in creating new jobs (DOE 1977b, 1978a, 1980a; see Ch. 1). The extent to which a conflict will emerge between green belt restraint and jobs is unclear. It depends in part on the aggressiveness of developers, on the rate and extent of national economic recovery, and on the degree to which improved transportation itself leads to a net gain in total economic activity as well as the encouragement it gives to the relocation of existing activity. In the short term, industrial plant is highly immobile but in the longer term the M25 could well undermine the Docklands Programme and other attempts to resuscitate the decaying inner-city areas of the capital. The M25 will increase development pressures in the MGB area, especially to the west of London, but it may prove possible to accommodate these largely on the land already identified for development (see Fig 2.2). Unemployment is now significant in some OMA centres (see Elson *et al.* 1981) and OMA labour markets might be able to meet the employment needs of the high technology, low labour demanding industries attracted by the M25. This would avoid the need for local authorities to house an expanded population of working age, especially if local authorities were to continue to give priority, if not exclusive rights, to the needs of local firms.

What is missing from this discussion is any sense of an overall strategy to take advantage of the motorway now that its construction is beyond doubt, although Standing Conference (1982) has recently sought to assess its regional impact. Some sense of central government purpose and direction over what new economic opportunities should be encouraged, what housing implications these might have and where they should be located would provide a framework within which local authorities could plan and which they *could not avoid*. Otherwise, random releases of land may occur on appeal, the surrounds to the motorway may not be effectively used and land speculation will be encouraged. There is in these circumstances a strong case to be made for positive planning emanating from, and controlled by, central government, but there is no evidence of such an initiative. Central government obviously believes that in financing the construction of the motorway it has done its job.

Summary

Although differing in detail, all the major studies of non-conforming land uses in the Green Belt lead to a similar conclusion. They all show that these land uses are expanding slowly but consistently and conclude that it would be impossible, even undesirable, to attempt to stop this growth altogether. At a strategic scale the rate of growth is acceptable, although this is not so locally just to the east and west of London where the urbanisation of the Green Belt has been most rapid. What development is occurring in the Green Belt is mostly near to existing settlements and largely at the expense of farmland. Overall and given the demand for development in the OMA, then the historic rate of growth of non-conforming uses *within* the MGB must be regarded as small, and in many authorities inconsequential, although in the medium term the M25 motorway may alter this.

Land-use change is but one expression of development pressures acting on the MGB, and because restraint is being imposed firmly, at least on private initiatives, a fuller explanation of the development process itself has proved necessary in order to obtain a complete picture of the demand for development land in the Green Belt. The free market in development land, and the very substantial capital gain net of tax that is realisable by landowners, accounts for the speculative activity occurring right on the urban edge. From the interviews with farmers it became apparent that most had sought planning permission at some time during the 1970s, sometimes in association with developers, for much of their land adjacent to existing residential development. There is little evidence to support the view that landowners now accept green belt restraint and behave accordingly. They behave largely as landowners do on the edge of any dynamic city, because the hope that they might obtain planning permission is constantly fuelled by a small number of successful applications – sometimes the result of changed circumstances stemming from other planning decisions over new roads and public utilities.

Hope is also kept alive by the spasmodic demands of central government for the release of green belt land for housing. Local authority reaction to these proposals has been strongly critical, and a lowering of trust between local and central government has been one of the main outcomes of these initiatives. The need to rebuild confidence over central government intentions towards the Green Belt helps to explain the firm support for restraint by DOE at the present time, although this may be undermined in due course by the secondary effects of the M25 for which central government has failed to develop a planning strategy. On the other hand, the negative strategy of many local authorities has to date been based on ignoring the motorway as far as they can and on seeking to minimise its environmental impact, but this may be adjusted if *local* unemployment continues to rise.

4   The changing extent and form of approved uses

Introduction

The land-use statistics presented in Chapter 3 show the great majority of land in the Green Belt still to be in an approved use. At current rates of change this will remain so for a long time to come and DOE takes great satisfaction from this state of affairs. It is necessary, however, to examine more closely what forms these approved land uses take, as it is no longer sufficient to maintain that, provided land use in the MGB is of an open and rural character, then green belt restraint is being satisfactorily applied. Local residents and planners expect the land to be used positively and standards of amenity to be upheld.

The planning context in which the effectiveness of restraint is being assessed today is quite different from that of a quarter of a century ago. Structure plans generally reflect a much greater concern for the countryside than the development plans that preceded them (DOE 1977c) and most structure plans contain a range of policies for the future use of all land not wanted for development (NEDO 1977, Hebbert 1979). These policies frequently include proposals for the management of urban-fringe environments, for reducing land-use conflicts and for ensuring the reclamation of derelict land. Furthermore, it can no longer be assumed that the approved land uses themselves are not in conflict with each other.

In order to debate these matters further a fuller description is required of the extent and character of the main approved land uses in the MGB – agriculture, recreation and mineral working – and the following description is based on a number of sources, including the Agricultural Census, the collation of statistics on mineral working by Standing Conference (Standing Conference 1975, 1979a,b) and the results of a study of informal recreation in the Green Belt conducted at University College London (Ferguson 1979, Harrison 1981a, Munton 1981a). These data provide a much better basis than has been available hitherto upon which to examine the opinions of local planners and politicians, and the opinions of officials of central government departments, as to the purposes of these approved land uses, over and above the fact that they are to be preferred to non-conforming uses. They also help to identify a number of green belt planning problems, which lead on to the further question of whether local planning authorities and other public agencies have the necessary powers and resources to achieve their objectives (see Ch. 5).

As far as agriculture is concerned there are two main issues. First, it is necessary to ascertain what goals, implicit or explicit, are being attributed to farming in the MGB and by whom. Secondly, what is the effect of green belt restraint on reducing the effects of urban intrusion on the efficient functioning of the farming industry? In the case of recreation there is one overriding question. Arguments in favour of green belts have always stressed the important role they could play in meeting some of the recreational needs of the urban population as a whole. Is this role being realised in the MGB today? Finally, mineral working is an approved land use but presents a number of planning problems. In particular, it leads to conflict between the amenity interests of local residents and the need for profit among mineral companies. The conflict centres around the twin issues of how much land in the Green Belt should be used for extraction, and the need to ensure high standards of land reclamation once extraction is completed if the amenity and after-use requirements of local residents and farmers are to be met.

Agriculture

Extent and character   Agriculture has always been regarded as an acceptable use of green belt land and certain agricultural developments, if they had the support of MAFF, have always been exempt from restraint. Housing for agricultural workers is a case in point. Without doubt agriculture remains easily the single largest user of land in the MGB (see Table 3.2), but establishing the exact proportion of land in agricultural use presents difficulties in the absence of a field or aerial photograph survey. There is no statistical source for the Green Belt itself as the MGB does not abide by administrative boundaries. The most straightforward approach is to employ the parish summaries of the Agricultural Census, and data from all 243 agricultural parishes with more than 50% of their area within the statutorily approved Green Belt in 1976 are included in the following figures used to describe some of the basic characteristics of the farming pattern. The data are aggregated at least to the district scale so that no individual data unit contains less than 900 ha of farmland (see Appendix). The reasons for this aggregation are well known and stem from the problems of trying to study agricultural parishes of very differing size (Coppock 1960, 1978). Some parishes are very small (less than 200 ha) and with the growing size and fragmentation of farms (see MAFF 1977a, Edwards 1978) have become unreliable data units. Many farms now straddle parish boundaries but the parish return allocates all the land for a particular farm to the parish in which the farmhouse is located.★

The parish data record a total area of 190 684 ha of agricultural land, which represents about 63.5% of the area of the MGB. This figure includes, however, the woodland for which the occupiers are responsible. This amounts to 3.5% of the total area and means that in round terms about 60% of the Green Belt was being farmed in 1976. Direct comparison with the figures of Thomas and

★ The June Agricultural Census data refer to holdings which may not be the same as farms as commonly understood (see Ch. 6).

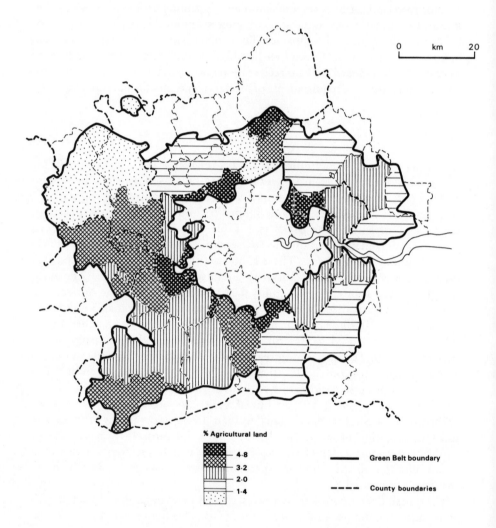

Figure 4.1 Percentage of agricultural land in rough grazings in the Metropolitan Green Belt, 1976. (Statistical source: unpublished parish returns from the Annual Agricultural Census 1976, MAFF.)

Standing Conference is impossible because the data sources are different and the area of the MGB changed between 1960 and 1976 (to include the extensions to the approved MGB shown in Fig. 1.1), but the census information suggests that the amount of farmland is continuing to fall. Thomas (see Table 3.1) gives a figure of 69.5% for agricultural land, excluding all woodland, for 1960.

The census data also allow a partial description of some of the industry's key characteristics. These show that 91.9% of the farmland in the Green Belt is under crops and grass with only 2.7%, or about 5000 ha, in rough grazings. The proportion in rough grazings is small, as would be expected in lowland Britain where land is rarely held in common, and can be taken to mean that most land is intensively farmed and well maintained. But this conclusion may be misleading. Farmers themselves decide how to define the use of their land when completing their returns, although the Ministry of Agriculture, Fisheries and Food gives them detailed instructions on how to do so. Farmers may be disinclined to record the full extent of rough grazings in case this is seen as a reflection on their standards of husbandry. Some rough grazings are probably returned as permanent pasture. The GLC has the highest proportion (6.7%) of rough grazings of any county in the MGB (see Fig. 4.1) and rather more rough grazings occur in the inner than the outer parts of the Green Belt. There is no obvious environmental reason for this and rough grazings are noticeably more apparent just to the east and west of London where the rate of growth in Developed Areas has been most rapid (see Fig. 3.2). Hounslow and Richmond together record a staggering 46.3% of farmland as rough grazings and the boroughs of Barking, Redbridge and Waltham Forest combined return a figure of 14.2%. There is some reason to believe, therefore, that despite the likely

Table 4.1 Percentage of holdings by type by county in the MGB.

County	dairying	cattle and sheep	Type[1] Group pigs and poultry	cropping	horti-culture	mixed	part-time
Berks.	12.3	5.7	5.3	3.9	11.4	4.8	56.6
Bucks.	10.9	6.4	7.2	3.1	9.4	1.5	61.5
Essex	6.4	1.9	5.6	8.9	29.4	1.5	46.2
Herts.	13.2	4.0	5.5	5.5	17.6	2.6	51.6
Kent	8.8	3.6	5.9	3.1	18.6	1.8	58.2
Surrey	15.2	4.8	4.3	2.2	12.9	2.3	58.3
GLC	7.2	2.8	5.2	2.6	26.3	1.1	54.8
total	11.2	4.2	5.4	4.0	17.8	2.0	55.5
England and Wales	20.7	12.7	4.3	10.1	6.4	3.9	42.0

Source: Agricultural Census, parish summaries June 1976.

[1] Type groups relate to the following MAFF categories: dairying 1–2; cattle and sheep 3–5; pigs and poultry 6–7; cropping 8–9; horticulture 10–12; mixed 13; part-time 14.

understatement of the area of rough grazings in the figures, land close to the urban edge is often poorly maintained (see Ch. 6).

The overall pattern of agricultural production is better illustrated by the distribution of farm types. All full-time holdings★ are classified by MAFF on the basis of the standard labour requirements for each of their enterprises (MAFF 1977a,b). The percentage of holdings falling into seven main categories are shown by county for the MGB in Table 4.1. The figures for the MGB depart from the national average in a number of ways. In particular there is a substantially higher percentage of part-time farms (55.5% compared with 42.0%) which helps to explain why, with the notable exception of horticultural holdings and to a lesser extent pig and poultry holdings, the percentage of other farm types is less than the national average. In area terms, farms in the MGB are small. Nearly half the farms are less than 10 ha in extent and only 11.5% exceed 100 ha. In 1976, the MGB contained approximately 2.2% of all holdings in England and Wales but only 1.7% of the agricultural area.

Within the Green Belt there are also marked differences in the spatial pattern of the different types of full-time holding. For example, Surrey has more than twice the proportion of dairy holdings of Essex, but Essex has many more cropping holdings than all the other counties. Most spectacular, however, is the concentration of horticultural units in the GLC and Essex. Two general observations may be made. First, the farm-type data indicate a gradation in the farming pattern from the north-east to the south-west with arable farming becoming less predominant in the south-west. Secondly, the measurement of holding size by its labour requirement is based solely on the data collected in the Agricultural Census. These data only include traditional farming enterprises and may be misleading in an urban-fringe context. Other farm-based enter-prises, such as farm shops and the keeping of horses,† are ignored. Thus in terms of total entrepreneurial activity, and whether the holdings provide full-time employment for the occupier, the statistics overestimate the number of part-time units and are in danger of presenting a false picture about the nature of farming generally.

Finally, not much is known about the ownership of farmland in the Green Belt. The Agricultural Census only records occupation, dividing this into rented and owner-occupied land. The area in owner-occupation has increased consistently during the 20th century (see Northfield committee report 1979) and by 1978 only 43% of farmland in Great Britain was rented. This percentage is almost certainly too high. Some forms of occupation recorded as tenancies in the census are effectively *de facto* owner-occupation (see Rose *et al.* 1977, Lund & Slater 1978, 1979). These 'tenancy arrangements' are separately identified in the Scottish Agricultural Census and in Scotland they account for 8% of the

★ Until 1976, 275 Standard Man Days labour requirement was used as the measure of a full-time farm. This figure was reduced to 250 in 1977.

† The 1979 Agricultural Census reintroduced a question on the number of horses kept for both farming and pleasure purposes (MAFF 1981a).

agricultural area. Keeping this point in mind, 48.4% of farmland in the MGB was recorded in the census as rented in 1976, 4.5% more than the national average. The figure for the Green Belt conceals significant local variations (Fig. 4.2) and especially the very high levels of renting within some parts of the GLC. This reflects the large amounts of land in public and semi-public ownership close to the urban edge and has implications for the current management and future use of this land (see Ch. 6).

These data suggest important differences in the farming pattern within the MGB. For example, the area of rough grazings and the proportion of rented land declines with distance away from London – confirming the findings of other surveys conducted in the MGB (Gasson 1966, Low 1973, MAFF 1973, Countryside Commission 1981) and in other urban fringes in Britain as well (Davies 1953, University of Reading 1975, MAFF 1976a, Rettig 1976). On the other hand, the pattern of farming varies significantly between the north and east of the MGB, with its greater emphasis on arable farming, and the south and west. There is as a result no clearly defined urban-fringe type of farming. Following his exhaustive analysis of the Agricultural Census data for 1967, 1972 and 1974 around all the major conurbations in England, Thomson came to a similar conclusion (Thomson 1981). For while he felt able to conclude that farms close to the urban edge were small, had a low proportion of cropped land, a high proportion of permanent grass, rough grazings and land in non-agricultural uses, and low stocking rates – probably the effect of the census failing to record the number of horses kept on farms – all of which might be seen as 'urban' farming features, he went on to note the importance of variations in land quality (see pp. 79–81) in determining the spatial pattern of farming activity around London (Thomson 1981, p. 95).

Restraint and urban impact The continued close adherence of DOE to the principles contained in Circular 42/55 means that DOE is content for green belt restraint to maintain the existence of agriculture in some unspecified form. What kind of agriculture this should be is for national agricultural policy to determine and that is the province of another central government department (MAFF). The only area of explicit co-operation between MAFF and DOE which directly relates to the implementation of green belt restraint concerns their joint commitment to limit the loss of farmland to urban development (DOE 1976b).

Co-operation is achieved through consultation and not through any statutory right of MAFF officials to determine the outcome of planning applications affecting agricultural land. Nevertheless, MAFF officials have had the right of consultation on certain kinds of planning application since 1947. The kinds of application referred to them have been changed as national concern over the loss of farmland to urban uses has varied. Until 1971 all applications affecting more than 2 ha of farmland and which departed from approved development plans were automatically referred to MAFF, as well as other applications on which the

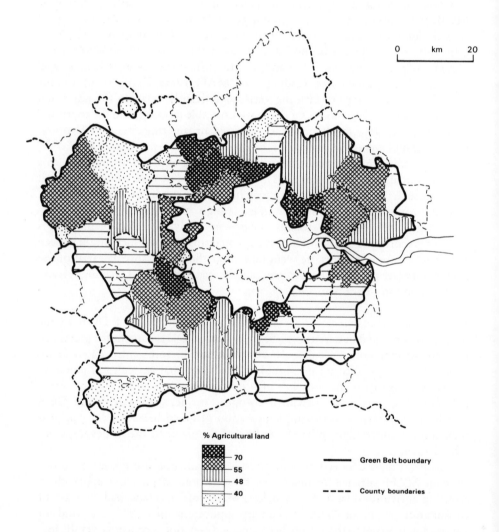

Figure 4.2 Percentage of let agricultural land in the Metropolitan Green Belt, 1976. (Statistical source: unpublished parish returns from the Annual Agricultural Census 1976, MAFF.)

local planning authority felt in need of specialist advice. Between 1971 and 1979 the cut-off point was raised to 4 ha in order to speed up the processing of small applications, only to be lowered again to 2 ha following the report *Agriculture and the countryside* (ACAH 1978) which expressed concern at the rate of loss of farmland in the early 1970s. It is now agreed that MAFF 'Should take a more active part in the planning process but without disturbing the present responsibilities of central and local government' (DOE 1979d). The final say thus remains in the hands of local planning authorities. In the context of the Green Belt, MAFF officials maintain that not all local planning officers seem to understand MAFF's priorities, and especially its concern to protect high quality farmland (see below). Green belt restraint, they point out, is a planning concept and MAFF cannot be expected to object to an application unless the site consists of Grades 1, 2 or possibly 3 agricultural land (ADAS 1976). On occasion, they felt that planning authorities have sought an agricultural objection in order to sustain green belt restraint.

More precise policy guidelines exist over the loss of farmland of high quality. In Circular 75/76 it is stated that 'Government policy for the protection of agricultural land is to ensure that, as far as possible, land of a higher agricultural quality is not taken for development where land of a lower quality is available and that the amount of land taken is no greater than is reasonably required for carrying out the development in accordance with proper standards' (DOE 1976b, p. 1). A literal interpretation of this statement would mean that MAFF's support for the MGB was conditional upon the quality of farmland being developed elsewhere as the result of urban growth being directed away from the MGB. It would be extremely difficult to determine whether the Green Belt had either a positive or negative effect in this regard especially as the quality of farmland in the MGB in aggregate is similar to that in the rest of the South East Economic Planning Region (see Table 4.2).

Using the 1:50000 land classification sheets, an estimate has been made of the proportion of agricultural land in the MGB falling into each of the five grades

Table 4.2 Agricultural land quality in the MGB, the South East Economic Planning Region, and England and Wales.

	% agricultural land area Grade				
	1	*2*	*3*	*4*	*5*
MGB (as approved in 1976)	3.3	16.1	69.8	10.7	0.1
SE Economic Planning Region	3.1	21.0	59.8	14.7	1.4
England and Wales	2.8	14.6	48.9	19.8	13.9

Sources: Agriculture EDC (1977); the MGB figures have been calculated from the published 1:50000 Agricultural Land Classification sheets.

recognised by MAFF. Almost 70% falls into Grade 3, about 10% into Grade 4 and nearly 20% into Grades 1 and 2. Land in Grades 1 and 2 imposes few, if any, limitations on arable cropping and is protected from urban development whenever possible. MAFF accepts that the definition of Grade 3 is unsatisfactory. Its present definition leads to a large proportion of the total farmed area being included within it (Carter & Sayce 1979) and MAFF are presently reclassifying land in Grade 3 into 3 subclasses. This is only being done on demand to meet specific requests for more detailed information and insufficient reclassification has been completed within the MGB for useful conclusions to be drawn about the nature of Grade 3 land around London. Figure 4.3 depicts the distribution of land in Grades 1 and 2 over the area of the approved and interim green belt as of 1976 (Standing Conference 1976). A significant proportion of this lies in north-east Hertfordshire, west Essex and west Kent. With local exceptions, such as around Harlow and Southend, it can be argued that most of this land is not under serious or widespread pressure for development. Much greater pressure is being exerted on the limited areas of Grade 1 land within or close to the GLC boundary immediately to the east and west of London. These small pockets of Grade 1 land, amounting to 6300 ha, most of which is in horticultural use, are threatened by speculative land market activity around Heathrow Airport (Hillingdon LB 1973) and gravel extraction in Havering (Countryside Commission 1981).

MAFF officials also expressed concern over any general lowering of agricultural productivity as a result of urban proximity or recreational activities. Thus insofar as green belt restraint reduces urban sprawl and scattered development, which it undoubtedly does, then it is regarded as advantageous. Likewise, if farmers acquire a sense of security from green belt designation, which seems more doubtful on the basis of their replies (see below), it is also seen as helpful. But MAFF no longer has statutory powers with which to tackle the poor maintenance of farmland as a result of intrusion, low managerial ability or any other cause. For although the supervision and dispossession provisions of the Agriculture Act 1947, themselves a survival from the emergency powers taken by central government during World War II, had permitted the ministry to act directly in cases of poor farm management until 1958, they were repealed under the Agriculture Act of that year. They were repealed on the assumption that the cost-price squeeze being imposed by central government on the farming industry would eliminate farming inefficiency (see Bowler 1979). Those making this assumption had not taken into account the wide range of market opportunities available to farmers in the urban fringe or the variety of motives for their ownership of green belt land. The repeal also means that MAFF are unable to control the spread of riding stables or other recreational enterprises which conflict with its primary objective of promoting efficient food production. In this sense, to MAFF the use of farmland for the keeping of horses is a misuse of national resources, even if the promotion of recreational activities is a perfectly legitimate planning objective in green belts.

Objectives for agriculture By largely ignoring amenity questions in green belts DOE avoids the need to take a position over the current conflict between contemporary forms of agricultural production and their impact on wildlife conservation and the landscape. There is a wide measure of agreement that most modern farming practices are inimical to the wellbeing of wildlife, even if the extent of the problem is still disputed, and that these practices often lead to more

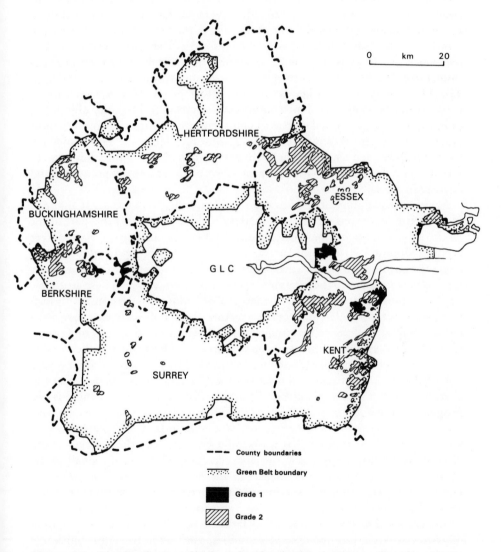

Figure 4.3 The distribution of high quality farmland in the Metropolitan Green Belt. (Source: 1:50000 Agricultural Land Classification Sheets, MAFF.)

open and less interesting rural landscapes (for discussions of these issues, see, from among a large literature, Westmacott & Worthington 1974, MAFF 1976b, Countryside Commission 1977, Shoard 1980, Goode 1981, Green 1981). Even the Ministry of Agriculture, Fisheries and Food's own advisory council states that 'there is evident concern about the harmful effects of many current farming practices upon both landscape and nature conservation, coupled with a widespread feeling that agriculture can no longer be accounted the prime architect of conservation nor farmers accepted as the "natural custodians of the countryside"' (ACAH 1978, p. 26). But the council adopts a rather different position when it examines the role of farming in the urban fringe, a location in which it is still concerned to promote continued efficient food production. It concludes that there is 'a growing awareness that a healthy farm economy is fundamental to the maintenance of landscape quality within the fringe' (ibid., p. 42). The council must either be assuming that given the characteristics of urban-fringe farming there is no conflict between them and amenity objectives, or be suggesting that even if there is a conflict commercial agriculture is the most practicable and preferred way of realising landscape objectives. The council fail to specify, however, exactly what forms of commercial agriculture they want to see. What, in these circumstances, are the views of local planners, politicians and farmers in the MGB?

Many local planning officers lacked confidence, but not necessarily interest, in answering questions on farming matters with the result that this part of the discussions with them either elicited considerable comment or was passed over rapidly (Munton 1981b). In the latter case, having noted the limited powers they held over farming activities, which seemed to define the extent of their interest, these officers suggested the interviewer seek advice elsewhere. These attitudes, expressed most noticeably at district level, are at odds with the emphasis given to policies for farmland in most of the structure plans. Policies in structure plans indicate a clear preference for 'traditional' or 'conventional' forms of agriculture. Modern systems of intensive, housed-livestock husbandry and extensive areas under glass and plastic are not wanted. Modern farm buildings are regarded as visually intrusive, indicative of industrial activity and not of a rural character. In the Buckinghamshire Structure Plan, for example, there is the proposal that the 'erection of buildings for intensive farming unconnected with the agricultural use of a substantial area of adjoining land' (Buckinghamshire CC 1976, p. 80) be refused. Yet this would seem to deny the position of the ACAH. A healthy farm economy, and especially if the many small farms identified by the Agricultural Census in the MGB are to survive, must be permitted to adapt to changing economic and technological conditions (Dexter 1977). Local planners do not seem to appreciate the long-term agricultural consequences of their position for small farms, especially as they do not approve of farm-based recreational enterprises either, such as farm shops and horse grazing. They frequently seek to inhibit the development of these enterprises but not always with much success (Turrall-Clarke 1981). Many local planners concur with the view of the Agriculture Economic Development Council which claims that the grazing of horses leads to pasture which 'is not managed in accordance with the best principles of grassland husbandry. As a result its productivity is low and weed infestation increases' (NEDO 1977, p. 11). No evidence is produced in support of this assertion.

Similar views are expressed by the chairmen of local planning committees. Most speak strongly in favour of promoting full-time farming in the Green Belt. Their views are doubtless strengthened by the fact that a significant proportion of them are either farmers or have a professional interest in the countryside as chartered surveyors, architects and estate agents – an urban-fringe equivalent to the domination of local government in rural Suffolk by farmers and landowners (Newby *et al*. 1978). But the determination to promote agriculture is not a function of how rural the authority is, some of the industry's strongest protagonists being councillors living on the edge of London. Farther away from the capital there is less need to emphasise the desirability of farming – it is taken for granted.

Precisely why full-time, commercial farming should be seen as so desirable is less clear from the replies. Often, it seemed, it is simply regarded as preferable to the alternatives. For example, only 4 chairmen out of the 38 interviewed would endorse a land-use policy that regularly put recreational needs before those of farming, as indicated by a preference for farms over golf courses, food production over horse grazing or modern farming practices over public access. The great majority are unequivocably in favour of full-time farming and would like to take vigorous steps to stop the spread of horse grazing, riding stables and hobby farming. Only a small number accept that present-day farming methods detract significantly from the quality of the landscape, and most of these would assert that any reduction in quality from this source is distinctly preferable to that resulting from mineral working, horse grazing, or the poor maintenance of land by hobby farmers.

Farmers were also asked for their views about their long-term farming prospects in the Green Belt. They would no doubt express surprise had they known of the amount of political support they seem to have in many planning authorities. Instead, they complain of being beleaguered, part of an isolated group in the community whose problems are neither shared nor understood by the majority. To them, farming in the urban fringe presents more problems than advantages, and green belt restraint makes little difference to this. It is important to be aware, however, that farmers regularly promote this view, expressing helplessness, frustration and even hostility towards townspeople (Elliott 1979, Blair 1981). Being part of the urban community during the week does not endear the hobby farmer to that same community at the weekend.

Contained within this general context of frustration, farmers' views vary as to their own prospects. For example, over 60% of the 185 interviewed expect to retain their farms intact over the next 20 years in the face of outside pressures.

The remainder feel more immediately threatened, especially by mineral extraction and the construction of the M25 motorway, and a clear difference of views emerges between the family farmer who rents his land and the owner-occupier, whether he be a large commercial producer or a hobby farmer. Owner-occupiers feel less aggrieved by urban development for they can always sell their land and buy again elsewhere. However, all the respondents qualified their answers by making the assumptions that restraint would be maintained *at least* as firmly as it had been in the past and that planning applications for recreational developments, farm shops and new farm buildings would be *more* favourably received. Indeed, other than the perennial problem of trespass (see Ch. 6) the most frequently mentioned disadvantage of farming in the Green Belt is the level of ignorance among local authority planners of farming problems. The restrictive approach to agricultural development adopted by planners in the MGB is regarded as a threat to the prosperity of farmers and the long-term efficiency of agriculture. Structure plan policies in support of agriculture are meaningless if farm-related developments fail to obtain planning permission.

Finally, many farmers fail to see the connection between their husbandry practices and landscape change, and others do not want to see it. The latter group often accept that their actions do not create attractive landscapes or protect wildlife but claim that the economics of farming today do not allow for such side-shows (see also MAFF 1976b, Newby *et al*. 1977). Only 15 of the 185 farmers had received grants for landscape improvement or tree planting from either their local authorities or the Countryside Commission, and many of the remaining 170 were not even aware of the existence of such monies.

It is inevitable that if asked, farmers will complain of any perceived threats to the security of their livelihoods, and will doubtless tend to exaggerate their importance and to underestimate the degree of protection from urban development afforded to them by green belt restraint. They will also oppose any form of planning intervention that restricts their range of business activities. Their position is clear-cut and well known. But the response of local politicians and planners to farming in the MGB is confused and ill informed. On the whole, planners and councillors seem to want to encourage an efficient agriculture that is uncluttered by recreational enterprises, modern farm buildings and hobby farms, yet at the same time they fail to appreciate that full-time farmers on small units must intensify and diversify their on-farm activities if they are to survive. Moreover, the planners in particular have yet to clarify their thinking over the conflict between modern farming methods and the level of amenity and access to land demanded by local residents. At present, they tend to give priority to farming considerations, something that would no doubt come as a surprise to many farmers, because an efficient agriculture at least maintains food production, which is seen as being in the national interest (MAFF 1975, 1979), and retains a 'tidy' landscape which is preferable to under-used farmland.

Recreation and amenity

As observed in Chapter 1, in almost every case made out in support of green belts it has been argued that they should contribute to an improvement in the recreational opportunities available to the urban population, and especially to those living in the inner city. Only recently has the level of achievement of this goal been assessed empirically and in some respects to be found wanting. Research shows, for example, that inner-city residents make up a disproportionately small number of users (GLC 1975–6, Fitton 1976). The most recent study, based on a very substantial on-site survey in the Green Belt, reveals that over half the visitors come from the borough or district in which the site is located, over 70% live within 10 km of the site on which they were interviewed, and few sites attract even 5% of their visitors from the inner city (Harrison 1981a,b). Whether the proportion is small because of the cost and time incurred getting out to the sites from central London, or whether the kinds of recreational opportunity on offer in the Green Belt – very largely open spaces dominated by semi-natural vegetation and with few facilities – do not meet the demands of inner-city residents, is less clear. Home-based interviews suggest that members of *all* socio-economic groups wherever they live enjoy visiting the countryside, but infrequent and costly public transport severely restricts the opportunities of inner-city residents who do not own or have access to a car (Fitton 1979). Indeed, the sheer size of London even inhibits the visiting of those who do own a car (see low visiting figures for the residents of the GLC, Countryside Commission 1979). Site surveys also reveal that members of all social groups and ages visit the countryside, even if low-income groups are underrepresented (Harrison 1981b). The implication must be that the inaccessibility of the Green Belt acts as a significant deterrent to inner-city residents and it would be naïve to assume that the MGB can ever meet their needs.

Nevertheless, clamour continues for more public open space and greater public access to private land in the MGB. Both Thomas and Standing Conference comment to the effect that comparatively little land is in public open space (see Table 3.2, Thomas 1970, Standing Conference 1976), and this position has been implicitly supported by the results from the *Study of informal recreation in south east England* (SIRSEE) carried out in the early 1970s (GLC 1975–6, Standing Conference 1977c, Fitton 1979). Home interviews were included in the SIRSEE study and these revealed considerable latent demand for countryside recreation, while SIRSEE's on-site surveys recorded congestion at peak times and in some instances ecological damage as a result of intense recreational use. Since the early 1970s, however, rising unemployment, slower growth in real earnings and a falling population in parts of the OMA (see Ch. 2) have meant that this latent demand has not been fully realised. The later study (Harrison 1981b) also makes it clear that SIRSEE's site studies are misleading, at least to the extent that they emphasise peak levels of use and concentrate their attention on a few of the best known sites of regional importance while ignoring the many more numerous but smaller and less used open spaces. As a result the SIRSEE study does not address itself to other possible solutions to the apparent shortage of open space, such as the feasibility of transferring demand from heavily- to under-used sites. It also largely avoids the question of whether 'more of the same', that is more sites with few built structures and limited management input catering for informal, outdoor activities, best meet the recreational needs of Londoners. This question has not been addressed by many of the sites' managing bodies either for they are largely satisfied with present arrangements (Ferguson *et al.* 1980). There is little evidence to suggest that urban-type facilities will be permitted in the Green Belt by local planning authorities anyway. This is in spite of Standing Conference's wish for local authorities to adopt a positive approach to providing a range of recreational opportunities in the MGB (Standing Conference 1979e). Indeed, many local authorities shun investment in major schemes designed, as they see it, to satisfy regional rather than local needs.

This selfish outlook is criticised by the Countryside Review Committee in its discussion paper *Leisure and the countryside* (CRC 1977, see also Elson 1979c, d) as a large proportion of local finance comes from non-local sources. Over half local authority income comes via the Rate Support Grant from central government and, following the Countryside Act 1968 and the Local Government Act 1972, a significant proportion of any major expenditure in the area of countryside recreation can be grant-aided by the Countryside Commission. Outside the national parks the Countryside Commission gives priority to urban-fringe projects and especially to major schemes of benefit to a wider range of users than local residents. But if facilities are not to be promoted with public money in the present period of expenditure cuts, then private entrepreneurs could be encouraged and a few authorities have been prepared to assist the private sector, as in Buckinghamshire, to the extent of pump-priming schemes. But more often than not, and in order to meet the objections of local residents, local planning authorities insist on extremely low levels of recreational use of green belt land thus making the proposals uneconomic.

Research also suggests that the amount of land in public, semi-public and charitable ownership already in public use for informal countryside recreation in the Green Belt is more substantial than had been previously appreciated. At least 9.0% of all land in the MGB in 1978 consisted of informal recreation sites (Ferguson & Munton 1978, 1979), amounting to over 26 000 ha of land on 390 separate sites (Table 4.3). These figures relate only to sites predominantly used for informal recreation and make no allowance for the extensive network of public footpaths and bridleways. The distribution of this land is uneven, with Surrey containing 45.4% of the sites and 50.1% of the area (Fig. 4.4). By contrast, parts of Kent, Hertfordshire, Essex and some boroughs in the west of London are poorly served (Law & Perry 1971).

What this research has done is to throw considerable doubt on the validity of the congestion and ecological damage arguments, at least for the average open

Table 4.3 Informal recreation sites in the London Green Belt, 1978[1].

	Area of MGB (ha)	Area of Sites (ha)	Sites as % MGB area
Berkshire	16 150	891	5.5
Buckinghamshire	48 450	2 231	4.6
Essex	35 400	2 725	7.7
Hertfordshire	33 350	1 616	4.8
Greater London	38 950	3 932	10.1
Kent	25 300	1 041	4.1
Surrey	94 800	14 003	14.8
total	292 400[2]	26 439	9.0

Source: Ferguson and Munton (1978, p.11).
[1] The interim green belt contained a further 101 sites covering 4617 ha.
[2] Total area is slightly less than that used elsewhere in this book.

space in the Green Belt. High density use and environmental deterioration are extremely peaked in time and are restricted to small zones on the most popular sites, and those who employ these arguments as a means of deterring attempts to increase the use of the MGB should be rebuffed, especially as the capacity of sites within the Green Belt to absorb greater use can be readily increased through improved management (Harrison 1980–1). This analysis also indicates that the case for acquiring more public open space in the Green Belt for informal recreational use needs careful examination, and that it may well prove a better use of public monies to improve the facilities on existing sites, despite the obvious advantage of bringing under-used or semi-derelict land into recreational use. The interviews with local planning officers do not, however, suggest that many new initiatives of any substance will go ahead in the near future.

The responses of local planning officers to questions on the promotion of recreation in the MGB were both variable and in general lukewarm. Only about half of them (27) indicated that their authorities had a policy of encouraging the greater recreational use of Green Belt land, in spite of the fact that 41 had expressed the view that recreation should be treated as a strategic green belt issue (see p. 34). Generally, authorities in the inner half of the MGB and in the GLC especially are most committed to sponsoring recreational opportunities. Local authorities in Essex and Buckinghamshire are cautiously in favour, views in Hertfordshire and Kent are mixed, and in Surrey and Berkshire the majority of officers say that their members exhibit little enthusiasm for any kind of recreational development. In all counties, however, considerable variations of view are to be found. The only widely held opinion is that informal, passive recreational pursuits are to be preferred to organised sports activity (see Elson 1979c). Planning committees invariably raise objections to all applications that include sports buildings, such as squash courts, that could be equally well accommodated within the urban area.

Three main reasons can be put forward to account for the indifference of local authorities. First, many believe that present arrangements are satisfactory. They will be supported in their views by most site managers and most visitors. A

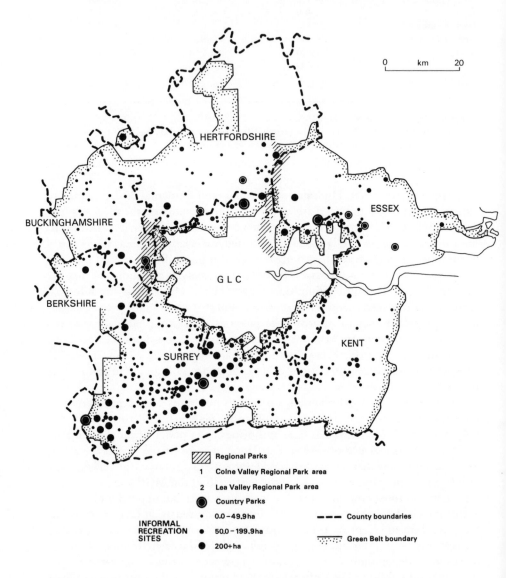

Figure 4.4 The distribution of informal recreation open space in the Metropolitan Green Belt, 1978. (Source: Ferguson & Munton 1978, p. 11.)

great majority of visitors speak positively of the site at which they are being interviewed, almost irrespective of the site's characteristics. The site is simply different from the urban environment, encouraging a feeling of spaciousness, solitude and relaxation (Harrison 1981b). But this is an almost inevitable finding if one seeks it by interviewing those who currently visit the Green Belt. Secondly, many authorities complain of budgetary restraint, noting that this is an area of spending not statutorily required of them (Munton 1981a). What is spent thus seems to depend largely on established practice and commitments. Thirdly, there is significant resistance among the members of planning committees to increasing public access to private land. At interview only 8 out of 34 chairmen indicated any real determination on their part to ensure that public access is either maintained by stopping farmers, developers and mineral operators from closing public rights of way, or enhanced by extending the existing network of footpaths. Although none oppose the right of public access to the countryside, six chairmen suggest that too many rights have already been conferred and often to the detriment of farming operations.

Planning officers in 19 out of 48 districts claim to have serious landscape problems of one kind or another and a further dozen experience minor difficulties. With the exception of a few districts with well known and widespread damage resulting from mineral extraction, industrial and urban-fringe dereliction (see Fig. 1.2), most problems are highly localised. They also exist in the eye of the beholder. One county planning officer reported problems associated with mineral extraction, motorways, the undermanagement of woodland and urban intrusion, while every single district planning officer in the same county denied the existence of any such difficulty.

Despite the emphasis placed by Standing Conference on landscape mainten-ance and restoration in their reports on London's Green Belt (Standing Conference 1976, 1978), few districts have been prepared to commit sizeable resources to restoration schemes (Standing Conference 1977a). At the county level, activity varies quite significantly. Surrey County Council, for example, argues that landscape improvements could prove an expensive exercise for the tangible benefits derived from them. Nevertheless, it established a Green Belt Fund to facilitate landscape improvements in the Green Belt (Surrey CC 1978), although the precise purpose of the fund is not clear and its size has been reduced to a point of insignificance (£5000 per annum). Hertfordshire CC has been much more active. The county has already received grant aid from the Countryside Commission for an urban-fringe management experiment in the south of the county (Countryside Commission 1981) and has drawn up countryside management and landscape development plans as part of its structure planning process. The county foresees the use of a county-wide ranger service, tree planting schemes, planning and management agreements with private land-owners, further land management experiments and a budget to fund the public acquisition of land if this is felt necessary. The GLC likewise have enterprising plans for the development of their estate and a once and for all reclamation scheme to restore old mineral workings; but funding in the present economic climate remains problematic.

Only faltering steps in favour of a more positive approach to recreation and landscape improvement are being made at present. Much depends on the view of the individual planning officer and his committee towards expenditure in this area. Some officers see it is an optional luxury that can be conveniently forgotten during the current period of budgetary restraint, whereas others who have acquired the necessary resources and expertise for active pro-grammes will do more. They are more than satisfied with the returns to their initiatives.

Mineral extraction

The catalytic effect of mineral extraction on land-use change in the urban fringe can only be understood if the process of mineral extraction is seen in its totality. There are at least four stages to mineral exploitation and each contributes to the overall profitability of the enterprise. The stages include the purchase of, or the taking of an option in, mineral-bearing land with a view to realising its mineral hope value when planning permission is obtained. The second stage is extraction, the third reclamation or the profitable filling of a pit if it is dry, and the fourth is the seeking of a profitable after-use for the land if the freehold has been acquired. The latter may even include housing development on the reclaimed site. The second stage often receives most attention but much of the operator's profit and many of the planning problems may result from the subsequent stages. These problems are often associated with the inadequate reclamation and aftercare of the land.

Major sand and gravel deposits lie within the MGB, as valley gravels along the Thames Valley to the east and west of London, and as 'high level' plateau deposits leading to dry workings, mainly in Hertfordshire, Kent, Essex and Buckinghamshire. There are also significant chalk workings in north Kent and south Essex. London is the largest single market in the UK for aggregates and high transfer costs in relation to product value mean that gravel has been worked close to the capital over long periods. Some of these reserves, especially those within the GLC boundary, have been exhausted. Nevertheless, extraction continues to be widespread within the MGB (see Fig. 4.5). It occurs on a significant scale in nearly 20 districts and boroughs in the Green Belt, and in every single case the local planning officer commented on the planning problems this particular use of land brings. As an approved use, green belt restraint is not a valid source of objection to extraction, but in the wider sense that extraction conflicts with other approved uses, creates environmental problems and affects public attitudes towards green belt generally, it is necessary to examine the impact on the Green Belt of past and present workings and the prospects for future extraction.

Standing Conference estimates that some 3360 ha were being worked for

Standing Conference estimates that some 3360 ha were being worked for
minerals in the approved and interim green belt in 1975 and permission had been
granted on a further 3075 ha (Standing Conference 1975). It also suggests that
the area being worked, or in an inadequate state of reclamation, is in the order of
2% of the total MGB area (11 350 ha), and that the environmental impact of
extraction is much greater than this percentage would suggest (Standing
Conference 1976). Mineral working is concentrated in urban-fringe areas,

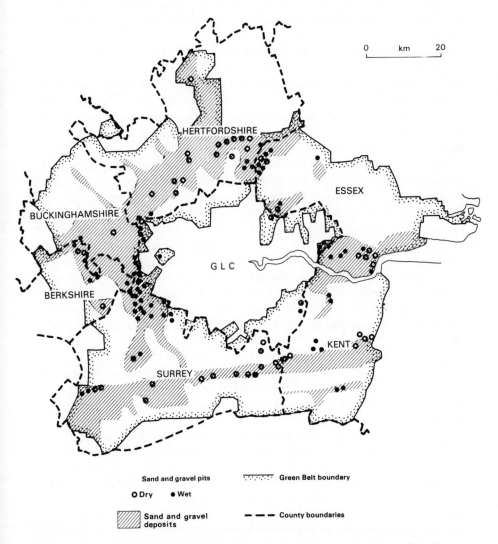

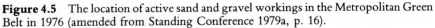

Figure 4.5 The location of active sand and gravel workings in the Metropolitan Green
Belt in 1976 (amended from Standing Conference 1979a, p. 16).

creating additional development pressures on land adjacent to it and causing serious nuisance to local residents. Moreover, commercial deposits of aggregates are often found in association with high quality farmland and the standard of past reclamation by mineral operators has been poor. In its view extraction is the primary cause of 'damaged landscapes'.

It is important to acknowledge that continued mineral extraction can be expected in the MGB and that restoration problems are yet to be overcome. There have been a number of recent analyses of the regional supply and demand situation for sand and gravel, easily the most important minerals, and they all conclude that extraction from land-based sources must continue at present rates for at least the next 10–15 years if a shortfall in supply or a marked increase in price for aggregates is to be avoided (Standing Conference 1975, Verney committee report 1976, Standing Conference 1979a). In the period 1974–6, consumption of aggregates in the South East averaged 64 million tonnes per annum of which 35 million tonnes per annum were met by land-based supplies. The shortfall was made up from marine-dredged gravels, manufactured aggregate and other waste material, and imports by road and rail from adjoining regions. The shortfall was greatest in the London area.

Expected rates of growth in demand for aggregates have been substantially lowered during the 1970s in line with reduced economic activity in the region, although the construction of the M25 motorway will continue to make substantial demands. Nevertheless, until recently demand was expected to remain at the 1974–6 level into the 1980s (DOE 1978e, f; Standing Conference 1979a). This forecast may now prove unfounded, but in any event a sizeable shortfall between regional demands and those supplies that can be won from land-based sources in the region can be expected to persist. Standing Conference does not expect supplies from other sources to increase markedly, especially as new investment in marine dredging is at present unprofitable and rising transport costs are reducing the competitiveness of imports into the region. Based on the 1978 situation, DOE estimates that the region's total demand for the period 1977–87 will be 701 million tonnes. Returns to Standing Conference suggest that the potential of permitted reserves (i.e. working pits and sites where planning permission for extraction has already been given) amounts only to 365 million tonnes. This is an upper figure for these reserves and in all probability some pits will not be worked during this period. It follows that almost inevitably 600 ha of land will continue to be excavated each year in the region and, for the medium term, further permissions will have to be granted to maintain output near this level. The MGB may well contribute a falling proportion of this because of the exhaustion of some deposits within it but its ideal location close to London suggests that extraction will continue as close to present levels as operators can achieve. This also means that land of high agricultural quality and land in areas of high landscape value will be increasingly threatened. Some areas of Grade 1 agricultural land within the GLC have already been released for mineral working (on appeal) and it will be impossible to protect all Grades 1 and 2 land overlying gravel in the MGB indefinitely (Verney committee report 1976, Standing Conference 1979a).

It is extremely important to mineral companies that they retain a land bank with planning permission for extraction. Otherwise they cannot plan their operations efficiently or with any degree of security. They prefer a land bank amounting to 10 years' supply and this they presently maintain in the region (i.e. 6000 ha with outstanding permission). Some companies operate on a much tighter basis than this and are unhappy about some aspects of the present situation. At interview, company representatives argued that their competitiveness in the MGB land market had declined during the 1970s. On the one hand, stringent planning conditions, planning delays and high interest rates had lowered the price they were able to offer for land, while on the other hand the general rise in agricultural land prices (see Fig. 3.3), and especially competition for land from hobby farmers, had worked against them. The theoretical basis for this argument is the fact that, ultimately, the price they can afford to pay for mineral land is determined by the delivered price of minerals imported into the region. In practice this argument is undermined by the rising real cost of transport and the rising real value of land in various aftercare uses close to London. This complaint is also dismissed by district valuers who say that in their experience mineral companies are almost always able to outbid at auction other non–urban land-use competitors where average quality gravel deposits are concerned.

Turning specifically to the MGB, mineral operators point out that green belt restraint itself makes little difference to the granting of permission for extraction, and as an approved use of green belt land that is how it should be. This does not mean to say that permission is readily granted. The numerous amenity societies in the MGB often try to use green belt restraint as a basis for refusal. In the companies' experience, however, other environmental impacts are more serious obstacles, especially those relating to the nuisance caused to local residents by noise, traffic and dust. These often present intractable difficulties whereas amenity objections can often be overturned by agreeing to landscaping programmes. Planning permission is, however, increasingly difficult to obtain, or so the companies argue. Public participation in planning and a basic unwillingness of county planning committees to comply have created delays and a generally negative attitude towards the industry. Nonetheless, it can be argued that caution is a justifiable response to minerals applications. The fact that, in the past, planning committees did not stipulate stringent planning conditions on the phasing of extraction or on the kind of reclamation required, does not wholly exonerate those companies that left land in a derelict condition. Thus although the companies complain that their present applications and promises of reclamation to a given standard are being unfairly assessed, that is, on the basis of their past performance, on what other basis are they to be judged?

Central to this debate is not only the substantial amount of derelict land

Table 4.4   Land affected by sand and gravel workings[1] in south–east England, 1948–75.

	ha	%
satisfactorily restored[2] and in an acceptable after-use	7 539	40.7
satisfactorily restored but not in an acceptable after-use	860	4.6
restored unsatisfactorily	1 383	7.5
undergoing restoration	2 637	14.2
worked out but not restored	4 208	22.7
	16 627	89.7
being worked in 1975	1 895	10.2
	18 522	100.0

Source: Standing Conference (1979b, p. 7).
[1]   Includes industrial and soft sand workings.
[2]   'Restoration' is defined as 'to comply fully with the restoration conditions [as laid down in the planning permission] or [to a state] otherwise acceptable to the local planning authority' (p.6).

created by companies in the past but also their ability to restore agricultural land to its original productivity now that most poor quality farmland overlying gravel has been worked. Information on restoration has been collected by Standing Conference county by county for the whole South East region, but not for the MGB specifically. Between 1948 and 1975, approximately 14 000 ha had been worked for sand and gravel in the region, but only 54% of this had been restored and put to an acceptable after-use (Standing Conference 1979b). In addition, a further 4500 ha was either being worked or actively restored at the end of 1975 (see Table 4.4). A careful examination of county data gives the distinct impression that mineral working in the MGB has been associated with lower restoration standards than in the region as a whole. Standing Conference says that 'significant concentrations [of unrestored land] are to be found to the west of London on the London, Buckinghamshire, Surrey and Berkshire borders, and to the north east of London on the London/Essex border' (1979b, p. 11). This concentration can be explained by the longer historical association of mineral working close to London than in areas further away, leading to a disproportionate amount of land in the MGB that has been subject to less stringent restoration standards than those required of operators today. It can also be attributed to the attempts of operators to acquire planning permission for urban development on sites close to London. It is arguable that the poor restoration of land on the urban fringe may improve their chances of getting the planning permissions they seek. Of the restored land that has been returned to a satisfactory use, 41% is farmed, 46% is in leisure uses (including wet pits used for sailing and fishing), 7% has been developed and 6% is heathland or afforested.

One of the major problems lies with the 41% in an agricultural after-use.

Much of this land has not been returned to its original level of productivity, and work by Lowe *et al.* (1977) in Havering questions whether it is ever possible to return Grades 1 and 2 agricultural land to its original productivity (see also Countryside Commission 1981). Much semi-restored gravel land can at best be used only for rough grazings (Grade 5) and some lies derelict. Such states of restoration, or non-restoration, conform with the impressions of MAFF officials for those pits worked prior to the 1960s when few, if any, restoration conditions were imposed. Today, many more conditions are laid down and land can often be restored to Grade 3 standard. But this can be a slow process, sometimes the result of the shortage of appropriate fill, and it makes mineral extraction much less of a transient landscape feature than operators often maintain. Attention is currently focused on the agricultural land restoration experiments at Papercourt Farm, Ripley and Bush Farm, Upminster where means of restoring Grades 1 and 2 farmland to their original productivities are being tested (DOE *et al.* 1977). The mineral companies are hopeful that the experiments will prove successful but MAFF officials are less optimistic. These are important experiments as much of the remaining gravel-bearing land in the MGB is under agricultural land of Grades 1 and 2. Even if, following the experiments, guidelines can be agreed for model restoration agreements, doubts remain as to whether they can be made effective. More suitably qualified staff are required even now to supervise restoration, both in local authorities and in mineral companies, especially as restoration activities themselves can constitute a nuisance to local residents (Lowe *et al.* 1977). This is a critical point because the introduction of a statutory financial penalty on those operators who do not ensure satisfactory standards of restoration (a bonding system) was not recommended in the Stevens committee report (1976), by central government in its response to it (DOE 1978g), or by the Verney committee report (1976). A tighter application of existing planning powers and higher professional standards was thought to be sufficient.

To sum up, mineral extraction remains a matter of concern to planners, councillors and the public alike. It is inevitable that the historical record of poor or non-existent restoration will continue to be held against companies until they have demonstrated that they have put their house in order to the satisfaction of local residents, planners, farmers and MAFF. The record also indicates that the environmental impact of extraction lasts much longer than the period of active working. Many pits have been poorly restored and yet requests are now being made to extract on better quality farmland, and often in areas where the local population is especially conscious of the quality of its environment. Nevertheless, most planning officers accept that aggregate extraction will have to continue in the MGB, but they accept this grudgingly. They are sceptical about their ability to enforce detailed restoration conditions. Threatening not to grant operators further planning permissions is also seen as something of a hollow threat. Central government is committed to a cheap gravel policy and may be prepared, as it has been in the past, to give the necessary permissions on appeal. Under these circumstances, and often against the wishes of their members, most planning officers feel it essential to try to retain local discretion over where and when mineral extraction takes place by granting at least some minerals applications.

Summary

This review of the three major approved green belt land uses reveals self-interest and serious land-use competition. This is only to be expected in the urban fringe. What is of greater concern are the inconsistent positions of individual local planning authorities and the few positive attempts they are making to resolve the conflicts illustrated here. Many planning staff have only limited experience of rural planning problems, especially those raised by agricultural development, and a lack of familiarity leads to a lack of confidence and to conservative attitudes. The weakness of the control powers they hold over farming and forestry (see Ch. 5) contributes to their lack of confidence, and where authorities have acted decisively it is often more a reflection of the enthusiasm and commitment of the officer concerned than the local severity of the conflict. Some planning officers, and rather more elected representatives, do not seem to be aware of the difficulties created for policy implementation by the gap between those that insist upon the full commercial use of rural land in the Green Belt and those that insist upon the maintenance of amenity at all costs. The middle ground, so far as it can be determined – and what follows is an oversimplification – is based around the positions that mineral working, if it is to be permitted in the MGB at all, must be carried out discreetly and the land must be returned to its former use and productivity; that public open space must be used only for informal, outdoor recreational activities; and that farming should be conducted by efficient, full-time operators without the undue assistance of large, modern buildings, farm shops and pony paddocks.

The Agricultural Census reveals a changing pattern of farming across the Green Belt from an arable north-east to a mixed farming south-west. It also records a decline in the proportion of rented land and rough grazings away from the immediate edge of London and an increase in the stocking rate of grassland with distance from the capital – partly the result of excluding horses from the statistics. At the same time the large number of horticultural units inside the GLC boundary (Table 4.1) contrasts with the evidence for poorly maintained land close to the urban edge, indicating the existence of marked interfarm differences about which the published statistics cannot inform (see Ch. 6).

The preference for commercial agriculture over recreational developments among planning committee chairmen, and to a lesser extent among planning officers too, in spite of their commitment in principle to recreation provision in green belts (see p. 34) is an interesting comment on local attitudes. The importance of this point is highlighted by recent research into the use of open land in the MGB. This shows quite clearly that most public open space in the Green Belt as presently promoted and managed is not intensively used and does not meet more than marginally the recreational needs of inner-London residents, primarily for reasons of its inaccessibility. Green belt open spaces are an additional amenity for the outer-suburban population (Harrison 1981a), and there is little evidence to suggest that most local authorities have the political will to alter the situation. The better promotion of sites, their more intensive use and their recreational development all add up to increased expenditure and external disbenefits to neighbouring residents and are strongly opposed by local amenity and residents' associations.

The conflict between mineral working, local amenity and high quality farmland is giving planners increasing cause for concern. In the face of what Standing Conference sees as the cheap gravel policy of central government (Standing Conference 1979a), local planners and MAFF officials often find themselves in agreement in opposing minerals applications and in struggling to ensure effective land reclamation and after-use. There are no simple solutions to this conflict as the extraction process has a number of stages *each* of which may lead to disamenity while contributing to the overall financial success of the enterprise. It is inevitable that extraction will continue in the Green Belt, whatever the wishes of local politicians, and dispute over the desired standards of land reclamation will continue while the present atmosphere of mistrust persists between the mineral operators on the one hand and local planners and MAFF officials on the other. Only the gravel companies themselves can reduce this tension through improved reclamation standards and until this happens their argument that extraction is a temporary, even ephemeral, adjustment to the landscape needs to be treated with the scepticism it deserves.

Conflicts between the interests of agriculture and all other land uses, conforming and non-conforming, are endemic in the MGB, and local planning authorities will become increasingly involved in these conflicts as policies for farmland are included in development plans and as increasingly strident demands are made to bring certain farming operations within the scope of development control (e.g. see Shoard 1980). And in this context it is worth reminding ourselves of the two main, related agricultural land-use issues in the MGB. First, should efficient food production be the primary goal of agriculture in the urban fringe even if this conflicts with broader amenity objectives? Secondly, even if the case for this goal can be sustained, is farmland in the MGB being maintained in such a way as to realise it? It is to these questions that this book returns in Chapter 6.

5 Planning powers and the implementation of green belt restraint

Introduction

The previous chapters have sought to elucidate the objectives of green belt restraint as seen by local and central government. Attempts to examine whether restraint is being effectively implemented are hampered by the range of objectives now being espoused for it by local authorities. Assessment is also complicated by the view that planners do not have the necessary powers to achieve their green belt objectives and that this difficulty has become more evident in recent years as amenity issues have assumed greater importance in local planning. Restricting the growth of non-conforming uses, difficult though this may be in the MGB, is at least an agreed goal among all local authorities, and between them and central government. Although dispute arises over individual cases, the purpose of restraint in this sense is well understood and local authorities have a long-established tool in development control, which is designed specifically to stop unwanted changes in land use.

Indeed, in the post-war period local authority planners have relied heavily on their development control powers to enforce restraint, and the need to bring large areas of urban-fringe land into public ownership along the lines promoted by the Green Belt (London and Home Counties) Act 1938 has seemed unnecessary. More generally, it is also agreed that the development control system is successful in limiting urban sprawl and scattered urban growth in the countryside (Hall *et al*. 1973, Best 1981, Blacksell & Gilg 1981). On the basis of the evidence contained in Chapter 3 it can also be argued that development control is successfully limiting the growth of non-conforming uses in the MGB. Nevertheless, these plaudits should not conceal the criticisms that are levelled at the system. The system is accused of being regressive in its effects (Simmie & Hall 1978), being an inefficient bureaucratic process (DOE 1975c, House of Commons 1977, 1978) and being mindlessly effected without thought for its purpose (Harrison 1972, Davies 1980). It does not escape criticism in its ability to enforce green belt restraint either (see below).

In some ways the problems associated with non-conforming uses and their control are straightforward when compared to the difficulties facing planners wishing to promote particular objectives for the main approved land uses (see Shoard 1979). Some of these problems, such as the acceptable reclamation of worked mineral land and the inability to ensure that agricultural land remains fully productive, have already been referred to. Planning powers have always been weak in this area, especially as agricultural and forestry operations lie very largely outside the scope of development control. Effectively, agricultural and forestry developments are determined by central government through its policies for these industries. These policies are promoted by the very substantial public monies made available to farmers and foresters as businessmen in the form of support prices and capital grants (Morris 1980), and the fiscal concessions available to rural landowners as owners of substantial capital assets (see Northfield committee report 1979, pp. 71–90, 354–69; Sutherland 1980). The total amount of subsidy received by farmers from consumers and taxpayers is disputed – it has been put as high as £8500 million per annum (Shoard 1980) – but what is indisputable is that in 1980/1 farmers received £1012 million in cash before other forms of tax relief and indirect assistance were taken into account (MAFF 1982).

In the face of increasing pressure from amenity interests, and as a response to the inadequacies of development control, planners have developed new skills, such as countryside management, and extended the use of existing powers, making more use of planning conditions for example. It is the purpose of this chapter to consider the relevance of these control powers in achieving some of the key objectives espoused for green belt land. Of particular concern is the ability of local authorities to restrict the growth of non-conforming uses, to minimise the loss of amenity resulting from the intensification of rural land uses, and to prevent the under-use of farmland and the inadequate reclamation of mineral workings. These matters are considered under three broad headings – development control, management schemes and the public acquisition of land. But before doing so a number of general principles are discussed concerning public intervention in the use and management of privately owned land.

Intervention

Intervention in the rights of private individuals, whether by the Crown, the state or a public agency, in respect of some higher national, collective or public good, is traditional in the area of property. English common law has never recognised absolute ownership by individuals. Even freehold ownership only bestows a bundle of rights and not absolute control. The most important of these rights confer upon the holder the power to occupy and to use the land, to improve it, to lease it to others, to sell it or to pass it on to one's heirs and, in the latter three situations, to determine which rights are to be transferred, at what price, when and to whom. It follows that land should be regarded as having a dual nature. It consists of physical attributes, such as topography, mineral deposits and buildings, *and* the legal rights attached to these. The object of ownership should thus be viewed as the acquisition of the rights that go with the land (Pearce 1980). It is from the ability to exploit the resource, as conferred or constrained by rights of ownership, that power, financial benefit and pleasure are derived; and it is in this context that public bodies have had powers delegated to them by society which they can then exercise over private individuals.

Traditionally, the ownership of land led to obligations as well as to rights (Denman & Prodano 1972, Denman 1978). Such obligations were more in evidence under feudal land law with its collective outlook than are evident under capitalism with its emphasis on private, personal and material considerations (Massey & Catalano 1978). With capitalism, owners have become increasingly concerned with the profit that can be made from the land, and Newby *et al.* now maintain that property law 'is concerned, not with obligations, but with rights. Indeed, the only significant legal obligations regarding property ownership today fall, not on the owner, but on the non-owner – those who do not own land are obliged not to trespass, but those who do are not obliged to distribute the benefits' (Newby *et al.* 1978, p. 337).

This view can be contested in detail and in its emphasis but it does indicate why planning controls, which are regulatory, can be regarded as a weak means of redressing the balance between public and private interests (Boynton 1979). In other words, planning authorities are unlikely to be able to *insist* on any particular course of action by the owner, they can only seek to influence or to prohibit. Indeed, it can be argued that the use of the term 'intervention' in this context implies that private individuals have acquired the basic rights to land. And in Britain it is the practice to define the nature of the public interest, to determine how important this is and to measure the degree to which private actions do not meet it, before the necessary mechanisms to accomplish the desired change are put into effect.

A very wide range of statutory instruments have been employed by the governments of Western countries, including the making of information publicly available (land registration), preferential taxation, planning controls on changes in use, laws of nuisance, the compulsory purchase of specific properties and the nationalisation of development rights (Pearce 1980, Lichfield & Darin-Drabkin 1980). Neutze argues that the key distinction between countries depends on the degree to which they leave the rights to property in private hands while employing other deterrents and inducements, or take the land into public ownership (Neutze 1973). The importance of this distinction should not be underestimated, not least because of its political and ideological significance, but it is in danger of oversimplifying a complicated tenurial situation. Most Western countries, including Britain, employ a battery of measures that cross this divide, and they rightly recognise that controls impose public and private costs as well as creating public benefits. Moreover, in a democratic society considerable effort needs to be made to persuade rather than to coerce owners into accommodating the needs and wishes of non-owners (and other owners) via information, advice and other forms of practical and financial assistance. And this co-operative or consensus approach underlies most attempts to resolve conflicts in the British countryside today. Nevertheless, this approach incurs a cost, often very largely met out of general taxation, and unless it is seen to be effective then opinions polarise. This has occurred in the case of the conflict between agriculture and wildlife conservation, drawing attention to the allied question of compensation for the loss of development rights (DOE 1972b, Bell 1979).

Development control

As the underlying social and economic objectives of development plans have been made more explicit so development control decision making has changed. The change has not been so much in the system itself, except for increased public participation, but in the way it has been applied (Alder 1979, DOE 1980b). The system remains responsive in that it only comes into play when an owner wishes to change the use of a piece of land in such a way that the change transgresses the areas of permitted development allowed under the General Development Order (DOE 1977a), but decisions are now taking longer to reach and having more planning conditions attached to them. These conditions must relate to matters encompassed by the Town and Country Planning legislation and, in an attempt to get round this limitation, planning authorities are increasingly using Section 52 Agreements (Town and Country Planning Act 1971). These Agreements are struck with developers before they submit their applications and they regulate either temporarily or permanently the future use of the land concerned. This approach emphasises bargaining, secrecy and the concept of planning gain, aspects of planning procedure that do not attract universal acclaim (Jowell 1977, Loughlin 1978, Heap & Ward 1980), and doubts remain as to the legality of some of these Agreements where their terms stray far from statutorily defined planning matters (Tucker 1978, Hawke 1981a,b). One of the grey areas concerns amenity. Strictly speaking, development control is concerned with changes in land use and not the appearance of land, and because aesthetics are a subjective matter there is a danger of inequity between applicants in different planning authorities.

In discussing development control procedures and their effectiveness in implementing restraint, local planning officers make a number of points in support of the present system. They argue that it has general public acceptance and endorsement, essential ingredients for it to work at all. They believe it to be an effective system in keeping scattered urban development to a minimum and in maintaining the openness of green belt, and that there is a workable degree of agreement between local and central government over the interpretation of restraint in particular cases. Over 80% of officers are satisfied with the appeals decisions given by the DOE's inspectors. Only three are wholly dissatisfied, the remaining seven accepting that their concern stemmed from an 18-month period following the publication of the white paper *Widening the choice: the next steps in housing* (DOE 1973b). During this period, they claim, neither the secretary of state nor his inspectors could be relied upon to make consistent decisions. This is interpreted as the result of political pressures and not inadequacies among the inspectorate or in the appeals system.

Planning officers also list a number of problems with the system. The one causing widest concern is the need to avoid the setting of precedents which in turn leads to the refusal of applications that are acceptable on their own merits, or are acceptable but only with the addition of unenforceable planning conditions. Agricultural occupancy conditions for farm cottages are an often quoted example of this problem, but in the area of environmental impact generally enforcement is difficult. In the view of planning officers the financial penalties imposed on defaulters are ridiculously small. Conditions relating to landscape appearance, which inevitably depend on personal judgement, are not matters on which enforcement can be assured. In some cases the cost that would fall on the authority were a Stop Notice decision to go against it on appeal, is sufficient to dissuade the authority from pursuing such matters. Mineral companies, small industrial enterprises and riding schools are often well versed in the difficulties facing planning authorities and are regarded as the worst offenders.

Three other major problems are raised by local planners and all are associated with approved land uses. One of these is the inadequate definition in the General Development Order (GDO) of what constitutes recreational development on agricultural land. At present this leaves planners in a position of being unable to limit the spread of horse grazing, stabling and riding schools, a position that has recently been confirmed in a judgement on a planning decision in Oxfordshire (Turrall-Clarke 1981). Secondly, planners complain that they cannot stop the intensification of existing land uses and often refer specifically to the growth in number and scale of intensive livestock units. This brings them into conflict with MAFF officials and farmers over the interpretation of permitted development within the Agriculture Use Class (Class VI, No. 289, GDO 1977) as to when an agricultural use becomes an industrial use of land. The present wording of the GDO does not restrict unduly the farmer's operations and seems not to have kept abreast of modern farming technology (Royal Commission on Environmental Pollution 1979, Ch. 7; Dolman 1981). Finally, there are the problems noted in Chapter 4 concerning the reclamation of mineral land. Planning officers are keen to retain the control of mineral operations under their jurisdiction and when interviewed in 1978 wanted to be able to specify the after-use of sites as a condition for planning permission. At that time, however, such a condition was *ultra vires* (Standing Conference 1979b) and could only be included as part of a Section 52 Agreement, something operators wanted to avoid. Since then the Town and Country Planning (Minerals) Act 1981 has given local authorities a number of increased powers. One of these is the ability to impose an aftercare (method of land reclamation) condition with a *particular* after-use in mind (Eve 1981).★

Management schemes

The inadequacies of development control as a means of promoting the positive management of green belt land have led to increased interest among local authorities in differing methods of countryside management. There are at least four separate but overlapping methods. One concerns the removal of eyesores and other one-off remedial treatments, usually on land within the public domain. A second consists of long-term management, again normally on publicly owned land, such as is carried out on public open spaces used for recreation. A third is associated with area-wide management experiments promoted by the Countryside Commission in association with local authorities and covering all kinds of rural land. And, finally, there are management agreements struck between public bodies and private owners, usually on a voluntary basis and at the initiative of the public body. In this sense they lie outside the immediate confines of the development control system and the making of Section 52 Agreements.

The term 'management agreement' can mean just about anything, but it is employed here in the specific sense used by the Countryside Commission as 'A formal written agreement between a public authority and an owner of an interest in land . . . who thereby undertakes to manage the land in a specified manner in order to satisfy a particular public need, usually in return for some form of consideration' (quoted in Feist 1978, p. 1). The value of such arrangements lies in the fact that they can be tailored to the exact circumstances of the situation and permit the public authority to take the initiative. Their basic weakness is that they are usually voluntary and depend for their success on the compensation clauses of the agreement. The principle of compensation to cover any additional management costs incurred by the owner in meeting a specified programme of management is only fair and reasonable. Compensation stemming from the loss of development rights, which in the broadest sense includes additional income from another conforming use, is more controversial. Critics point to the fact that applicants in urban areas can no longer claim compensation for planning refusals. In principle it would also seem to be unacceptable where compensation is given to owners for *not* carrying out developments that they had not intended to do anyway, or would have only been able to do as a result of other public spending, such as MAFF grant aid (see MacEwen & MacEwen 1982). Compensation is also unacceptable if it were to be used to encourage occupiers of perfectly normal farmland to bring it in to full

★ The more general issue of the development decisions of central government departments and agencies lying outside local jurisdiction has already been discussed in Chapter 2.

production, when other occupiers already do this as a matter of course. A further weakness with management agreements, although this is much more fully appreciated today following the debates surrounding the Wildlife and Countryside Act 1981, is the limited financial resources often put into public hands to back up agreements where strong commercial interests are involved (see below). This is especially evident in the urban fringe where mineral deposits and the hope of residential development affect land values (Countryside Commission 1981).

Management agreements should not be confused with the area-wide countryside management experiments initiated by the Countryside Commission and funded jointly by it and the relevant local authorities. These experiments began in the Lake District (Countryside Commission 1976a) but were quickly extended to the urban fringe, first to Manchester (Countryside Commission 1976b) and then to London's Green Belt. Experiments have been conducted in the south Hertfordshire–Barnet LB and Havering LB areas (Countryside Commission 1981) and in the Colne Valley. The Commission sees countryside management as a flexible, low-cost approach to the positive management of land that operates within the context of local planning policies and as a complement to the negative powers of development control. Through the use of limited financial inducements to landowners, the mobilisation of voluntary effort, the taking of educational and publicity initiatives, and personal contact between the project officer, interested groups and local authority officials, these experiments seek to resolve local land-use conflicts and to change the attitudes of conflicting user-groups.

These schemes have achieved a degree of success. They have reduced overt conflict and made people talk to each other, and these gains should not be minimised. But the whole approach is largely dependent upon informal agreements worked out on a personal basis and is hamstrung by its limited financial resources and its short duration (initially for three years). There is the real danger that the approach will prove cosmetic, obscuring the real difficulties by tackling the effects and not the causes of inadequate land management.

This conclusion also sets in context the findings of Standing Conference. Following the publication of its report *The improvement of London's Green Belt*, Standing Conference encouraged its members to draw up landscape development strategies, to make further use of countryside management experiments and to conduct tree planting schemes. It recommended that all these activities be drawn together into annual programmes of action in order to establish 'a pattern of behaviour by local authorities: and a conscious decision on their part to make improvements in the Green Belt and maintain the impetus of their decisions. To do this we consider that the DOE should issue a circular to all Green Belt local authorities calling for such programmes to be prepared and submitted to them and the Countryside Commission' (Standing Conference 1977a, p. 25). Discussions with officials reveal that DOE has never addressed itself to the question of incentives specifically for improving green belt land. The Green Belt

Working Party of Standing Conference also looked into the sources of central government finance that its members might tap to help them with their programmes. Sources do exist but the legislation from which they derive is widely scattered and directed at specific *land-use* goals rather than at the comprehensive improvement of *areas*.

These difficulties may help to account for the limited commitment of local authorities in the MGB to landscape improvement through management schemes (Standing Conference 1977a, p. 21). Frequently, management activity consists of no more than small tree planting exercises, the maintenance of rights of way and country park management, an obligation that would follow anyway if grant aid had been received from the Countryside Commission to establish the park. Other reasons for limited activity emerge from the interviews with planning officers. Some officers are simply unwilling to commit resources to land management projects and argue that land management lies beyond the statutory remit of the planning legislation and responsibility for it therefore falls to their estates departments. Many officers are loathe to operate outside a consensus model and their activities are thus heavily constrained by the willingness of owners to co-operate. This problem is often side-stepped by only conducting management work on their own land. Finally, both Standing Conference and individual member authorities constantly emphasise the low cost of such management activity, a point they feel obliged to stress if they are to obtain any resources for it at all. But by so doing they severely restrict the range of management options open to them and focus their members' attention on the cost of management rather than on what they would like to achieve.

The public ownership of land

The public acquisition of land has often been regarded as an action of last resort. The circumstances under which it should be conducted and the level of compensation that should be paid to existing owners still arouses considerable debate. Some bodies with compulsory purchase powers, such as the Nature Conservancy Council, rarely use them; others like the Forestry Commission can only purchase land when it is made available for sale. However, the purchase of land in the urban fringe, either to ensure that development takes place efficiently and equitably or that land is secured for amenity or public utility purposes, occurs quite regularly. The MGB contains perhaps three or four times the national average of publicly owned rural land (see Ch. 6).

One reason for this large area is the purchase of land for green belt purposes (see Ch. 1), although this is only one pretext under which open land has been acquired by local authorities. Within the context of green belt, the home counties and their districts have regularly purchased or protected land by covenant since the 1920s and have been aided in this by the LCC and the GLC. In 1935 the LCC set aside £2 million to grant aid (up to 50% of their cost) the

Table 5.1   The Green Belt Estates: area and number of properties.

County (pre-1965)	Properties bought					
	with LCC aid		without LCC aid		Total	
	no.	area (ha)	no.	area (ha)	no.	area (ha)
Bucks.	33	2 226	38	2 658	71	4 884
Essex	21	2 347	13	1 643	34	3 990
Herts.	28	2 082	14	384	42	2 466
Kent	13	1 091	9	151	22	1 242
Middlesex	23	2 692	74	2 830	97	5 522
Surrey	31	1 642	66	3 926	97	5 568
(Croydon)	4	247	?	?	(4)	(247)
total	153	12 327	214	11 592	367	23 919

Source: Sharp (in preparation).

acquisition of properties to which Londoners would have access for recreational purposes, the LCC itself having very little undeveloped land left within its own boundaries. The area acquired or protected is shown on Table 5.1. It amounts to almost 24 000 ha and most of it was purchased before 1947. Nearly half attracted LCC grant aid, and at the time of purchase over 50% of the land was in agricultural use and only some 20% was public open space with a further 3.4% in use as golf courses (Sharp, in preparation).

These 'green belt' properties only constitute a small part of the public estate in the MGB and what is important is not that land is publicly owned but that the management objectives of the various public owners comply with the objectives of green belt. The proprietary powers held by the owner that go with freehold ownership are sufficient to ensure that public access and reasonable standards of farming husbandry and amenity can be maintained in situations where development control and management agreements are inadequate. Public ownership should stop speculative land market activity for example. Yet control through ownership does not ensure in practice that all the management objectives of the owner are met, especially where the land is let on full, secure agricultural tenancies. The needs of the tenant have always to be taken into account. But changes to the lease, in order to admit public access for example, can always be made when occupiers change or even when the rent is reviewed (triennially), perhaps in exchange for a rent reduction (Williams 1979). Likewise, public ownership can provide an effective control over non-conforming land uses. But it will only do so if the public owner does not have to meet a superior statutory requirement, such as waste disposal, and if public land is not regarded as an amenable resource upon which to effect public sector developments, such as new roads, which might otherwise prove more difficult to achieve, or more expensive, on private land. Those owners with a superior statutory requirement cannot, in implementing that function, always be expected to meet the high amenity standards of outer-suburban residents, but they do have to 'have regard to the desirability of conserving the natural beauty and amenity of the countryside' under Section 11 of the Countryside Act 1968. To sum up, at the level of principle, freehold ownership offers the means of meeting the amenity and land-use objectives of local planning authorities in the MGB, but in practice, unless owned by the local authority, the jurisdiction of local planners over this land may be limited and tenuous.

The whole question of public ownership was raised with both planning officers and planning committee chairmen. Some officers argued that increased public ownership is essential if certain intractable environmental problems are to be resolved. The kinds of situation they had in mind are sites where the cost of restoration will exceed the value of the reclaimed site and where small plots of land are cut off by new roads from the remainder of the farm. The estates department of the GLC, for example, was convinced that the public interest, however defined, is best served on land owned by the council, and this view, it is fair to say, is slowly gaining ground in other authorities. Standing Conference also concluded that in general there is less risk of 'damaged' or 'threatened' landscapes on large units of land in public ownership (Standing Conference 1976). Planning committee chairmen, all but three of whom were from Conservative-controlled councils, expressed surprisingly mixed views. Only 14 were opposed to public ownership as a matter of principle. They felt that existing planning controls were sufficient to achieve green belt restraint objectives. The remaining 24 were prepared to consider each case on its merits and despite local political difficulties would purchase on a small scale to meet particular problems. Examples given included the purchase of derelict glass-houses so as to maintain agricultural use, of scrubland to be managed as public open space, of run-down farmland for reletting to other farmers, of land for golf courses and of land near the M25 motorway to prevent speculative activity. A pragmatic rather than an ideological perspective predominated, with ownership being seen as a means to an end but not as an end in itself.

Summary

The problem with trying to decide whether local authorities have insufficient powers and resources to achieve their green belt objectives, or whether they lack the political will fully to effect the powers they already have, stems from the diffuse objectives local authorities often attribute to green belt. Broadly, however, objectives are increasingly emphasising the maintenance and en-hancement of amenity, and this change demands a reassessment of the relative value of the different control measures available.

Local planning officers are largely in agreement that development control is quite effective in minimising the spread of non-conforming land uses. It is a system of control in which they, their members and DOE are well versed. The ongoing problems of how to avoid setting precedents and alleviating tensions between local authorities and statutory undertakers are unavoidable. At least they are familiar problems. The use of planning conditions has become more widespread in recent years, as has the use of Section 52 Agreements, but the danger with the latter is that they encourage secrecy. Development control is less effective in promoting particular forms of conforming land use, such as higher standards of gravel land reclamation, or preventing others, such as the industrialisation of farming. Protecting landscapes and enhancing amenity is the most difficult area of all (see Shoard 1981). Within the confines of the existing system the best hope lies in redefining the Use Class Orders to exclude certain kinds of permitted development, such as horse grazing on agricultural land (Standing Conference 1977a).

Management agreements and the public ownership of land allow a much more positive stance to be taken by local authorities. They provide the authority with an opportunity to take the initiative, but only do so at a cost. The cost consists not only of transfers of public money to private individuals, both as investments in capital assets and as recurrent management expenditure, but also in the employment of skilled manpower and in the mobilisation of political will within local authorities where the predominant ethos is one of reducing local taxation and promoting individual freedoms. As a result, action, as reflected in countryside management schemes, is often limited in scope, and the public acquisition of land for green belt purposes has been largely confined to the inter-war period.

Greater public control thus imposes increased public and private costs, and will only be endorsed if the problems are seen to warrant it. Opinions as to the importance of amenity in the MGB are varied in this regard and it is sensible to proceed from a position that endorses common sense, flexibility and a range of initiatives designed to meet specific situations (e.g. see Shoard 1979). The force of this point is illustrated by the case study of poorly maintained farmland contained in Chapter 6.

6 The maintenance of agricultural land in the Green Belt

Introduction

On many occasions the discussions with local planning officers and planning committee chairmen led back to the run-down condition of stretches of open land in the MGB. Much of this land is either unreclaimed mineral workings or is nominally in some form of agricultural use. Given the views expressed about the preferred nature of farming in the Green Belt (see Ch. 4), it is not surprising to record that respondents felt that farmland was being misused if its productivity was low, that farmland should produce food and not support recreational activities (including horses), and that under-used farmland represented a loss of amenity. Not all local planners and chairmen hold these views but the majority that do are supported in their opinions by MAFF officials. Land with an untidy or run-down appearance has few supporters, a matter to which Standing Conference drew attention when it mapped the extent of 'threatened' landscapes (see Fig. 1.2).

In recent years Standing Conference has not been alone in commenting on this phenomenon, nor in making the allied point that the amount of land lost from agriculture is considerably greater than that transferred to a purposeful urban use (Low 1973, Coleman 1976, 1977; Elson 1979a, Countryside Commission 1981). Coleman, for example, measured land-use change in the Thames estuary area between 1962 and 1972, and in a zone of 850.5 km^2 she recorded a loss of improved farmland amounting to 42.0 km^2 but a gain in total settlement of only 18.5 km^2, and that included a net increase of 4.5 km^2 in derelict land. She further recorded an increase of 30.5 km^2 in the area of waste land, and went on to argue that too much development occurred on productive farmland and not enough on existing derelict, scrub and waste land within the urban area.

Her work raises a number of important issues as significant areas of derelict land undoubtedly exist both within and on the edges of our major cities (Civic Trust 1977, Burrows 1978, Moss 1981). Nevertheless, her studies can be criticised on a number of grounds. First, some critics question whether her definitions of such terms as 'waste land' are sufficiently precise to be consistently applied in the absence of other information. On its own, untidy appearance is an insufficient criterion (see the discussion in Rogers 1978). Secondly, in projecting her findings forward to future states of land use in Britain, Coleman suggests, without providing supporting evidence, that the growth in 'waste land' is a cumulative process and not a once-and-for-all adverse effect stemming from the development of land. Thirdly, and most important, critics object to the crisis-orientation implicit in her evaluation of her land-use findings. Her evaluation implies that farming is good and the built environment is bad, but at no point does she conduct a full social cost–benefit analysis of the consequences of urban growth. If she were to do this then others maintain that the benefits to be gained by the urban population from a generous lay-out of new development would more than offset the additional farming land and productivity losses that would result from this approach to development (Best 1981, Boddington 1973, Wibberley 1959, 1981).

It is fair to say that the debate surrounding the under-use of farmland is clouded by imprecise statements over what is being measured and why, and in the absence of any rigorous investigation into why land is being maintained in this condition. Most analyses depend upon secondary sources of data, or even anecdotal evidence (Elson 1981), and not surveys designed specifically to examine the issue. Unfortunately, the only comprehensive study in the MGB that is relevant, the mapping of 'threatened' landscapes by Standing Conference (see Fig. 1.2), consists of a broad classification of areas of not less than 1 km² in extent and does not allow for local change. Yet data from the Agricultural Census (see Ch. 4) strongly suggest that intensive (horticultural units) and extensive (rough grazings) uses of farmland exist side by side in the inner half of the MGB. It follows that a full understanding of the causes of poor land maintenance will only be established within the context of individual farm circumstances, i.e. the level at which land management decisions are taken and to which remedial measures will have to be addressed.

Of course, more general levels of explanation for the presence of run-down farmland can be postulated on the basis of the uncertain planning environment of the urban fringe. But it can be argued from the findings of other empirical studies that a specific type of urban-fringe farming remains more clearly postulated in theory (Sinclair 1967, Boal 1970, Bryant 1974a) than is discernible on the ground. Empirical studies support some hypotheses about urban impacts on agriculture, but not others (e.g. see Bryant 1974b, 1981; Moran 1978, 1979; Berry 1979), and suggest that those assumptions that hold good around one city do not necessarily hold good elsewhere (Bryant & Greaves 1978, OECD 1979). There is nothing surprising about this conclusion given the wide variety of institutional responses to the impacts of urban areas on farming, and the varying degree of severity with which these pressures operate. Farming is characterised by an intrinsic heterogeneity, which is often exaggerated in the urban fringe. Those writers who imply that farming patterns in the urban fringe should be explicable in terms of immediate urban influences also underestimate the degree to which *all* farmers respond to technological and managerial innovations introduced to meet changing economic and political considerations quite unrelated to urban proximity (Munton 1974).

That said, it is possible to generalise about the causes of poor land maintenance and from this to draw up a list of specific hypotheses to be examined in the context of the MGB. There are three main related causes. These are, first, the effects of urban intrusion on farming decisions such as result from mineral extraction, road construction, the siting of public utilities and trespass (MAFF 1973, Rettig 1976, Hearne *et al.* 1977). Secondly, there is the lack of long-term security for agricultural occupiers in the face of urban expansion. This leads to a reluctance to make long-term improvements to land and buildings, to the speculative purchase of property and to the short-term letting of land. Both farmers and developers allow holdings to run down in the hope that this will increase their chances of gaining planning permission (Low 1973, University of Reading 1975, ACAH 1978). Thirdly, there is the presumed lack of experience (even disinterest) among urban-fringe hobby farmers in the management of their land (CRC 1978, Countryside Commission 1981).

These notions are examined here through a survey of land maintenance standards on 185 farms, carried out in conjunction with interviews held with the farms' occupiers. The interviews with occupiers (see Appendix) were designed to elicit information about their farming circumstances which was not available in any published source, and which would permit the general causes of run-down land noted above to be addressed in the context of specific farms. The data collected are sufficient to improve our understanding of the problem well beyond that so far achieved, and a number of hypotheses are tested. They are explained more fully later in the chapter but in brief it is assumed that poor standards of land maintenance are positively associated with:

(a) outlying parcels of land detached from the main holding;
(b) owner-occupation;
(c) the ownership of land by public bodies;
(d) the ownership of land by development (including mineral) interests;
(e) land let short-term and without security;
(f) attempts by the occupier to gain planning permission for development;
(g) land immediately adjacent to urban development;
(h) the importance of off-farm sources of income; and
(i) the keeping of horses.

These hypotheses cut across the three areas listed above and take account of the fact that occupiers of green belt land have widely differing motives and will respond in differing ways to the constraints and opportunities of farming in the urban fringe. The farm data collected focuses on the pattern of ownership and occupation of the farm, the sources of income of the occupier and the location of the farm in relation to existing development, as well as the attitudes and recent investment decisions of the occupier. Clearly, some of the 'explanations' are to be regarded as surrogate measures of attitudes towards land maintenance. The keeping of horses, for example, should not of itself lead to poor land maintenance.

Methods of survey   All attempts to assess the standards of land maintenance on a farm are bound to include an element of subjectivity, but that does not mean to say that the process need be inconsistent. It is impossible to define precise and absolute standards against which to relate field data. What is required of land by one farming enterprise is not necessarily required of it by another, and there is no agreement as to what are appropriate farming enterprises in the MGB (see Ch. 4). Nevertheless, this study does not seek to discriminate against farm-based recreational enterprises because they are not producing food, and it does not start by trying to establish any desired aesthetic standard for the countryside. Instead, it endeavours to determine whether the occupier is maintaining his land in such a way as to realise satisfactory levels of production, and in such a manner as to avoid any long-term deterioration in the condition of the land such that some enterprises will be impossible to pursue in the future in the absence of major capital expenditure on improvements.

To be certain of a high level of accuracy in determining standards, a detailed analysis of farm accounts and past investment decisions is in principle necessary. Experience shows that this approach would be impracticable in the urban fringe where most farmers do not keep records of this kind (see below). Those that do and who would be prepared to discuss them would not be representative of the farming community. Moreover, this level of detail is probably only necessary when seeking to resolve a particular farm problem and not, as here, when trying to reach an informed view about the general standards of land maintenance on urban-fringe farms. It was decided, therefore, that a sufficiently reliable assessment could be achieved based on a visual evaluation of certain estate management and husbandry features, cross-checked against the other data collected at interview.

This approach represents a major advance on previous studies. First, it considers land maintenance in the context of the agricultural land that occupiers themselves return as such in the Agricultural Census. The results cannot be dismissed as being related to open land in the urban fringe generally. Secondly, maintenance standards are assessed in the context of farms about which much else is known. Thirdly, information collected for other purposes, such as the land-use category 'waste land' as defined in the Second Land Utilisation Survey, is not used as a surrogate for standards of land maintenance. Finally, as a detailed study based on farm situations it avoids making general judgements on landscape quality that are divorced from how landscapes are actually being made.

CLASSIFICATION OF MAINTENANCE STANDARDS   Given the problems of assessment, simplicity was the primary guide to procedure both in terms of the number of categories used (there are only three) and in the criteria employed to allocate land to them (see Table 6.1). On the one hand, the general condition of growing crops, grazings and woodland has been examined to gain an impression of husbandry standards. On the other, the state of repair of farm

Table 6.1 Land maintenance categories.

Category I	Areas exhibiting high standards of crop husbandry and farm maintenance. Rough margins to fields, small patches of weeds or thin areas in standing crops are ignored. Field boundaries and farm roads are well maintained, and hedges fully stock-proof where appropriate. Woodland is managed; few signs of poor field drainage.
Category II	Areas indicating management problems. Crops may be thin and weedy, with permanent grass deteriorating to rough grazings for no apparent environmental reason. Signs of poor field drainage and farm 'infrastructure' inadequately maintained. Woodland receiving little or no attention.
Category III	Derelict or semi-derelict land either with no, or extremely limited, agricultural value at the present time. Occasional grazing and, where the field is flat enough, the odd hay crop taken. Field boundaries and farm roads badly maintained unless for the benefit of a neighbouring field.

Most areas exhibit more than one attribute characteristic of its category.

roads, hedges and field boundaries, and evidence of poor field drainage, have been assessed. Judgements on these elements were combined qualitatively by the surveyor to produce a single value.* Category I land gives the appearance of good or even adequate maintenance, the benefit of the doubt always being given to the occupier. Category III land, or land of extremely limited or no agricultural value in its present state, is only assigned sparingly. The amount of land in this category should be seen as a minimum estimate of the area experiencing wholly negligent maintenance. All the land in Category II, the most difficult to assign, is regarded as 'under-used'.

THE FARM SAMPLE   In 1976 there were approximately 4500 holdings in the MGB. Only a small proportion of these are included in the farm survey. One hundred and eighty-five occupiers with 4 ha or more land were interviewed following a pilot survey in Spelthorne, Surrey. The sample contains 14 810 ha of farmland or approximately 7.5% of the farmland in the MGB at that time. The farms are located in three carefully selected areas (see Fig. 6.1). All three areas are in the inner half of the Green Belt and experience some degree of urban penetration. Two of these (north Surrey and adjoining London boroughs, and south Buckinghamshire and east Berkshire) have been chosen because they contain significant areas of 'threatened landscape' (see Fig. 1.2). The third, part of west Essex and north Havering LB,† does not. Although it is impossible to select three identical areas they are similar in terms of total size, proportion of

---

* The survey was conducted by a single surveyor between June and September 1978 following a careful reconnaissance of the study areas to assess the range of conditions.

    † From now on, these areas will be termed the Surrey, Bucks. and Essex areas respectively.

part-time farms and percentage of rented land. They have a similar proportion of horticultural holdings but are dissimilar in terms of their other farm types and average size of farm (see Table 6.2). Approximately 40% of holdings with more than 4 ha of land were randomly selected, including replacements for refusals (see Appendix). The final sample contains 69 farms in Bucks. (covering 4420 ha), 65 farms in Surrey (4687 ha) and 51 farms in Essex (5703 ha).

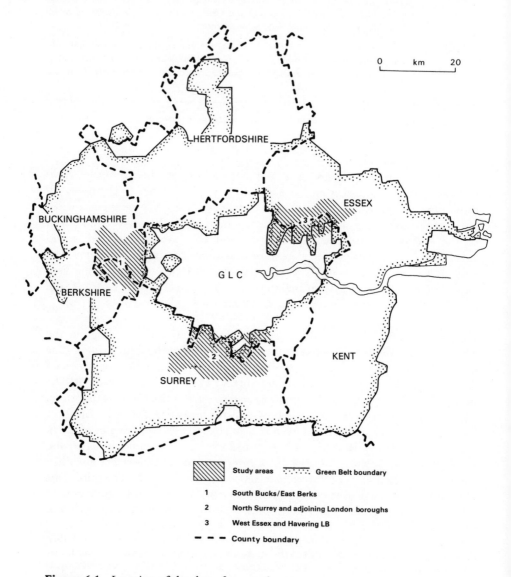

Figure 6.1   Location of the three farm study areas.

General findings

A small proportion of the total area (696 ha, 4.7%) has not been surveyed because of problems of gaining access to it. Over the remainder (14 113 ha) nearly two-thirds of the land exhibit few if any maintenance problems (Table 6.3). Major areas do not lie derelict but substantial tracts are poorly maintained. Nearly 30% of the area falls into Category II and 5.5% into Category III. To the extent that 'threatened' landscape consists in part of areas of poorly maintained farmland (see p. 26) then the existence of such landscapes is reaffirmed. But Standing Conference's map (see Fig. 1.2) of 'threatened' landscape is not an especially reliable indicator of the distribution of poorly maintained farmland as defined here. For example, although the proportion of land falling into Category II is significantly less in Essex than either Bucks. or Surrey, as would be expected from Figure 1.2, the map does not suggest that as much as 20% of farmland would fall into this category.

A careful examination of the findings farm by farm also shows that land on most farms falls largely into one category or another. The main exceptions arise where difficulties exist for clearly defined reasons on odd parts of the farm, such as where land is let short-term or is adjacent to housing. The usual effect is to lower the standards of maintenance by one category. In other words, the occupier of a well run farm is able to minimise the effects of such difficulties. Even so, small parcels of land – outlying, awkwardly shaped fields for example – fall into Categories II and III on even the best maintained farms, and there is no reason to assume that a proportion of all farmland in the countryside generally is not poorly maintained for reasons quite unrelated to urban proximity. In the absence of a control survey, however, it is impossible to assess how significant these findings are. It is clear, however, that even within the MGB farms away

Table 6.2 Agricultural characteristics of the farm study areas.

	Bucks.	Surrey	Essex	Total
total agricultural area (ha)	7692	7586	7359	22 637
number of holdings	226	223	145	594
average size of holding (ha)	33.7	34.0	50.8	38.1
% agricultural land in owner–occupation	39	40	37	39
Farm types (%)				
dairying	5	23	—	9
livestock	12	3	—	5
mixed	12	13	17	13
crops	—	2	11	4
horticultural	17	15	16	16
pigs, poultry	6	—	—	2
part-time	48	54	56	52

Source: Agricultural Census, parish returns 1976.

Table 6.3 Area by maintenance category.[1]

Maintenance category	Bucks.		Essex		Surrey		Total	
	ha	%	ha	%	ha	%	ha	%
I	2 413	58.7	4 038	73.3	2 680	59.7	9 131	64.7
II	1 606	39.0	1 092	19.8	1 502	33.5	4 200	29.8
III	95	2.3	379	6.9	308	6.9	782	5.5
total	4 114	100.0	5 509	100.0	4 490	100.0	14 113	100.0

Source: farm survey.
[1] Area represented by missing values (696 ha) excluded from this and all subsequent tables.

from the immediate urban edge have higher standards of land maintenance than those close to it (see below).

The occupation, ownership and maintenance of farmland

Merely calculating the area occupied by each respondent, or in which the respondent had an interest, proved complicated and a few words of explanation are necessary. Information in the Agricultural Census refers to *holdings*, or the area of land returned on each census form. A holding may not be the same as a *farm*, or that area of land managed as a single unit on the basis of day-to-day farming operations. In recent years, the Census and Surveys Branch of MAFF has sought to minimise this distinction so as to base the census on *farms* as defined here, but it has not been helped by the growth in numbers of large units. Some of these have several occupiers, who may be different members of the same family, each returning a separate census form for a part of the whole, all parts of which may *also* be managed together as a single *business* or financial entity (Harrison 1975). In this survey, the interviewer first established the size of the *business*, sometimes including land a considerable distance away from the

Table 6.4 Area occupied and rented out, 1977.

	Bucks.		Essex		Surrey		Total	
	ha	%	ha	%	ha	%	ha	%
Total area	5 141	116.3	6 226	109.2	5 252	112.0	16 619	112.2
land rented out	603	13.6	327	5.7	189	4.0	1 119	7.6
land away from main holding but *not* farmed with it	118	2.7	195	3.4	377	8.0	690	4.7
area occupied and farmed as single enterprise	*4 420*	*100.0*	*5 704*	*100.0*	*4 686*	*100.0*	*14 810*	*100.0*
land away from main holding but farmed with it	470	10.6	857	15.0	994	21.2	2 321	15.7

Source: farm survey.

Table 6.5 Pattern of farm occupation.

Category	No. of occurrences	Total area (ha)	%	Sub total %
Owner-occupation				
respondent owned	83	2 984	20.1	55.1
joint ownership	25	979	6.6	18.1
family farming company	6	286	1.9	5.3
trust	11	1 168	7.9	21.6
subtotal	125	5 417	36.5	100.0
Full tenancies from				
private landlords	54	2 664	17.9	31.0
companies	22	784	5.3	9.2
public landlords	61	2 348	15.9	27.6
charities, traditional institutions	26	2 746	18.5	32.2
subtotal	163	8 522	57.6	100.0
Rented on short-term agreement	46	871	5.9	
total[1]	334	14 810	100.0	

Source: farm survey.

[1] Only 184 farms included as one occupier rents out all his land.

MGB, but then concentrated his attention on the *farm* at which the interview was being conducted.

The area eventually identified, and italicised in Table 6.4, amounts to 14 810 ha. This includes over 2300 ha farmed in separate blocks away from the main holding but as part of the *farm*. Less than 60% of the farms in the sample consist of a single block of land, even though many of the farms are very small, and some of these are crossed by major roads. The degree of fragmentation, however, is not extreme when compared with other cases in Britain (Jones & Simmons 1965, Edwards 1978), although the amount of traffic on roads around London may exacerbate its effect on farming operations. A further 690 ha can legitimately be added to the 14 810 ha as part of these farm *businesses*, and a further 1119 ha are rented out sometimes to other occupiers in the sample.★ The total figure (16 619 ha) thus contains an element of double-counting. The average size of all *farms* is 80.5 ha varying between 111.8 ha in Essex, 72.1 ha in Surrey and 64.1 ha in Bucks.

Respondents were asked to allocate each parcel of land they occupied into one of nine categories (Table 6.5). By national standards the proportion of land that is owner-occupied (36.5%) is low. The Agricultural Census for 1977 indicates an overall percentage for England and Wales of 56.5% (MAFF 1980), although

★ One 'farmer' in Surrey let all his land.

land rented on short-term agreements is recorded as owner-occupied in the national figures. Non-corporate, private landlords only let one-third of the tenanted land and only 17.9% of the total area. The company category of landlord is dominated by developers and mineral extractors. Gravel companies own 311 ha and hold extraction rights over a further 200 ha, and five builders and developers own 152 ha between them.

Public and institutional landlords are the most important, owning one-third of the total area between them. This illustrates a further, important difference between the MGB and the country as a whole. In 1978 only about 8.5% of agricultural land in Great Britain was owned by public, semi-public and institutional landlords (Northfield committee report 1979). The figure of 34.4% returned here is also higher than those recorded by Thomas (12.9%) and Standing Conference (13–15%) for the Green Belt as a whole (Thomas 1970; calculated from the map in Standing Conference 1976, p. 14),* and reflects the extensive area of non-private ownership in the inner half of the MGB (see p. 106). The Crown Estate Commissioners and the Church Commissioners own over 1600 ha in only 10 farms (largely in Essex) and Merton College, Oxford owns 560 ha in three farms in Surrey. Five major public landlords are included in the sample. The GLC has interests in 14 farms (483 ha), Surrey CC in 15 farms (486 ha), Essex CC in five farms (221 ha), Redbridge LB in five farms (258 ha) and Reigate and Banstead DC in six farms (107 ha).

The pattern of occupation by farm is extremely complex. Over half the tenants have more than one landlord and 23 have three or more. One-third of occupiers rent all their land and one-third own it all. Over 9% of the rented land (871 ha), or 5.9% of the total area, is let short-term and without security. There is no national figure available for this category of tenure but it is thought to be much smaller (1–2%). About half of the 871 ha is let on 364-day leases and much of the rest is let informally for the taking of a half crop or the summer grazing of horses. This is a form of letting that occupiers are reluctant to discuss, and certainly do not want revealed to MAFF, and this figure must be seen as a minimum estimate. Much of this land is leased by developers, gravel companies and other farmers (part of the 1119 ha recorded in Table 6.4), and if the returns from this sample are regarded as representative of all farmers in the MGB then 60–65% of land let short-term is let by other farmers.

Many of these short-term lets consist of informal or casual arrangements. In a situation of land shortage such arrangements are acceptable to both parties. The landlord finds this situation convenient as he can repossess the land quickly. But it would be a mistake to assume that all these lets are linked to speculative land market activity, for as retirement approaches some 'farming' landlords seek to run down the size of their businesses by leasing out their land in this way. Most full-time farmers avoid depending on such insecure leases if they can,

* Thomas and Standing Conference employ a slightly more restrictive definition of non-private land, excluding religious and educational ownerships for example, and are concerned with rural land generally rather than farmland.

and few rent as much as one-quarter of their land on this basis. The only exceptions are new full-time entrants to farming who are desperate to expand their operations. Most of the large blocks of short-term lease land (i.e. over 30 ha) are occupied by large, established farmers owning or leasing substantial areas of land on secure tenancies. Some of the short-term let land is occupied in small fragmented pieces by hobby farmers or the proprietors of riding stables.

It also proved possible from respondents' replies to establish changes in occupation between January 1970 and December 1977. Net change in total area is very small (a net gain of 40 ha) once the 16 new occupiers arriving since 1970 are excluded. The figures conceal, however, large numbers of small changes at the individual farm level that frequently cancel each other out over the sample as a whole. In line with national trends, owner-occupation increased slightly but average farm size remained the same. Thirty-two farmers bought land on 41 separate occasions, 12 buying all or part of the freeholds to their properties. Over and above the 37 farmers who *admitted* selling land for non-agricultural use (see Ch. 3), there were at least 17 sales of farmland, amounting to 291 ha, to other farmers. Many small sales and minor adjustments to the pattern of occupation typify urban-fringe agriculture.

In the light of this evidence on the pattern of ownership and occupation it is possible to return to some of the hypotheses listed on page 111. Taking the question of farm fragmentation first, it is hypothesised that land detached from the main holding will, on average, be maintained less well than that located within a ring fence. This position is taken on two grounds. First, outlying, detached fields are difficult to reach and as such will receive less attention than land close to the farmhouse (Chisholm 1962). In their replies, respondents lent support to this view. Secondly, fields distant from the farmhouse are away from the watchful eye of the farmer and are subject to increased problems of trespass and vandalism (Elliott 1979). Nearly one-quarter of the land in the sample of farms does not lie within a ring fence and there is some evidence to support the view that it is less well maintained than the land that does (Table 6.6). The difference is not substantial but a higher proportion of land falls into Categories II and III on fields away from the main holdings.

In examining the relationship between form of occupation and land

Table 6.6 Maintenance category and farm fragmentation.

	Maintenance category							
	I		II		III		Total	
	ha	%	ha	%	ha	%	ha	%
main holdings	7 360	67.8	3 069	28.3	432	4.0	10 861	100.0
detached fields	1 771	54.5	1 131	34.8	350	10.8	3 252	100.0
total	9 131	64.7	4 200	29.8	782	5.5	14 113	100.0

Source: farm survey.

maintenance, the first question must concern possible differences in approach between owner-occupiers and tenants on either secure or insecure leases. When asked their views on whether they felt the MGB offered more advantages than disadvantages as a place to farm, the primary split in opinion came between tenants and owner-occupiers, and not between full- and part-time farmers (see Ch. 4). Tenants approve of the additional security from urban development brought about by green belt restraint, whereas owner-occupiers are prone to complain of their loss of development prospects which in itself is indicative of their motives for owning land in the Green Belt. Financially, tenants have little to gain and potentially a great deal to lose from the sale of their land for development, whereas the reverse is true for landlords and owner-occupiers (see Ch. 3). Tenants receive comparatively small amounts of compensation, at present four years' rent plus an amount for disturbance, and many will find it impossible to acquire another tenancy in today's letting market (Northfield committee report 1979, Ch. VIII). They may well be forced out of farming altogether. And in this situation many are well aware that if they can demonstrate their farming efficiency and the serious consequences for their livelihoods at a planning inquiry, then their landlords may experience increased difficulty in acquiring planning permission. Many are prepared to appear at inquiries and to speak against their landlords, and some have already done so. The incentive in this situation is for the tenant to maintain his land, whereas the owner-occupier may feel he improves his chance at an inquiry by allowing his land to run down. In spite of their attempts to avoid run-down appearance working in favour of the applicant, local planning officers admit that from time to time this does strengthen the applicant's case.

If this phenomenon were to be at all widespread it should be reflected in lower standards of land maintenance on owner-occupied land. The results are shown in Table 6.7 and they do show a small difference in favour of tenants, but the difference is almost wholly accounted for by the figures for the Surrey sample, and it has to be agreed that this result may stem from other considerations, such as the fact that most hobby farmers are also owner-occupiers (see below). Among reasons for the absence of a more clear-cut finding can be included the general effectiveness of restraint in reducing the rate of growth of non-conforming uses and the considerable security of tenure available to the majority of tenants with full leases under the Agricultural Holdings legislation. Those with short-term leases would not have anything like the same degree of security in practice,* and there is no incentive for the tenant to invest his time, effort or money in making improvements. There is every reason to believe that land let short-term will be poorly maintained.

A report on changes in occupation on Humber Bank in Humberside,

* Planning permission for development forms a valid notice to quit for any kind of lease under the Agricultural Holdings legislation, but a full lease provides the tenant a better basis – morally if not legally – upon which to object to the planning application in the first place.

Table 6.7 Land maintenance and form of occupation.

	I		II		III		Total	
	ha	%	ha	%	ha	%	ha	%
Owner-occupation								
Bucks.	1 299	61.9	729	34.7	70	3.3	2 098	100.0
Essex	1 388	75.6	359	19.5	90	4.9	1 837	100.0
Surrey	596	44.3	620	46.1	129	9.6	1 345	100.0
subtotal	3 283	62.2	1 708	32.3	289	5.5	5 280	100.0
Tenanted (full tenancies)								
Bucks.	1 068	60.6	683	38.3	10	0.6	1 761	100.0
Essex	2 624	77.2	617	18.1	160	4.7	3 401	100.0
Surrey	1 998	66.1	863	28.6	161	5.3	3 022	100.0
subtotal	5 690	69.5	2 163	26.4	331	4.0	8 184	100.0
Short-term lets								
Bucks.	47	18.4	193	75.7	15	5.9	255	100.0
Essex	26	9.6	116	42.8	129	47.6	271	100.0
Surrey	85	69.1	20	16.2	18	14.6	123	100.0
subtotal	158	24.3	329	50.7	162	25.0	649	100.0
total	9 131	64.7	4 200	29.8	782	5.5	14 113	100.0

Maintenance category spans columns I, II, III.

Source: farm survey.

produces startling evidence in support of this view (ADAS 1977). Following the designation of two Special Industry Areas and an Area of Port Development on the south bank of the Humber, much of the site was purchased by industrial companies and leased by them on 364-day tenancies without security to the occupier. According to ADAS, half the remaining farmland area (360 ha) is now seriously under-used and 8% of the total area lies derelict or vacant. Comparable figures are given in Table 6.7. One-quarter of the total area falls into Category III. There is no readily available explanation for the range of values between the three study areas. Without doubt, however, insecurity significantly lowers the maintenance standards of land.

The figures for full, secure tenancies are broken down by type of landlord in Table 6.8. Landlords, both individually and by type, have different objectives for owning farmland and have varying financial circumstances, particularly as regards taxation. For example, charities and traditional institutions such as the Crown and the church experience preferential fiscal treatment by comparison with private landlords (see Northfield committee report 1979). Many private owners, despite their traditional commitment to the full maintenance of their estates, now complain that marginal rates of revenue and capital taxation often

Table 6.8 Land maintenance standards by type of landlord.

	I		II		III		Total	
	ha	%	ha	%	ha	%	ha	%
Land let on full tenancies from								
private landlords	1695	68.9	703	28.6	62	2.5	2460	100.0
companies	338	47.4	329	46.1	46	6.5	713	100.0
public landlords	1433	62.1	716	31.0	160	6.9	2309	100.0
charities and traditional institutions	2224	82.3	415	15.4	63	2.3	2702	100.0
total	5690	69.5	2163	26.4	331	4.0	8184	100.0

Source: farm survey.

make it impossible for them to meet their traditional, long-term maintenance obligations. That they are now taxed more heavily than either other kinds of landlord or owner-occupiers is not in doubt, but the extent to which this leads to a poorer quality of land maintenance would be difficult to prove. Nevertheless, Table 6.8 records that private landlords as a group have figures for their land close to the average but of a lower standard than for charitable and institutional owners.

It was hypothesised that the maintenance of land in public hands would fall below the average. This position is taken on the grounds that much publicly owned land is held for non-agricultural reasons and public landlords may as a result not be overly concerned for, or be knowledgeable about, farming and its needs. The ACAH, for example, is not impressed by the standards set by the regional water authorities (ACAH 1978). In the event, the overall figures in Table 6.8 show public land to be maintained to almost the average standard, and this reflects the high standards achieved on the smallholdings and Green Belt Estates managed by the local authorities. As anticipated, land owned by companies is not so well maintained even where it is on secure leases. This is predictable as gravel companies have an interest in two-thirds of this land and some of it has been poorly restored.

In broad terms, the results are as would be expected but, in the case of different types of landlord especially, it is not possible to press the findings further as the interviews were conducted with the occupiers and not the owners.

Urban intrusion, planning permission and land maintenance

Many of the farms are located close to the urban area. It is well recognised that farms near to new urban development especially are subject to trespass and

Table 6.9 Urban interference with farming activities.

	No.	%
number of occupiers affected by interference during 1977	131	71.1
interference since 1970 leading to		
adoption of new farming enterprises	75	40.8
taking of additional precautions	120	65.2

Source: farm survey.

other forms of intrusion including the realignment of roads, installation of public utilities and the dumping of rubbish (University of Reading 1975). Establishing the frequency of occurrence and the severity of these difficulties for farmers presents problems. Nobody would deny their existence but much evidence is anecdotal and some would argue that the main effect is psychological (Hellard 1976). Only when the problems become especially severe do occupiers adapt their farming systems to meet these difficulties.

Farmers were questioned about interference with their day-to-day farming operations (Table 6.9) and over 70% claimed to have suffered difficulties during 1977 alone. The figures are remarkably even between all three study areas and they are not out of line with those obtained in other urban-fringe farming surveys (MAFF 1973, 1976a; Rettig 1976, Countryside Commission 1981). Only 40% of occupiers have found it necessary to adjust the mix of their farming enterprises since 1970, but others noted that they included intrusion as a factor in deciding their mix of activities in the first instance. Rather more (65.2%) have taken other precautions to minimise damage, such as extra fencing, the careful siting of buildings so that they were visible from the farmhouse and the keeping of guard-dogs. It is difficult, however, to escape the impression that intrusion is a widespread nuisance creating additional stress rather than a major financial burden, but its severity as a problem increases markedly right on the urban edge (Countryside Commission 1981).

All fields adjacent to existing development or to new trunk roads and

Table 6.10 Maintenance standards on land adjacent to residential development and new roads.

	Maintenance category							
	I		II		III		Total	
	ha	%	ha	%	ha	%	ha	%
land adjacent to								
housing	724	35.2	929	45.1	406	19.7	2 059	100.0
new roads	158	28.3	300	53.7	101	18.1	559	100.0
all other land	8 249	71.8	2 971	25.8	275	2.4	11 495	100.0
total	9 131	64.7	4 200	29.8	782	5.5	14 113	100.0

Source: farm survey.

Table 6.11 Maintenance standards on land adjacent to sources of urban intrusion and let short-term.

	I		II		III		Total	
	ha	%	ha	%	ha	%	ha	%
land adjacent to sources of urban intrusion	882	33.7	1 229	46.9	507	19.4	2 618	100.0
land let short-term	158	24.3	329	50.7	162	25.0	649	100.0
land in both categories	28	8.2	152	44.4	162	47.4	342	100.0
all other land	8 249	71.8	2 971	25.8	275	2.4	11 495	100.0

Source: farm survey.

motorways (constructed since 1970) have been identified and their maintenance standards compared with the rest of the sample. Trespass and vandalism from housing estates, and disturbance and severance from road construction are expected to lower standards, and this is confirmed (Table 6.10). Much higher proportions of land on the edge of urban development fall into Categories II and III than on the remaining area. About 18.5% of the total land area of the farm sample lies in fields adjacent to housing and new roads and two-thirds of this consists of land in Categories II and III. As with mineral extraction, the secondary effects of road construction can be long-lasting, if not permanent, and the impact of the M25 motorway will need to be carefully monitored in this regard.

Nevertheless, as the field survey regularly demonstrated, the determined occupier can maintain vulnerable areas close to urban development quite satisfactorily, but he must have a feeling of security. This is quite apparent from the analysis of land that is both adjacent to one of these possible sources of urban intrusion *and* is let short-term (see Table 6.11). The evidence is overwhelming, with only 8.2% of the land in Category I, 44.4% in Category II and 47.4% in Category III. Moreover, *every hectare* of land let short-term that is in Category III lay adjacent to these sources of urban intrusion.

The effect of uncertainty on maintenance standards, where attempts have been made to obtain planning permission since 1970, does not produce quite as dramatic a result. This may be partly explained by data problems. As noted in Chapter 3, tenants are often poorly informed about their landlords' intentions and some owners are reluctant to release details of their attempts to develop their land. Although it has proved possible to ascertain which farmers have been approached by developers or have put in a planning application, they were often unprepared to specify precisely which fields were involved. Experience indicates, however, that in the MGB permission is only ever sought for land immediately adjacent to existing development. In the absence of further detail, all it is possible to do is to compare the standards of maintenance of all land next

Table 6.12 Maintenance category, urban edge land and attempts to develop the land since 1970.

	I		II		III		Total	
	ha	%	ha	%	ha	%	ha	%
Land on the urban edge farms where approach made								
by developer	489	41.9	538	46.1	140	12.0	1 167	100.0
where no approach made	393	27.1	691	47.6	367	25.3	1 451	100.0
All other land	8 249	71.8	2 971	25.8	275	2.4	11 495	100.0
total	9 131	64.7	4 200	29.8	782	5.5	14 113	100.0
Land on the urban edge farms where owner has sought planning permission	331	31.7	570	54.7	142	13.6	1 043	100.0
where no permission sought	551	35.0	659	41.8	365	23.2	1 575	100.0
all other land	8 249	71.8	2 971	25.8	275	2.4	11 495	100.0
total	9 131	64.7	4 200	29.8	782	5.5	14 113	100.0

Maintenance category

Source: farm survey.

to existing developments, on those farms where the occupier has admitted either to discussions with developers or has attempted to gain permission on his own account, with all other land on the urban edge on farms where development has not been sought, and to compare these results with those for all remaining land.

The findings are shown in Table 6.12. As would be expected from the results contained in Table 6.10, all land on the urban edge, irrespective of whether attempts have been made to develop it or not, is much less well maintained than other land. Within the differing categories of urban-edge land the results are less easy to interpret. Standards are marginally worse on land where the owner himself has sought planning permission. This could be anticipated because a developer's approach to an owner cannot be taken to mean that the owner wishes to develop his land, although developers with local knowledge will have a shrewd idea of those who might be tempted into an arrangement. As both developers and mineral companies made clear at interview, identifying those owners with parlous financial circumstances or who wish to retire is often critical to the success of their land market activities.

Of equal significance, the findings in Table 6.11 do not suggest that attempts to develop the land necessarily lead to lower maintenance standards than for land on the urban edge generally. Indeed, although poorly maintained, land on the urban edge, where developers have made an approach to the owner, is better maintained than land similarly located on other farms. Inadequately precise data may be concealing the full effects of attempts to acquire planning permission. But on the information available, the hypothesis that owners run down their land in order to improve their chances of getting planning permission is not disproved, but neither is it sustained. Urban intrusion may lead farmers to seek planning permission because they no longer feel able, in the circumstances, to maintain high standards of land management.

Sources of farm income and land maintenance

Certain enterprises and types of farmer are, it is regularly asserted, associated with indifferent farming competence. Among these are farmers who gain most of their income from off-farm sources. They are said to have little knowledge of farming and to be more concerned for their country lifestyle than the needs of their farms. Those that keep horses are also often regarded as being ignorant of pasture management and estate maintenance. These views are based on a particular perspective of the purpose of farmland – efficient food production – and may not be upheld in the broader sense that the land maintenance categories are being employed here. But before the hypothesis concerning the relevance of different income sources to land maintenance can be examined some means of classifying farm types is needed.

Most analyses of farm type are based on returns made by occupiers to the

Agricultural Census (e.g. see MAFF 1977a, Bowler 1981a). The census concentrates almost exclusively on conventional farming enterprises, data on other farm-based activities, such as agricultural contracting and farm shops, and the occupier's off-farm sources of income not being recorded. These other areas of activity are frequently suggested as being of particular importance to farmers in the urban fringe but they have yet to be described in any detail. An attempt must be made to measure them if the true extent and nature of part-time and hobby farming* are to be established. The importance of these activities can also be taken as indicators of the adaptability of urban-fringe farmers to the opportunities as well as the difficulties of farming on the edge of the city.

Farm types are usually defined by the presence or absence of particular enterprises, and when some measure of the relative importance of the different enterprises is needed it is usually calculated in terms of labour requirements, or occasionally, gross output per hectare. The calculation of labour input is usually based on standard figures for full-time farming of average efficiency (MAFF 1977a). This is an inappropriate approach for urban-fringe farms, many of which provide only part-time employment for their occupiers, whose enterprise structures are strongly influenced by outside sources of income (Gasson 1966), and to which conventional standards of economic efficiency often do not apply. Instead, the proportions and not absolute amounts of *gross income*, i.e. pre-tax income, received by the occupier throughout the range of his income sources have been recorded. These sources have been classified into farming, farm-based and off-farm.† By seeking proportions and not absolute amounts it was hoped to achieve a high level of co-operation. In one important sense this was realised. Only 2 out of the 185 interviewees refused to indicate their main sources of income, but fully quantified information that could be treated as reliable – a qualitative judgement based on the conduct of the interview as a whole – was only obtained from 120 respondents.

In some cases the sheer complexity of income flow militated against a comprehensive return, leading some occupiers to argue that they were unable rather than unwilling to assist. Some were clearly reticent and in the case of farm managers were unable to comment on their employers' off-farm sources of

---

* Hobby farming can be defined in many ways (see Gasson 1977, Layton 1978). Here the term will refer only to occupiers who acquire an *incidental* quantity of income, less than 10% of the total, from farm sources of *all* kinds.

† More detailed information on individual enterprises within each category was collected but this is not discussed here, as it is not to be linked to land maintenance standards, except in the case of horse keeping.

Farming enterprises included dairying, beef-rearing and fattening, sheep, pigs, poultry, horticulture, cash-cropping, hay crops.

Farm-based enterprises consisted of agricultural contracting, woodland management, horse grazing, riding and stabling, camping and caravanning, farm shop, farmhouse holidays.

Off-farm income included both earned and unearned income. Income acquired by other members of the family was ignored.

Table 6.13 Classification of occupiers by source of income.

Source of income	No.	%
farming only	53	29.0
farm-based only	6	3.3
off-farm only	31	16.9
farming, farm-based	43	23.4
farming, off-farm	24	13.1
farm-based, off-farm	4	2.2
all sources	22	12.0
total	183	100.0

Source: farm survey.

income. A small number (14) claimed to receive no gross income at all, and a further 30 (for tax reasons) either said that their farms were loss-making enterprises or this could be adduced from their other replies. Only about half of these had conventional farming enterprises whereas the rest just grazed a few horses, produced some hay crops or did some agricultural contracting. At least 28 occupiers acquired more than 90% of their gross income from off-farm sources and if circumstantial evidence is employed, such as size of farm, nature of farming system and source of off-farm income, then a further 22 can *safely* be added to this group. These 50 respondents (23.3% of the total) are termed hobby farmers in this study. They occupy only 4.0% of the agricultural area with an average farm size of 11.8 ha.

Occupiers can be classified according to their sources of farm income (Table 6.13). Eighty-one (44.2%) receive at least some of their income from off-farm sources and 75 (41.1%) have farm-based activities on their holdings. Forty-one (22.4%) claim to receive no income from traditional farming enterprises and only 53 (29.0%) acquire all their income this way. Few occupiers (six) are wholly dependent on farm-based enterprises and even fewer (four) combine this source exclusively with off-farm income. Much more frequently, farm-based enterprises are linked to conventional farming activities, but usually in a secondary role. In only about one-quarter of cases do farm-based enterprises provide more gross income than conventional farming activities. Off-farm sources quite frequently generate more income than conventional farming sources. Only 12 of the 81 occupiers with off-farm sources of income claim these to be minor.

Fully quantified data on the proportions of gross income from different sources was only forthcoming from two-thirds of the respondents, and these occupiers are probably unrepresentative of the sample as a whole. There is no satisfactory way of confirming this but their average size of farm is significantly greater than that of non-respondents. This difference in farm size could be taken to mean that the proportion of income allocated to off-farm sources in the sample as a whole is an underestimate and that allocated for farming enterprises is an overestimate (see Table 6.14). The second important point about the data in Table 6.14 is that they are compiled from the proportion of income received by each respondent irrespective of the absolute amount received. This overweights the effect of small farms on the aggregate figures. Nevertheless, the data permit a broad assessment to be made of the relative importance of different income sources. Income from off-farm sources represents about 30% of the total and from farm-based enterprises a further 11%. Most income still comes from conventional farming operations. There are noticeable but not always easily explained differences between the three study areas. Off-farm sources contribute twice the proportion in Surrey to Bucks., for example. The higher proportion of farm-based income in Essex reflects the important 'pick your own' fruit and farm-shop enterprises in the county (Blair 1978) but given the growth in other forms of farming activity in recent years, especially from farm shops and horse grazing (Bull & Wibberley 1976, Bowler 1981b), higher proportions than 7.3% and 9.8% might have been expected from the Bucks. and Surrey samples respectively.

Finally, a record was taken of the numbers of horses kept on these farms. In 1977, 113 out of 183 respondents (61.7%) kept a total of 1062 horses. This is known to be an underestimate as five occupiers with significant numbers of horses refused to indicate how many they kept. Eleven occupiers keep nearly half the total number with 30 or more horses each. About one-third have no more than two horses, almost always kept for pleasure. Only 41 claim to keep horses in order to supplement their income from other farming enterprises, but on 14 farms specialised activities (livery stables, riding schools, studs, etc.) represent the single most important source of income. Most startling, however, is the rate of increase in numbers, the total having risen from 664 to 1062 between 1970 and 1977.

The hypotheses to be tested here concern the commitment to farming of the occupiers, as reflected in their sources of income, in relation to the standards of land maintenance achieved on their farms. The first hypothesis asserts that land will be less well maintained by those occupiers who obtain much of their income from off-farm sources because they are less dependent on their farms financially and consequently take less interest in them. Testing this hypothesis requires two

Table 6.14 Proportion of gross income by source area, 1977 (%).

	Bucks. (43 farms)	Essex (35 farms)	Surrey (42 farms)	Total (120 farms)
farming enterprises	70.9	52.2	48.2	57.5
farm-based enterprises	7.3	18.4	9.8	11.4
off-farm sources	21.9	29.4	42.0	31.1

Source: farm survey.

Table 6.15   Land maintenance standards by type of farm.

					Maintenance category			
	I		II		III		Total	
Type of farm	ha	%	ha	%	ha	%	ha	%
1	3 283	64.8	1 510	29.8	274	5.4	5 067	100.0
2	20	15.9	53	42.1	53	42.1	126	100.0
3	517	56.6	342	37.4	55	6.0	914	100.0
4	2 720	60.4	1 500	33.3	280	6.2	4 500	100.0
5	1 492	81.6	264	14.4	72	3.9	1 828	100.0
6	5	14.7	21	61.8	8	23.5	34	100.0
7	1 094	66.5	510	31.0	40	2.4	1 644	100.0
total	9 131	64.7	4 200	29.8	782	5.5	14 113	100.0

Source: farm survey.

The same farm types as are used in Table 6.13 based on sources of gross income.

Key: 1.   farming income only,
2.   farm-based income only,
3.   off-farm income only,
4.   farming and farm-based income,
5.   farming and off-farm income,
6.   farm-based and off-farm income,
7.   all three sources of income.

steps. First, standards of land maintenance are separately identified for each type of farm, based on income sources, as defined in Table 6.13. The results are shown in Table 6.15. From these it can be seen that those occupiers whose only source of income is from traditional farming enterprises (Type 1) have almost identical maintenance standards to the sample as a whole, as do those in Type 4 (farming and farm-based income) and Type 7 (all three sources of income).★ Those that combine farming and off-farm income (Type 5) record the highest standards, but those with off-farm income only (Type 3) record standards that are significantly below the average. These apparently contradictory results suggest the possibility of a major difference in outlook between those that need to combine on- and off-farm income (the part-time farmer) with those who do not need, or do not bother about on-farm income (the hobby farmer). The second step is thus to examine the performance of the hobby farmer, defined earlier as acquiring 90% or more of his income from off-farm sources. This definition is different from that for occupiers of Farm Type 3 in Table 6.15 who are wholly dependent on off-farm income. The results in Table 6.16 show hobby farmers to be associated with much poorer overall maintenance

★ The two smallest categories (Types 2 and 6), with operators who are either dependent wholly on farm-based enterprises for their gross income or combine this income with that from off-farm sources, have by far and away the worst maintenance standards.

Table 6.16 Land maintenance standards on hobby farms.

| | Maintenance category | | | | | | | |
| | I | | II | | III | | Total | |
	ha	%	ha	%	ha	%	ha	%
hobby farms	360	41.8	442	51.3	60	7.0	862	100.0
all other farms	8 771	66.2	3758	28.4	722	5.4	13 251	100.0
total	9 131	64.7	4200	29.8	782	5.5	14 113	100.0

Source: farm survey.

Table 6.17 Land maintenance standards and the keeping of horses.

| | Maintenance category | | | | | | | |
| | I | | II | | III | | Total | |
	ha	%	ha	%	ha	%	ha	%
0–2 horses	5 121	68.6	2 100	28.1	247	3.3	7 468	100.0
3–9 horses	2 998	66.5	1 227	27.2	286	6.3	4 511	100.0
10–29 horses	557	50.5	438	39.7	108	9.8	1 103	100.0
> 29 horses	455	44.1	435	42.2	141	13.7	1 031	100.0
total	9 131	64.7	4 200	29.8	782	5.5	14 113	100.0

Source: farm survey.

standards than other occupiers, with over half their land falling into Category II. Hobby farmers, as opposed to part-time farmers, thus meet the expectation of the hypothesis.

In the minds of many local planners and councillors the keeping of horses on a commercial scale is associated with run-down farmland. This association is examined in Table 6.17 in which four categories of occupier are defined based on the number of horses they graze. Those with two horses or less have above average standards of maintenance, but so do those with less than 10 horses. It is only those that keep horses in large numbers that have land with below average maintenance standards.★ To this extent a link may be established between the keeping of horses and run-down land. But it is difficult to draw any conclusions based on causation, for why should large-scale horse keeping lead to inadequate land maintenance? It is equally possible that some horse grazing is conducted on poorly reclaimed mineral land not capable of supporting the grazing needs of more intensive sheep, beef and dairy enterprises (Lowe *et al.* 1977). In other words, horse grazing is as much a symptom as a cause of poor land maintenance and is a response to uncertainty in a situation in which the owner does not want to give the occupier a secure lease. The demand for horse grazing land is known to be considerable, and on the basis of reliable anecdotal evidence, is known to command a higher rent than more conventional farming enterprises, especially in areas close to the urban edge.

★ This point may be tied back to the footnote on page 130.

A continuing problem of poor maintenance?

The findings confirm substantial tracts of poorly maintained farmland but comparatively small areas of semi-derelict and derelict agricultural land. It must be repeated, however, that all this land occurs on farms with a minimum size of 4 ha and whose occupiers return an Agricultural Census form. The percentage of land that is under-used in the urban fringe as a whole is almost certainly greater than that recorded here. But taking the survey at its face value and making the assumption that these farms are representative of those in the inner one-third of the Green Belt today, then in this area alone there must be about 10 500 ha of Category III farmland and between 55 000 ha and 60 000 ha of Category II land. Given the importance of urban proximity to the presence of Categories II and III land then it would be reasonable to assume that these proportions would not hold in the remaining, less urbanised parts of the MGB.

Most of the hypotheses are confirmed. In particular, poor maintenance is associated with:

(a)   the short-term letting of land;
(b)   proximity to housing and new roads;
(c)   the ownership of land by companies, principally developers and gravel companies;
(d)   hobby farmers; and
(e)   occupiers who keep horses in substantial numbers and are dependent on farm-based enterprises for most of their income.

Some of these attributes are interrelated. The poor maintenance of land adjacent to housing is a reflection of the effects of both trespass and uncertainty stemming from the development potential of the land. A critical distinction seems to lie between the hobby farmer and the part-time farmer who is determined to make a financial success of his farming enterprises. And some occupiers right on the urban edge continue to farm well, whereas others maintain their land poorly for no apparent reason.

It is one matter to identify and to confirm the existence of poorly maintained land, it is another to propose measures to reduce its extent. Before attempting to do so it is necessary to decide whether this is an ephemeral problem, the result of some farmers still not having adapted to the stresses of urbanisation, or whether it is likely to be a permanent one in the absence of further measures to eliminate it.

It is difficult to argue that these extensive areas of poorly maintained farmland will diminish of their own accord. There are trends that might be regarded as encouraging but these are off-set by other developments. Taking planning matters first, on the credit side is the increased awareness today of farming matters among planners, but this awareness remains at the level of principle rather than the taking of action. Likewise, slow though the change may be, the quality of mineral land restoration in the MGB is improving, and speculation in residential development land is less in evidence today than in the early 1970s. On the debit side, it could be argued that development pressures in the MGB will remain intense. In the current recession central government is likely to place, if pressed, a higher priority on job creation than on environmental protection, and maintaining restraint will be made more difficult by the building of the M25 motorway. These pressures allied with uncertainty over green belt boundaries, local needs arguments, and differences of opinion between county and district authorities over restraint (see Ch. 2), will not encourage those owning land on the urban edge to overlook its development potential.

The effects of changes in farming are also difficult to predict, but again there can be no grounds for undue optimism. Statements of national agricultural policy provide few specific clues for the urban fringe although some intelligent guesswork is possible. Central government remains committed to a high level of self-sufficiency in food production and the protection of high quality farmland (MAFF 1979) and under the Common Agricultural Policy (CAP) farmers will continue to receive substantial financial support. But after a period of growth in real earnings in the first half of the 1970s incomes on full-time farms are now falling and may well continue to do so as consumers' interests strive to reduce agricultural surpluses. In particular, superlevies of various kinds may be introduced to penalise large producers along with a general move to adjust the CAP towards income support rather than price support (Commission of the European Communities 1980). This move might prove to be of advantage to small family farms in the MGB, but if the penalties imposed are too high, then they may only encourage larger producers to seek even further improvements in their efficiency to prevent significant reductions in farm income. What might such changes mean for land maintenance?

First, full-time farmers will want to invest further in buildings and other structures to improve their farming efficiency, but with declining real incomes and high interest charges they will seek low-cost investments, or make do. Were planning objections seriously to inhibit this investment, and in the absence of compensating sources of income, then a depressed farming economy could develop in the urban fringe, especially among smaller family farms, leading to the eventual sale of the land after a period of indifferent land maintenance. The land would in all probability be lotted, some of it being sold to hobby farmers. Secondly, if occupiers seek to compensate for a decline in farming income by increasing their dependence on farm-based enterprises, then this might imply a fall in land maintenance standards. On the other hand, the need for improved efficiency in a static market for such services, the result of the economic recession, could lead such farmers to maintain their land rather better than they have up to now. Thirdly, it is possible to anticipate a polarisation of farming into a small number of large, efficient units and a large number of hobby farmers. The hobby farms would be owner-occupied, whereas most full-time farms would contain a core of let land on secure tenancies, leased primarily from institutional and public owners. Hobby farmers would continue to maintain their land indifferently and full-time farmers to maintain it well. Land owned by institutional landlords is particularly well looked after (see Table 6.8), and where they have a commitment to the management of rural land, public owners can also be expected to ensure high standards of maintenance.

Any attempt to anticipate farming changes in the MGB and their effect on maintenance standards is clearly fraught with difficulties. But in the absence of specific policies to the contrary there is no clear evidence to suggest that the area of poorly maintained land will decline, especially in the light of the generally pessimistic replies given by farmers as to their future farming prospects in the Green Belt (see Ch. 4).

The need for well maintained farmland

Assessing the importance of this issue raises difficulties, especially as farming questions continue to stir deep emotions in Britain. These emotions feed on the fact that Britain is a crowded island which is not self-sufficient in food, and on the myth that our food supply could be seriously threatened if concessions are made by the farming industry to other legitimate users of rural land (Best 1981). Yet all the major studies of recent years show that the loss of farmland to other uses is not a critical issue in either the maintenance or the expansion of domestic food supply (Edwards & Wibberley 1971, Centre for Agricultural Strategy 1976, Wise & Fell 1978). Naturally, the loss of farmland reduces the potential for food production but those that support the preservation of farmland at all costs frequently do so at the expense of examining other factors affecting supply – especially technological change and levels of managerial efficiency – and ignore the potential benefits to the urban population of low densities of urban development.

That said, respondents in local authorities made it clear that, to them at least, the poor maintenance of farmland in the urban fringe is a problem, and one that requires their attention (see also Standing Conference 1977a). Poor mainten-ance, they point out, contributes to a reduction in food output over and above that resulting from the formal transfer of farmland to urban uses. Such land, it is argued, should be brought back into full agricultural production, despite our membership of the European Community – a community that is largely self-sufficient in food (Commission of the European Communities 1980) – on the grounds that rising energy costs, uncertainty over the international food supply situation outside Western Europe and increases in the price of food on world markets make it prudent to do so. Whether such a policy should be followed depends very largely on the degree of risk perceived to surround overseas food supplies in the future (from Western Europe and elsewhere), and whether any additional public money put into farming would not be better spent elsewhere within the economy. Ritson concludes that the matter of risk –

or security of food supplies – only becomes critical when it is impossible to meet the minimum food requirements of the nation at a time of emergency, and this includes 'the ability to *become* self-sufficient' if needs be (Ritson 1980). At present we produce about 60% of our total domestic food consumption at current dietary standards and 75% of temperate foods (MAFF 1981b) but most scientists agree that we could be self-sufficient if we were to accept a changed diet (Blaxter 1975, Mellanby 1975). As for food losses resulting from the poor maintenance of urban-fringe farmland, it is unlikely that these amount to more than a few per cent and much of the land is not permanently lost to food production anyway. Some of it is grazed by horses and some could be rapidly brought back into full production if necessary, as the improvement of run-down farmland during World War II showed. Even so, it might be a wiser use of national resources to increase output further on better quality land in eastern England rather than to endeavour to improve indifferent farmland on the urban edge.

The other objection to poorly maintained farmland is the one relating to amenity. Run-down land is often untidy and unkempt and this frustrates those who regard this as indicative of an uncaring attitude towards the countryside on the part of some of its occupiers. Articulating this concern in terms of specific environmental or land-use goals, and ways of achieving them, is less easy and it is necessary to examine further the assumption that the effective maintenance of farmland, and the efficient agriculture that often goes with it, can be equated with amenity objectives. As explained in Chapter 4, this assumption can no longer be sustained for the countryside generally, although it is still frequently upheld in the context of the special circumstances of the urban fringe. Efficient farming is seen as the least damaging way of creating an acceptable landscape.

Provided the risks entailed in this approach are appreciated then both pragmatically and politically this view has merit. One of the consequences of this approach is that planners must not inhibit the adoption of new farming methods. There is no reason to believe that farmers living on the breadline are more amenity conscious than those making an acceptable living. Differences in outlook among farmers depend rather more on their backgrounds and traditions (Newby *et al.* 1977), and those farmers that are in financial difficulties in the urban fringe may endeavour to resolve these by any means they can, including the running-down of parts of their farms in an attempt to acquire planning permission. But from the local authorities' points of view, this is a cheap way of 'maintaining' the landscape based largely on central government monies via the agricultural budget. This approach does not make a call on their resources and there is precious little evidence that local authorities are prepared to undertake landscape rehabilitation programmes in the present economic circumstances. Recent studies of informal recreation also do not indicate major sources of latent demand for the use of large areas of additional open space that would somehow pay for the transfer and improvement of poorly maintained farmland into informal recreational use (see Ch. 4).

However, any endorsement of this approach to land maintenance can only be made in the context of a number of caveats. First, it is quite possible that some agricultural landscapes in the urban fringe would deteriorate in the face of modern farming technologies. Secondly, it is desirable for ecological reasons, and possibly aesthetic ones too, to retain some poorly maintained land. Variety would be lost through the efficient management of every last agricultural hectare. Thirdly, the endorsement of an approach to landscape management through high standards of land maintenance must not be equated with the primacy of farming to the point where other legitimate uses of green belt land and public access to open land are seriously inhibited. Farming has an important role to play in the MGB, not least because a very substantial percentage of the land is farmed, but not a predominant one over the *whole* area. The zoning of preferred but conforming land uses within the Green Belt must be one concomitant of this approach.

A case can be made for the efficient maintenance of farmland in the urban fringe for food production and amenity reasons, but it is not a wholly convincing one. Any remedial measures put forward must, therefore, be assessed in this light (see pp. 145–9).

Review

Introduction

Green belts are now an established and widely employed planning instrument in local as well as regional planning. This has been confirmed time and again during the structure planning process, and the growth in area of the approved London Green Belt by nearly 50% is just part of a more general pattern. In these circumstances it is more important to inquire whether local and central government have the same objectives for this widely desired planning tool, and to examine whether green belt restraint is being effectively implemented, than to ask whether green belts should be retained as an instrument of planning policy. This is a valid question but one that loses sight of the local political and planning realities of the present situation, and it is not addressed here.

A common understanding of the purpose of green belt between local and central government does not exist. DOE sees green belt as an instrument, a means to an end, whereas district planning authorities see it as an end in itself. Faced with the demands of local residents and under the constant pressure of planning applications, green belts take on a concrete reality, an amenity to be defended. At the same time DOE continues to promote the urban restraint function of green belt almost to the exclusion of all other considerations, whereas many district authorities attribute much greater emphasis to the environmental benefits of green belts. To complicate matters further, local authorities do not agree among themselves and reconciling their views is made more difficult by the recent redistribution of planning powers. The need to produce local plans is making them think for the first time about what *they* want to achieve from green belt restraint.

The difficulties currently being experienced by local authorities in deciding what they want from conforming land uses, and more especially in discovering that they do not always have the means to achieve what they want, may confirm DOE in its view that environmental questions should be kept quite separate from the implementation of restraint. And where such questions impinge on the remits of other government departments, DOE may continue to believe that they are best left alone. This, however, would represent a backward-looking, bureaucratic response that places procedures before objectives and traditional attitudes before positive thinking. There is no doubt that in practice amenity and restraint are related matters and success in achieving the one impinges on success in achieving the other. Some guidance from DOE to local authorities on these issues is long overdue and it is one objective of this Review to indicate where such guidance seems necessary and of what it might consist. These observations necessarily derive from the circumstances of the MGB, but they are not unique to it. The other objective is to draw together the findings of the study and to indicate where further work is still required.

Local and central government: a matter of discretion or a conflict of views?

Differences in approach to green belt are evident from the responses obtained at interview and the published statements of local and central government. But to what extent is consistency of outlook either desirable or necessary? And does the DOE have the authority, not only through its powers but also in its understanding of local situations, to achieve sufficient consistency for the policy to be credible in strategic terms? After all, in its relations with local authorities central government encourages a degree of local discretion in planning matters, even if this is being reduced at present (McAuslan 1981), and an element of ambiguity as well (Rhodes 1980). The value of ambiguity is that it allows politicians and officers on both sides to blame the other when decisions go against them and this vagueness also helps to explain why strategic planning is so attractive in principle but may be regarded as so ineffective in practice (Solesbury 1981).

  Some insights into these interauthority relations can be obtained from a re-examination of recent experience in three areas where there have been inconsistencies in outlook.

Size of the Green Belt   Prompted by rapid economic and population growth in the region in the 1950s and 1960s OMA authorities pressed for extensions to the Green Belt. These requests led to an uncertain response from central government and to various categories of non-statutory green belt. But in an attempt to clarify this confused situation a largely consistent stand has been adopted to structure plan proposals. Successive secretaries of state have only conceded in part the extensions requested by local authorities, arguing that a green belt of 20–25 km width, with a few fingers of restraint beyond this along some of the main communication axes, was all that was necessary. Blanket green belt over whole counties was thought to weaken the concept. There is logic in a narrow green belt at a time of reduced urban growth, especially as central government wishes to retain what opportunities it can to create new jobs. Moreover, consistency of purpose is more easily achieved across a narrow green belt than a broad one within which there are numerous planning authorities experiencing widely differing pressures.

Determination of green belt boundaries   The devolution of plan making, development control and other planning powers to districts and boroughs has increased the problems of implementing strategic policies by raising the number of responsible authorities and by encouraging a local perspective. One illustration of this concerns the debate over which tier of local authority (county or district) should be responsible for determining the detailed alignment of green belt boundaries and how 'permanent' these boundaries should be. Again, central government has expressed itself clearly. Discretion in these matters has been effectively given to the districts and boroughs, with uncertain consequences for the statutorily approved structure plans. Emphasis is placed on meeting local needs, and by advocating a policy of 'loose but permanent' green belt boundaries around existing settlements central government has provided an escape route for those councillors who complain of having to maintain 'outdated and silly boundaries'. But what it has not done is to provide much guidance on where adjustments should occur. The danger must be that the cumulative effect of many small local decisions taken to meet local priorities will create a green belt unrelated to any strategic objective because of the mixed and confused aims put forward for green belt by local authorities (see Table 2.2).

DOE does not believe that this will occur on the grounds that it is difficult to prise *any* development land out of most local authorities in the MGB. Moreover, DOE maintains that the benefits of local discretion over centralised control outweigh any minor modifications to the strategic role of the MGB that may arise from local decisions. This position may prove to be complacent. The most recent data on residential development land allocations suggest the completion of more than 50 000 houses between 1981 and 1986 in towns within and close to the MGB (see Ch. 2, Standing Conference 1981b). Although the great majority of this building will not take place on land within the MGB, it will fuel pressures for the release of green belt land. Even more important, the strategic consequences for the region and the Green Belt of the construction of the M25 motorway are at present being largely ignored by local and central government alike (see below). In the light of recent events there is the need for a clearer and more up-to-date exposition by central government of its views on restraint policies in south-east England than is contained in its rather thin statement of 1978 (DOE 1978a).

Environmental issues   It is, however, in the context of incorporating environmental aims into green belt that DOE has been least forthcoming and one result of this is that local authorities are themselves confused. DOE is at least consistent in seeking not to combine an urban restraint objective with resource-use goals within a single policy. Nevertheless, these matters do inevitably get cross-linked at local level and they must therefore be treated as separate but *complementary* (see Ch. 2). It follows that central government as the initiator and continuing supporter of green belt should ensure that the appropriate countryside policies are included in local as well as structure plans, if the credibility of restraint is not to be undermined by an apparent lack of resolve among local authorities in tackling urban-fringe land-use problems. The particular countryside proposals for different parts of the Green Belt must be decided locally, but DOE must see that they are included in local plans and put into effect. This will encourage local authorities to believe that DOE is committed to green belt in a purposeful way while ensuring that local authorities cannot shelter behind a convenient development control device without themselves thinking positively about the purpose of green belt.

To conclude, at a strategic scale, and at the level of principle, central government had made its position over green belt much clearer in recent years. Nevertheless, questions remain over the future implementation of restraint and it is possible to argue that in the absence of effective policy making at district and borough level, then decisions by central government at appeal and in response to structure plans are, on their own, inadequate guides as to the purpose and performance of green belt as a strategic policy. Few planners outside DOE doubt that a new and clear statement on these matters by central government would be of considerable value to them. A revised circular would have to take a more positive stand on environmental issues. Its continuing absence reflects not only the current lack of commitment by the present (1982) government to regional planning but also a basic unwillingness on the government's part to provide local authorities with the necessary resources and powers to help them improve their environments, through the reclamation of derelict land for example, unless the improvement scheme is also linked to the identification of development land (DOE 1980c, 1981a).

The growth of non-conforming land uses

All studies of land-use change in the MGB show that restraint has not stopped the slow but continuous growth of non-conforming land uses. Road improvements and public utilities now consume more land than housing, both public and private, and the demand for planning permission for residential development is often a consequence of public sector investment. This familiar sequence of events helps to explain why local authorities are often angered by what they see as the insensitive siting of public sector development in green belts.

On its own, development control cannot stop speculative land market activity in the face of the slow but persistent release of green belt land and the large financial gains realisable by landowners (see Ch. 3). To be largely successful in halting development is not good enough. Landowners and developers do not accept that restraint eliminates all development interest in green belt land and this is a perfectly reasonable position since some development does occur. The effect of restraint is to confine 'hope' value in land to the immediate urban edge. Since the late 1970s central government, through its appeals decisions, has enforced restraint quite firmly, partly as a response to the criticisms it received from local authorities following the white paper *Widening the choice: the next steps in housing* (DOE 1973b). There are, however, a number of other pressures that might lead to the release of more land. These include the secondary effects of the building of the M25 motorway, the requirement laid on local authorities in Circular 71/77 (DOE 1977b) not to act in such a way as to inhibit industrial expansion, and the general approach to speeding up the supply of building land as outlined in Circular 22/80 (DOE 1980b).

Government policy does not encourage local authorities to release green belt land for any of these development needs. It suggests that such land should, and indeed could, be found elsewhere within urban areas and on land identified for development. Standing Conference (1981a) also believes that local authorities have identified enough land in their structure plans to meet the medium-term housing needs of the region without trespassing into the Green Belt. Nevertheless, the wider national economic need may become a higher order priority than maintaining green belt restraint once the economy begins to expand again, and the procedural approach outlined in Circular 22/80 will ease the implementation of such a change in policy. To date, the growth of non-conforming uses have been concentrated in the inner half of the Green Belt but this pattern may be changed by the M25 motorway. Along its length of 190 km, and especially around its 20 intersections, the pressure for development will be considerable. If the same kinds of effects of new roads on the maintenance of farmland, as are recorded elsewhere in the Green Belt (see Ch. 6), are repeated for the M25, then the motorway's environmental impact, even in these narrow terms, will be considerable.

As well as local environmental disbenefits, the motorway will create new economic opportunities (Manners 1981) upon which central government will surely wish to capitalise (see DOE 1978a). But DOE has not given any guidance to local authorities on how to take advantage of these benefits. The M25 is the largest public sector investment in south-east England for many years. It is deserving of a comprehensive and positive approach to its planning and economic consequences, including those for the MGB, and this needs to be conducted on a scale quite beyond the means of the individual local authority. Having disbanded the regional economic planning councils, the ball lies firmly in the central government's court. It is extremely doubtful, however, if central government knows except in the vaguest of terms what it wants, and the best that can be said is that the future rate and pattern of growth of non-conforming uses in the Green Belt is highly uncertain.

Conforming land uses

Attitudes among local planning officers towards the positive promotion of conforming land uses are extremely varied. Some officers, especially in county planning offices, take these matters seriously, but at district and borough level there is much talk but little independent action. All officers espouse high ideals for the environment but many retreat from effecting them in the face of difficulties (lack of money, skilled staff and statutory powers, and indifferent support from members). Most now recognise, however, that conforming uses may conflict with each other and the forms that some of them take are unacceptable. In particular, they are concerned about the poor reclamation of gravel pits, industrialised agriculture and buildings linked to sports activities. The terms 'openness' and 'of a rural character' used to exemplify the nature of conforming land uses in 1955 (MHLG 1955) are unhelpful in today's circumstances which often encourage the intensive use of rural land. These terms are open to variable interpretation and are largely meaningless outside the context of specific countryside policies. Yet they are still employed regularly by those local authorities determined to frustrate, where it is within their powers to do so, all changes in land use. Indiscriminate use of these terms would be less possible if local authorities were obliged to spell out *precisely* what their objectives were for open land in the Green Belt.

Recent research means that we are now much better informed about the nature of conforming uses and how land in the MGB is managed. Unfortunately, inquiry reveals a confusion of aims among local planning officers and their members while at the same time illustrating rather than repudiating some of the researchers' concerns. Recreation is a good case in point. A great deal of public open space is available but often it only acts as an additional amenity for outer-suburban residents and not as a realisable asset for the majority of those living in the conurbation. For reasons of accessibility it may well continue to lie beyond the reach of most inner-city residents, but it will certainly do so if more imaginative management schemes designed to attract those who do not participate at present are not implemented. District authorities, whose elected representatives reflect local concerns, are unlikely to alter current practice in the present economic circumstances unless pressed to do so by central government agencies.

Green belt restraint is not a valid planning objection to mineral extraction and it is inevitable that the working of aggregates will continue in the MGB at or near recent levels in the medium term despite the undoubted opposition to it of some planners and the public generally. The demand for aggregates in the region has fallen with the recession but other sources of supply cannot meet the region's needs on their own. In the area of the extended green belt, that is, on land in one or other category of green belt (see Fig. 1.1), more than 10 000 ha of land have been worked for sand and gravel between 1948 and 1976. Although it is impossible to give a precise figure for the MGB (see Ch. 4) several thousand hectares of land have not been satisfactorily restored, even to the standards laid down at the time of their working which were often much less stringent than those required today. In many cases past workings will need central government finance to put them right especially as the most profitable after-use – housing – is a non-conforming land use. The reclamation of current workings faces two particular difficulties, namely the increasing use of high quality farmland and the rising standards of reclamation now expected for amenity reasons. It is doubtful whether the planning system can meet these difficulties in spite of the increased powers contained in the Town and Country Planning

(Minerals) Act 1981. It certainly has been unable to do so in the past, and central government has turned its back on other tough control measures such as a statutory bonding system for extractors. This means that the DOE–MAFF–SAGA experiments assume a critical importance, but in the absence of additional qualified staff employed in local authorities and by mineral companies even those reclamation standards known to be practicable, technically and financially, may not be realised.

Difficult though the planning problems raised by mineral extraction are, they can be tackled more directly than those presented by agriculture. The main reasons for this are, first, agricultural policy is formulated partly in Brussels and implemented through another central government department; secondly, there is no clear view among local planners, or in DOE, as to what is wanted of farming in the MGB although it is the major user of land; and thirdly, agriculture furnishes the particularly difficult question of the 'under-use' of land (see below). Except over one comparatively minor matter, that of seeking to limit the loss of high quality farmland, the two responsible central government departments (DOE and MAFF) seek to avoid trespassing on each other's remit.

Standing Conference argues, with some justification, that there is a policy void between MAFF and local planning authorities over the use of farmland (Standing Conference 1977a). Neither the ministry nor the authorities have the necessary powers to act decisively. Agricultural land-use change is one example of permitted development, and the ministry no longer retains the supervision and dispossession powers granted to it during World War II which allowed it to intervene directly in cases of poor farm management. But this begs the question of what objectives farming is supposed to be meeting and whether any national objectives for the industry should apply equally in green belts, most of which experience severe urban-fringe pressures of various kinds. MAFF regards food production as the primary, and the ministry often means the exclusive, objective for the industry. Very few resources, in terms of staffing and cash for example, are allocated to combining the objectives of food production with those of recreation or wildlife conservation, or even the broader social needs of rural areas. Some local planners and planning committee chairmen in the MGB would agree with this state of affairs. To them, horses and even farm-gate sales where this leads to farm shops, are undesirable forms of development. But the importance of these enterprises to some farmers' incomes (see Ch. 6) should not be dismissed and attempts to inhibit their growth would not only conflict with the recreational purpose of green belt but would militate against the wishes of most planners for a viable, self-financing urban-fringe farm economy. It is at this point that MAFF and local authorities often part company, the ministry encouraging farmers through its various grant aid schemes and tax reliefs to invest in industrialised farming techniques, whereas local authorities would prefer a traditional, low input–low output form of mixed farming.

The antipathy expressed towards planners by farmers and mineral companies is not surprising given their different interests in the future of the MGB. But recognition of this fact does not help all the interested parties to arrive at agreed goals, and with their present powers it is impossible for planners to insist that *their* objectives are met. The development control system only regulates some of the effects (land-use change) and not the causes of change. Causes lie in national policies determined elsewhere, such as the Common Agricultural Policy, motorway construction policy and the wish for cheap aggregates. Furthermore, the development control system does not address the question of promotion as opposed to prevention. Management agreements and the public ownership of land do allow for promotion but require considerable resources and public will to put them into effect. Furthermore, in situations where the occupier holds the responsibility for promoting a non-conforming use, as in the case of a public utility, such measures may prove ineffective. Indeed, the farm study described in Chapter 6 makes it abundantly clear that rights to property are extremely complex and the motives of occupiers and owners are extremely varied. Thus although it is possible to draw generalisations about the use of land in the Green Belt and the reasons for it, it is also evident that particular land policy instruments (management agreements, capital grants, public ownership, and so on) are likely to be effective in only a proportion of cases, especially if they are employed as general planning tools and not tailored to the requirements of particular cases. Flexibility of arrangements, something that frequently fails to appeal to politicians and officials who favour simple, cheap and widely applicable measures, is essential and this point is followed up below in the specific case of farmland maintenance.

The poor maintenance of farmland

One of the less tractable problems concerns the poor maintenance of farmland. Its importance as a problem derives from the fact that at least 60% of the MGB is still farmed and the farmed landscape is thus a key component in maintaining the amenity of the Green Belt. Its interest lies in the fact that it is illustrative of the difficulties facing local planners trying to achieve amenity objectives.

The findings of the land maintenance survey reported in Chapter 6 confirm the impressions of other observers. Sizeable areas are poorly maintained from the point of view of both amenity and food production, even if only 5.5% of farmland can be classified as derelict or semi-derelict. Insofar as the benefit of the doubt over maintenance standards has always been given to the occupier and that all the land surveyed has been returned as farmed in the June Agricultural Census, then the survey probably underestimates the full extent of poor land maintenance in London's urban fringe, but not necessarily in the Green Belt as a whole as the study has been conducted within the inner one-third of the MGB. It is also concluded in Chapter 6 that the area of poorly maintained land will not diminish of its own accord although there is no reason to assume that it will increase substantially either, except possibly as one secondary consequence of the construction of the M25 motorway. Furthermore, the position adopted in Chapter 6 is that although it is possible to argue in favour of high standards of farmland maintenance in the urban fringe as one means of realising amenity objectives, the case is not an especially persuasive one. It is just the best of a set of indifferent alternatives. It is important to recall that domestic food supplies are *not* threatened by the poor maintenance of urban-fringe farmland, and that agricultural efficiency can conflict with broader amenity considerations. The promotion of farming efficiency can lead to restrictions on public access to the countryside, to a reduction in landscape diversity, and inhibit the development of other legitimate recreational uses of green belt land. Measures introduced to limit the area of poorly maintained farmland must keep these points in mind.

Before considering such measures it is important to remind ourselves of some of the main reasons for poor land maintenance. They stem from a variety of sources, some planning, some agricultural and some specific to the occupier. The poor maintenance of land is especially associated with the large-scale keeping of horses, the ownership of land by gravel companies and developers, proximity to housing and new roads, the short-term, insecure letting of land, and hobby farmers. Three broad areas of action to remedy this problem are considered here, none of which are mutually exclusive. Major changes in capital taxation, especially with regard to Development Land Tax and Capital Transfer Tax, are not examined although they could have a significant effect by themselves or in combination with the other proposals.

Possible amendments to the planning system   Vagueness over the future of farming in local plans will reduce commitment to high land maintenance standards, and for land on the urban edge the possibility of quinquennial adjustments to green belt boundaries each time local plans are reviewed could prove disastrous. This is not to suggest that green belt boundaries can be regarded as inviolate. It is impractical for planning committees to continue to defend green belt sites that for reasons beyond their control, for example motorway construction, have become indefensible. But building on the land does not solve the land maintenance problem, it just shifts its location. Some revision of boundaries could reduce urban intrusion but the process of boundary realignment itself has to be handled carefully. Otherwise, it will activate the kind of speculative activity that is a primary cause of poor maintenance. It would also need to be co-ordinated centrally. To meet these difficulties an initiative over boundary changes would:

(a)   have to be treated as far as possible as a once-and-for-all change, initiated and directed by DOE with reference to a clearly stated objective – in this case improving agricultural land maintenance standards – but be based on detailed proposals for boundary changes from local authorities;

(b)   require the public purchase of MGB land at existing-use values, that is, compensation for the loss of approved uses rights only, in order to minimise speculation; and

(c)   require the land purchased to be put to a use that meets local needs while effectively buffering farmland from the intrusive effects of development.

Even this proposal runs the danger of establishing precedents and it might be regarded as unduly complicated, expensive and politically contentious for such a limited objective as farmland maintenance, but anything less than this is unlikely to suffice, and would create as many new problems as it solves.

If planners believe that the best way of avoiding the under-use of land is to encourage a viable farm economy then they must take a more relaxed view towards farm buildings and improvements, and herein lies the potential conflict with public access and wildlife conservation. The conflict must be recognised and not concealed behind platitudes about the desirability of multiple land use. Such platitudes cut little ice among farmers who would respond much more positively to the identification of clear planning objectives in local plans for different zones in the urban fringe and some financial resources to help realise the objectives. Farmers react strongly against what they perceive as a lack of understanding and sympathy among planners for their position. This only encourages them to seek out alternative avenues of financial gain, including speculation in land with all its consequences for land maintenance. The frequently expressed wish among local planners to prohibit horse grazing also needs to be carefully examined. Attempts to enforce this could well be counter-productive, reducing farm incomes and not necessarily improving land maintenance. A better approach would be to encourage but regularise horse keeping with stricter controls over the hygiene standards of premises through a licencing system.

Land management agreements   Some success in achieving effective countryside management is claimed for land management agreements willingly entered into by the landowner in exchange for some form of compensation, consideration or practical assistance (e.g. Hookway 1977). These agreements should not be confused with area-wide land management experiments (see Ch. 5), three examples of which exist in the MGB (Colne Valley, south Herts–Barnet, Havering). There is no reason why management agreements and area-wide experiments should not go hand in hand to mutual advantage. Agreements represent an opportunity for public bodies to act positively, unlike the largely reactive posture of development control, although such agreements are by definition dependent upon the willing co-operation of landowners. Would they therefore be successful in reducing the poor maintenance of urban-fringe farmland? There are a number of complications.

First, current forms of agreement have not been designed to improve agricultural land maintenance but usually to minimise conflict between amenity and agricultural interests. Modifications in this direction would bring these agreements into close contact, if not overlap, with various forms of MAFF grant aid, and raise the important principle of equity. Would some farmers not then be paid for doing something they could reasonably be expected to do anyway? And what of those farmers who are revealed in the survey as continuing to maintain their properties well? Secondly, to date most agreements have led to little money compensation for owners, leaving the impression that this is a cheap solution to management problems in the countryside. But land prices, rents and maintenance costs have all risen rapidly in real terms in recent years and now create a level of recurrent costs that local authorities are keen to avoid. Moreover, following the Wildlife and Countryside Act 1981 and the precedents set by the very large amounts of indexed compensation awarded to farmers in Exmoor (MacEwen & MacEwen 1982), this whole approach is in danger of exploding in the face of its advocates. In the Green Belt, costs would prove considerable, especially as agreements of any significant duration are most unlikely to be entered into by owners of land right on the urban edge, just where they are most needed. In these locations the compensation that owners would require to forfeit voluntarily the chance of a development gain would be substantial. The success of agricultural land conservation measures of a similar nature in North America, and in areas where development pressures are strong, is now being seriously questioned (Hansen & Schwartz 1975, Carman 1977). Thirdly, the interviews with local planners (see Ch. 4) reveal inertia or even resistance on their part to land management schemes of a substantial nature. Given the genuine difficulties in making agreements work (Feist 1978), agreements would be more likely to be successful in difficult urban-fringe locations if implemented within the context of an urban-fringe experimental area where back-up advice is readily available. Unfortunately, the experiments are coming to an end and local authorities will now have to fund and organise such schemes themselves. Management agreements may well not be capable of resolving serious conflicts anyway and other reports conclude that in areas of severe land-use conflict compulsory powers may be necessary (Porchester 1977). These reports begin by recognising that the free market in land may have to be curtailed.

Land Boards and the public ownership of land   The right to sell land to whom one chooses, at a time of one's choosing, and to receive whatever price the market will realise, is a jealously guarded right among owners, public as well as private. But this right often conflicts with the need to ensure a secure farming environment in the urban fringe. To combat this a Land Board with similar powers to those given to the Rural Development Boards could be established in London's urban fringe. Although the Rural Development Boards have been disbanded the necessary legislation, based on provisions in the Agriculture Act 1967, is still on the statute book. The key powers given to the Rural Development Boards include those to acquire, compulsorily if necessary, manage, improve, sell or let land; and to intervene in land transfers in order to promote farm amalgamation (see Capstick 1978). If put fully into effect, this could stop the subdivision of farm properties, reduce the short-term letting of land and ensure that competent farmers occupy the land. But this could only be achieved at what some would regard as an unacceptable price. The board would intervene directly in the working of the land market and would exercise considerable discretionary power over who is worthy of more land and who is not (it judges people); and the board would be another body cutting across the jurisdiction of other agencies and local authorities.

In a rather different way, the public acquisition of land also interferes with the working of the market, especially if the land is acquired at existing use value only. It also leads to full proprietary control over the management of the land and could by this means prevent the fragmentation of properties and their occupation by incompetent tenants. It could prohibit the extensive grazing of horses, the short-term letting of land, make sure that gravel land is effectively reclaimed and provide full security for tenants. But as with a Land Board there are major objections including outright political opposition and the cost of land acquisition. Furthermore, given the problems of acquiring dispossession orders generally, there could be no guarantee that public landlords would be able to ensure higher standards of land maintenance in all instances than exist at present, partly because maintenance would remain to some degree in the hands of the tenant.

The preceding discussion illustrates the problems of achieving more than a partial solution. It is impossible to predict how effective any approach would be as we have no idea how much land is poorly maintained in the countryside generally. Moreover, to criticise the planning system for being inefficient in this regard (Coleman 1976, 1977) is wide of the mark. Farmers speculate in land as much as any other group of landowners and it is changes in land policy and fiscal policy that are most urgently needed if the planning system is to work effectively. Whether such radical changes are justified in order to meet the land maintenance issue is as much an ideological question as a practical planning one; but they hardly seem worth it. What is fairly certain, however, is that any relaxation of restraint, or the frequent adjustment of green belt boundaries, or any major reduction in the marginal rate of Development Land Tax will only make the situation worse.

There are no simple or universal solutions. The circumstances of neighbouring owners and occupiers vary considerably and the causes of poor land maintenance have been shown to have widely differing origins. The split in responsibilities in this area in central government between MAFF and DOE, and between departments of planning and estate management in local authorities, does not help. Neither does the absence of a land register. In these circumstances most official reports argue for a consensus solution based on the tightening-up of planning powers and an extension of management schemes of various kinds (Agriculture EDC 1977, ACAH 1978, CRC 1978). These reports fail to acknowledge, however, that these approaches are unlikely to be effective in the most difficult, and perhaps the most sensitive, planning situations. There is, therefore, no single means of eliminating inadequate land maintenance in the urban fringe and it is essential that local planners and their members recognise this. Having done so, if they wish to minimise the extent of poorly maintained land, then they must embrace as wide a range of measures as possible, treat each situation on its merits, and accept that successful rural land management depends on taking a long-term view that is both explicit and consistent.

Final comment

The implementation of green belt restraint raises many complex issues. This is partly because the purpose of green belt can be interpreted in widely differing ways and partly because today's substantial green belts encompass a great range of local planning situations.

One of the main objectives of this comprehensive, but by no means exhaustive, study of London's Green Belt has been to examine these differences and to get beyond the published statements of central and local government. Necessarily, these statements have been carefully analysed, as has the other literature on green belt, but the interpretation contained here has depended very largely on the views of numerous respondents who hold differing kinds of responsibilities for land use in the MGB. Many of the respondents hold firm but inconsistent views and their replies have often been confused; but this is the context within which restraint is actually implemented and it bears only limited relation to the broad principles laid down by central government. Nevertheless, within this mosaic of opinions it is possible to establish a feel for the forces that are currently amending the purpose of restraint and influencing the general pattern of land use in London's urban fringe.

As with any investigation, during its course new issues arise, gaps in our knowledge emerge and tantalising glimpses are provided of other fruitful avenues of research. Of the many avenues that could be listed three in particular are worthy of mention. What will be the strategic and local impact on the Green Belt of the M25 motorway when it is completed in the mid-1980s? How do local residents and amenity groups see the link between the maintenance of farmland and local amenity? And how, precisely, do property owners, some of whom may be in conflict with each other, act to protect their own interests and with what effect on the maintenance of restraint?

One gap to emerge that should be filled with some urgency is a revised statement on green belts by central government. With some difficulty it is possible to piece together an embryonic central government view based on successive secretaries' of state responses to structure plan proposals, including such matters as the size of green belts, criteria for green belts and which tier of local authority should implement restraint. But DOE responsibility does not stop there if green belt is to retain vestiges of its strategic function. DOE must provide local authorities with guidance on such specific issues as the M25 motorway, and on more general matters including the relationships between green belt restraint, job creation, amenity designations and the management of green belt land. It needs to adopt a much more positive and concerned outlook for the urban-fringe environment than is contained in Circular 42/55, and to reflect on the planning problems of the latter part of the 20th century. By doing so not only would central government indicate a concern for these issues, but it would also strengthen the positions of those local authorities that are keen to act positively while at the same time cutting the ground from beneath the feet of those authorities that employ green belt restraint as a means of avoiding the need to address them at all.

Appendix *Data sources and surveys*

Much of the detailed information in this book has been compiled from semi-structured interview surveys held with different groups with an interest in, or knowledge of, the Green Belt. This Appendix provides additional information on the surveys and how they were conducted to supplement that contained in the text. The surveys are divided into three groups, those concerned with current restraint policy, land market trends and farmers.

Green belt restraint – current policy

Information was obtained primarily from three semi-structured interview surveys, one with local planning officers, one with the chairmen of local planning committees and one with officials from the DOE.

The interviews with planning officers at both county and district level aimed to establish their views on:

(a)   the purpose of green belt restraint in their local authorities and its relations with other local environmental policies;

(b)   the sources of pressure on green belt and officers' attitudes towards the major approved land uses;

(c)   the appearance of green belt land;

(d)   the effectiveness of development control in implementing restraint;

(e)   land market considerations.

Chief planning officers in 49 districts and seven counties (including the GLC) were approached for interviews. The survey included authorities in the 'extended' green belt, as recorded in Figure 1.1. Only one officer (North Herts.) refused. All the interviews were arranged and conducted between August and November 1977 (Table A.1). With the preparation of structure plans under way, county planning officers were approached again in November 1978 to ascertain any changes in policy over the intervening period. The earlier discussions had raised a number of important points and four* new questions were put to them. They were:

(a)   What relationship, if any, exists in either policy or practical terms between the urban restraint function of green belt and countryside management policies for London's urban fringe?

* Only questions (a) and (b) were put to the GLC.

(b)   In our previous interviews many planners mentioned the lack of resources available to them to improve the amenity value of green belt land. Do you regard the lack of resources for landscape improvement to be a major constraint?

(c)   Several district planning officers thought that the M25 motorway and DOE Circular 71/77 *Local government and the industrial strategy* both presently and potentially would make the imposition of green belt more difficult. To what extent do you agree?

(d)   How, in association with your districts, have you agreed to determine green belt boundaries once your development plan is replaced by structure and local plans?

Table A.1 Local authority planning officers and planning committee chairmen giving interviews and those returning development control decision data.

Greater London Council	Hertfordshire County Council
*Barnet LB	Broxbourne
*Bexley LB	†*Dacorum
†*Bromley LB	*East Hertfordshire
†*Croydon LB	*Hertsmere
†Enfield LB	†*St Albans
†Havering LB	†*Three Rivers
†*Hillingdon LB	Watford
Redbridge LB	Welwyn–Hatfield
*Berkshire County Council	*Kent County Council
†Bracknell	Dartford
†*Slough	Gravesham
*Windsor and Maidenhead	†*Sevenoaks
†*Wokingham	*Tonbridge and Malling
	*Tunbridge Wells
*Buckinghamshire County Council	
†Aylesbury Vale	*Surrey County Council
†*Beaconsfield	*Elmbridge
†*Chiltern	*Epsom and Ewell
*High Wycombe	*Guildford
	†*Mole Valley
Essex County Council	†Reigate and Banstead
†*Basildon	†*Runnymede
†*Brentwood	*Spelthorne
Castle Point	*Surrey Heath
*Chelmsford	†*Tandridge
†*Epping Forest	†*Waverley
Rochford	†*Woking
Thurrock	
*Uttlesford	

Planning officers were interviewed in all these authorities.
*Authorities in which the planning committee chairman was interviewed.
†Planning authorities returning key development control decisions.

Those officers returning data on development control decisions are identified in Table A.1 (see Ch. 3).

The interviews with planning officers were designed to examine some of the technical aspects of restraint and to be supplemented by discussions with committee chairmen of the political aspects of green belt. The matters raised with the chairmen included local pressure group activity, the degree of public concern caused by green belt decisions, the public ownership of green belt land, public access to green belt land and potential conflicts between local housing needs and green belt. Interviews were successfully completed with 38 chairmen between October 1977 and January 1978 (see Table A.1).

In order to acquire a central government view, interviews were arranged with five DOE officials. Two of these were responsible for green belt policy in the context of local planning generally, and three were responsible for planning in the Eastern region, South East region and the GLC, the three DOE regions covering the MGB. As with the discussions held in local authorities an informal interviewing procedure was adopted based on a set of questions sent to respondents in advance. These related to strategic green belt considerations, green belt boundaries, land use within the MGB, the white paper *Widening the choice: the next steps in housing*, the Standing Conference 1976 report on *The improvement of London's Green Belt* and the Community Land Legislation. A follow-up letter was sent in October 1978 to ascertain whether any policy changes had occurred over the previous 12 months – none had.

Information on land market trends

Information on who holds interests in land is extremely difficult to acquire. For England and Wales there is no publicly available land register recording details of individual ownerships, occupancies or transactions. Information held by HM Registry describes legal title to, and not beneficial interest in, property, is incomplete and is not open to public inspection (see Northfield committee report 1979, pp. 109–16). Data are published on market transactions but in order to maintain confidentiality are highly aggregated. In order to collect as much direct evidence as possible, data were acquired through the survey of farming occupiers (see below) and from semi-structured interviews held with district valuers, developers and mineral operators.

Records held in Valuation Offices constitute a comprehensive and reliable source of information as details of all transactions are sent to them by the Inland Revenue. The Chief Valuer's Office agreed to support an approach to district valuers for non-site-specific information for transactions concluded since 1969. After discussions with the Chief Valuer's Office an approach was made to 16 district valuers, not all of whom were able to assist (Table A.2). Views were sought on the imposition of green belt restraint, valuations for seven types of predetermined property for 1969, 1971, 1973, 1975 and 1977, and information on the amount of land sold in each subsector of the market.

Table A.2 District Valuers and developers in the MGB.

District Valuers' offices with more than 40 km² of MGB land approached for information

Harlow	Medway[1]	Guildford[1]	S. Bucks.
Chelmsford[1]	Bromley	N. Surrey	Watford[1]
Basildon[1]	Tunbridge Wells[1]	E. Bucks.	St Albans[1]
Havering[1]	Reigate	Hillingdon	N. Herts.

Developers interviewed,	*Location of head office and*	*Main areas of activity around London's Green Belt*
Barratts (SE) Ltd	Wallington, Surrey	Surrey
Bovis (Bovis Homes Division)	Sidcup, Kent	Berks., Surrey, Kent
Cardinal Homes Ltd	Bromley, Kent	Bromley
Countryside Properties Ltd	Billericay, Essex	Essex, Herts.
Crest Homes Ltd	Weybridge, Surrey	Surrey, west of London
Croudace Ltd	Caterham, Surrey	Surrey
Fairview Estates (Enfield) Ltd	Enfield, Middx	Essex, Herts., Bucks., Berks.
French Kier Development Ltd	Buckhurst Hill, Essex	Essex
Higgs & Hill Property Holdings Ltd	New Malden, Surrey	Surrey
Moody Homes Construction Ltd	Brentwood, Essex	Essex, Herts.
New Ideal Homes Ltd	Woking, Surrey	Surrey
Wates Built Homes Ltd	Norbury, London SW16	Surrey, west of London
George Wimpey & Co. Ltd	Hammersmith, London W6	all areas

[1] Provided full information.

A number of 'typical' green belt properties were defined in advance. This was deemed necessary because of the comparatively small number of sales in the MGB within each of the District Valuation Office areas and in order to provide comparability between returns. Seven properties were defined, five agricultural and two for development land – one of the latter without current planning permission – and each district valuer was asked to provide a 'high' and 'low' valuation for each date. The difference was split and the figures averaged to arrive at the data in Table 3.6, the agricultural land prices being derived from Properties 1 to 4 and the building land prices from Property 6. The property particulars sent to district valuers were as follows:

Property no. 1. Arable farm of 100 ha: 50% Grade 2, 50% Grade 3 land; farmhouse (modernised) of average size plus two cottages; well equipped, land drained; no 'hope' value; vacant possession.

Property no. 2. Mixed dairy, livestock farm of 50 ha: Grade 3 land; farmhouse (modernised) of average size plus one cottage; well equipped; no 'hope' value; vacant possession.

Property no. 3. Part-time, hobby farm: 14 ha of Grade 3 land; 'desirable', modernised farmhouse/residence; 5 km from main line commuting station (20–30 minutes to main line London terminal); all land in pasture; buildings rather old and in poor condition – of limited value for modern agriculture; no 'hope' value; vacant possession.

Property no. 4. Pasture accommodation land: 12 ha; average drainage; not really suited to arable farming; no 'hope' value; vacant possession.

Property no. 5. Accommodation land: 8 ha of flat, poorly drained pasture adjacent to post-1950 private housing estate developed to 30 houses to the hectare; green belt land not regarded as 'infill' but could be said to have long-term 'hope' value. Assume all main services available, no abnormals, although normal estate roads and drainage within the site to be provided. No existing road frontage, but access easily available; 1 km from small town with commuter services to London main line terminal in approximately 20–30 minutes.

Property no. 6. 'Infill' farmland: 2 ha of land with inter-war private housing on both sides; main road frontage of 40 m; all services available; no abnormals but internal estate roads and drainage to be provided. Outline planning permission (OPP) for private residential development at 30 houses to the hectare refused once, but clear short-term 'hope'; 1 km from small town with commuter service to London main line terminal in about 20–30 minutes.

Property no. 7. Building land: 2 ha of land with 40 m frontage to existing estate road having all main services; no abnormals but internal estate roads and drainage to be provided; OPP for 30 houses to the hectare granted; 1 km from small town with commuter service to London main line terminal in about 20–30 minutes.

The main aim of the discussions with developers and mineral companies was to investigate changes in the MGB land market generally during the 1970s and to discuss the kinds of interests in land held by companies rather than to detail the green belt land holdings of these firms, although questions were asked about these. Of particular concern was the process of acquisition, including the taking out of options and conditional contracts, and the role adopted by the firm alongside private owners in preparing planning applications and fighting appeals. The interviews were conducted between October 1978 and February 1979. There are no perfect sample frames as, *in principle*, it is not known which companies hold interests in MGB land. Twenty-three developers were approached and interviews conducted with 13 medium- and large-scale developers known to be operating in all parts of the MGB (see Table A.2), and in round terms these firms built (on occasion by subcontract) and sold nearly 30 000 housing units in 1977. Of these, only one-third were built in south-east England. Of the 11 mineral companies approached only three agreed to an interview,* all of whom specialised in aggregate production in their south-east England operations. The interviews with them included discussion on:

(a)   the present and prospective markets for aggregates in south-east England;
(b)   land reclamation and conflicts in use with farming and amenity interests;
(c)   particular difficulties, if any, of operating within the MGB; and
(d)   land acquisition policy and practice.

Agricultural data sources

These sources included the use of parish summaries from the June Agricultural Census (1976), interviews with MAFF officials and the farm survey. The difficulties of using the Agricultural Census are noted in Chapter 4. One of these concerns the differing size of agricultural parishes and the need to aggregate them. The basic data unit became the district or London borough (or that part of them in the MGB) but even these have been aggregated to ensure no data unit has less than 900 ha of farmland within it (Table A.3).

In March 1979 a meeting was held with four MAFF officials to examine the ministry's view of agriculture in the MGB. A number of specific themes were pursued. These were (a) the effect of green belt restraint in mitigating urban-fringe pressures on farming; (b) the extent and causes of 'undermanaged' farmland in the MGB; (c) the view of MAFF on the use of farmland for recreational enterprises; (d) the lotting of farm properties for sale; (e) the amount of land leased on short-term lets, and (f) the way in which agricultural questions had been treated in the structure plans of the GLC and surrounding county authorities.

* The firms were Hoveringham Gravels Ltd, Beaconsfield, Bucks.; Ready Mixed Concrete (UK) Ltd, Feltham, West London; Redland Aggregates Ltd, Knebworth, Herts.

Table A.3 Agricultural area in the approved MGB by district.

District	Area (ha)	'New' ha	District	Area (ha)	'New' ha
Broxbourne	1 927		Slough	19	} 9703
Dacorum	1 344		Windsor and Maidenhead	9 684	
East Herts.	1 964		Wokingham	3 261	
Hertsmere	5 413		Aylesbury Vale	1 423	
St Albans	3 557		Beaconsfield	6 560	
Three Rivers	4 376		Chiltern	12 377	
Welwyn–Hatfield	5 415		Wycombe	7 127	
Brentwood	8 204		Barking	692	
Epping Forest	14 548		Redbridge	347	} 1055
Thurrock	9 247		Waltham Forest	16	
Dartford	3 299		Barnet	802	} 1291
Sevenoaks	13 480		Harrow	489	
Elmbridge	1 982		Bexley	400	} 5842
Epsom and Ewell	372	} 6151	Bromley	5 442	
Reigate and Banstead	5 779		Croydon	538	
Guildford	11 490		Kingston	526	} 1281
Mole Valley	13 514		Sutton	217	
Spelthorne	898		Enfield	1 936	
Tandridge	14 674		Havering	3 024	
Waverley	8 953		Hillingdon	2 055	} 2231
Woking	2 124		Ealing	176	
			Hounslow	384	} 977
			Richmond	593	

Source: Agricultural Census 1976.

Reference has already been made in Chapter 6 to the conduct of the farm survey and to the land maintenance survey in particular. No published source records the enterprise structure or ownership and occupation pattern of individual holdings. Such information can only be acquired through direct contact with occupiers. Prior to the full survey carried out during the first half of 1978, a pilot study was conducted in Elmbridge DC, Surrey during November 1977. At the outset of the interview the respondent was informed that he would be asked about matters that he might regard as confidential and that he could decline to answer questions about them. This open approach helped to create an atmosphere of trust and co-operation, and was reinforced by the recording of all answers in the presence of the respondent. A high level of response was achieved for most questions. Likewise, the response rate for interviews was high (74%). Thirteen per cent of the sample had to be redrawn because of failings in the sample frame and a further 13% declined to participate. Each non-respondent was replaced by an occupier of similar size and type of farming in the same general location.

There are over 4500 farms in the MGB and it was decided for practical and policy reasons not to draw a random sample from the whole MGB. Budgetary considerations restricted the sample to less than 200 occupiers and it was decided that at least 50 farms should be included in any sample area to account for local variability. Three areas were selected (see Ch. 6) with differing planning but fairly similar farming conditions. A 40% sample of farms of more than 4 ha was sought in each area. It was decided to exclude very small holdings. This was a difficult decision to make. For example, small holdings may be particularly attractive to developers, and hobby farmers may be especially susceptible to pressures to sell as their livelihoods are not dependent on their farms. But there is no evidence to support these assertations or evidence to disprove that parts of full-time farms are not equally ripe for development and their owners not equally willing to sell if the opportunity arises. Moreover, a random sample would have included within it more than one-third of all holdings with an area of less than 5 ha, the management of which contribute relatively little to the overall appearance of the green belt. Appearance will continue to depend largely on the long-term viability of much larger holdings and it was decided to weight the sample in their favour. Moreover, as the major operational restraint on farm surveys is the time taken getting to each interview, the inclusion of many small holdings would not release sufficient time to increase the overall size of the sample.

The interviews sought to ascertain information on:

(a)   the present location and area of each farm business and how these had changed since 1970;
(b)   the effects of various forms of urban intrusion on farm management practice;
(c)   the attitudes of the occupier to the appearance of the MGB;
(d)   the detailed pattern of ownership and occupation of the holding in 1970 and 1977;
(e)   whether any land had been bought or sold (and to whom) since 1970;
(f)   the combination of enterprises on the farm, including non-agricultural enterprises, and also non-farm sources of income;
(g)   investment in improvements since 1970; and
(h)   the occupiers' expectations as to the future of his business.

Some of the material collected in the farm survey is not discussed in this book and at no point is reference made to information specific to a particular farm, whether the occupier might regard it as confidential or not.

Bibliography

Abercrombie, P. 1945. *Greater London plan 1944*. London: HMSO.

ACAH (Advisory Council for Agriculture and Horticulture in England and Wales) 1978. *Agriculture and the countryside* (Strutt report). Chesham: Robendene.

ADAS (Agricultural Development and Advisory Service) 1976. *Agricultural land classification of England and Wales*. Tech. rep. no. 11/1. London: MAFF.

ADAS 1977. *Land use on Humber Bank*. Unpubl. report. Leeds: ADAS Research Group.

Agriculture EDC (Economic Development Council) 1977. *Agriculture into the 1980s: land use*. London: National Economic Development Office.

Alder, J. 1979. *Development control*. London: Sweet & Maxwell.

Anderson, M. A. 1981. Planning policies and development control in the Sussex Downs AONB. *Town Plann. Rev.* **52**, 5–25.

Bardach, E. 1977. *The implementation game: what happens after a Bill becomes Law*. London: MIT Press.

Barrett, S. and C. Fudge (eds) 1981. *Policy and action: essays on the implementation of public policy*. London: Methuen.

Barrett, S. and G. Whitting 1980. *Local authorities and the supply of development land to the private sector*. Work. Pap. no. 19. University of Bristol: School of Advanced Urban Studies.

Barrett, S., M. Boddy and M. Stewart 1978. *The implementation of the community land scheme: interim report*. Occ. Pap. no. 3. University of Bristol: School of Advanced Urban Studies.

Bather, N. J. 1976. *The speculative residential developer and urban growth*. Geog. Paps. no. 47. University of Reading.

Bell, M. 1979. Agricultural compensation: the way forward. *J. Plann. Environ. Law*, September, 577–96.

Bell, M., A. Hearne and D. van Rest 1978. Agricultural land taken for new roads. *Town and Country Planning* **46**, 164–7.

Berkshire County Council 1978a. *East Berkshire Structure Plan: submitted written statement*. Reading: Berkshire CC.

Berkshire County Council 1978b. *Central Berkshire Structure Plan: submitted written statement*. Reading: Berkshire CC.

Berkshire Planning Department 1979. *Green Belt Subject Plan* (draft for public consultation). Reading: Berkshire CC.

Berry, D. 1979. The sensitivity of dairying to urbanization: a study of north-eastern Illinois. *Prof. Geog.* **31**, 170–6.

Best, R. H. 1981. *Land use and living space*. London: Methuen.

Bexley, L. B. nd. *Green belt: discussion paper*. Sidcup: Borough Engineer's and Surveyor's Department.

Blacksell, M. and A. Gilg 1981. *The countryside: planning and change*. London: George Allen & Unwin.

Blair, A. M. 1978. *Spatial effects of urban influences on agriculture in Essex, 1960–1973*. Unpubl. PhD thesis. University of London.

Blair, A. M. 1980. Compulsory purchase: a neglected factor in the agricultural land loss debate. *Area* **12**, 183–9.

Blair, A. M. 1981. Farmers' attitudes to planning in the countryside. *Ecos* **2**, 6–11.

Blaxter, K. 1975. Can Britain feed herself? *New Scientist* **65**, 697–702.

Boal, F. W. 1970. Urban growth and land value patterns: government influences. *Prof. Geog.* **22**, 79–82.

Boddington, M. A. 1973. The evaluation of agriculture in land planning decisions. *J. Agric. Econ.* **26**, 37–56.

Bowen, M. J. 1974. Outdoor recreation around large cities. In *Suburban growth: geographical processes at the edge of the Western city*, J. H. Johnson (ed.), 225–48. Chichester: Wiley.

Bowler, I. R. 1979. *Government and agriculture: a spatial perspective*. London: Longman.

Bowler, I. R. 1981a. Regional specialization in the agricultural industry. *J. Agric. Econ.* **32**, 43–54.

Bowler, I. R. 1981b. Some characteristics of an innovative form of agricultural marketing. *Area* **13**, 307–14.

Boynton, J. K. 1979. Planning policy – its formation and implementation. In *Development control – thirty years on*. Occ. Paper, *J. Plann. Environ. Law*, 2–9.

Brazier, S. and R. J. P. Harris 1975. Inter-authority planning: appreciation and the resolution of conflict in the new local government system. *Town Plann. Rev.* **46**, 255–65.

Bryant, C. R. 1974a. The anticipation of urban development. Part I: Some implications for agricultural land use practices and land use zoning. *Geog. Polonica* **28**, 93–102.

Bryant, C. R. 1974b. An approach to the problem of urbanisation and structural change in agriculture: a case study from the Paris region, 1955 to 1968. *Geog. Ann.* **56**, Series B, 1–27.

Bryant, C. R. 1981. Agriculture in an urbanizing environment: a case study from the Paris region, 1968–1976. *Can. Geog.* **25**, 27–45.

Bryant, C. R. and S. M. Greaves 1978. The importance of regional variation in the analysis of urbanisation – agriculture interactions. *Cah. Géog. Québec* **22**, 329–48.

Buckinghamshire County Council 1976. *Buckinghamshire County Structure Plan: submitted written statement*. Aylesbury: Bucks. CC.

Bull, C. and G. P. Wibberley 1976. *Farm-based recreation in South East England*. Studies in Rural Land Use, no. 12. Ashford: Wye College.

Burrows, J. W. 1978. Vacant urban land – a continuing crisis. *The Planner* **64**, 7–9.

Capstick, M. 1978. Economic, social and political structures in the uplands of Cumbria. In *The future of upland Britain*, R. B. Tranter (ed.), vol. 2, 510–18. Centre for Agricultural Strategy, University of Reading.

Carman, H. F. 1977. California landowners' adoption of a use-value assessment program. *Land Econ.* **53**, 275–87.

Carter, E. S. and R. B. Sayce 1979. Conservation of agricultural land. *J. R. Agric. Soc. England* **140**, 22–33.

Centre for Agricultural Strategy 1976. *Land for agriculture*. Rep. no. 1, Centre for Agricultural Strategy, University of Reading.

Cherry, G. 1981. George Pepler 1882–1959. In *Pioneers in British planning*, G. Cherry (ed.), 131–49. London: Architectural Press.

Chisholm, M. 1962. *Rural settlement and land use*. London: Hutchinson.

Civic Trust 1977. *Urban wasteland*. London: Civic Trust.

Clark, D. J. 1974. London's Green Belt. *Greater London Intelligence Q.* **29**, 5–17.

Coleman, A. 1976. Is planning necessary? *Geog. J.* **142**, 411–30.

Coleman, A. 1977. Land use planning: success or failure? *Arch. J.*, **165**(3), 95–134.

Coleman, A. 1978. Agricultural land losses: the evidence from maps. In *Urban growth, farmland losses and planning*, A. Rogers (ed.), 16–36. Ashford: Wye College.

Collins, B. J. 1957. A talk on green belts. *Town Plann. Rev.* **28**, 219–30.

Commission of the European Communities 1980. *The agricultural situation in the community*. Brussels: The Commission.

Coppock, J. T. 1960. The parish as a geographical/statistical unit. *Tijds. Econ. Soc. Geog.* **51**, 317–26.

Coppock, J. T. 1978. The statistics of land use. In *Review no. 14, Reviews of United Kingdom statistical sources*, W. F. Maunder (ed.), vol. VIII, 1–101. Oxford: Pergamon Press.

Cornwall County Council 1976. *Structure plan topic report: environment*. Truro: Cornwall CC.

Correll, M. R., J. H. Lillydahl, and L. D. Singell, 1978. The effects of green belts on residential property values: some findings on the political economy of open space. *Land Econ.* **54**, 207–17.

Countryside Commission 1976a. *The Lake District upland management experiment*. CCP 93. Cheltenham: The Commission.

Countryside Commission 1976b. *The Bolin Valley: a study of land management in t emgban fringe*. Cheltenham: The Commission.

Countryside Commission 1977. *New agricultural landscapes: issues, objectives and action*. Cheltenham: The Commission.

Countryside Commission 1979. *Leisure in the countryside*. CCP 124. Cheltenham: The Commission.

Countryside Commission 1981. *Countryside management in the urban fringe*. CCP 136. Cheltenham: The Commission.

CRC (Countryside Review Committee) 1977. *Leisure and the countryside: a discussion paper*. Topic Pap. no. 2. London: HMSO.

CRC 1978. *Food production in the countryside: a discussion paper*. Topic Pap. no. 3. London: HMSO.

Dalton, H. 1939. The green belt around London. *J. London Soc.* **255**, 68–76.

Davidson, J. and R. J. Lloyd (eds) 1977. *Conservation and agriculture*. Chichester: Wiley.

Davidson, J. and G. P. Wibberley, 1977. *Planning and the rural environment*. Oxford: Pergamon Press.

Davies, H. W. E. 1980. Policy forum: the relevance of development control. *Town Plann. Rev.* **51**, 7–17.

Davies, I. 1953. Urban farming: a study of agriculture of the city of Birmingham. *Geography* **38**, 296–303.

Denman, D. R. 1978. *The place of property*. Berkhamsted: Geographical Publications.

Denman, D. R. and S. Prodano, 1972. *Land use: an introduction to proprietary land use analysis*. London: George Allen & Unwin.

Dennis, A. 1976. Agricultural land classification in England and Wales. *The Planner* **62**, 40–2.

Department of Health for Scotland 1960. *Town and Country Planning (Scotland) Acts 1947–1959: I: Green Belts*. Circular 40/60. Edinburgh: HMSO.

Dexter, K. 1977. The impact of technology on the political economy of agriculture. *J. Agric. Econ.* **28**, 211–20.

Dix, G. 1981. Patrick Abercrombie 1879–1957. In *Pioneers in British planning*, G. Cherry (ed.), 103–30. London: Architectural Press.

DOE (Department of the Environment) 1972a. *Land availability for housing*. Circular 102/72. London: HMSO.

DOE 1972b. *Development and compensation – putting people first*. Cmnd 5124. London: HMSO.

DOE 1973a. *Greater London Development Plan: report of the panel of inquiry*, (Layfield report). London: HMSO.

DOE 1973b. *Widening the choice: the next steps in housing*. Cmnd 5280. London: HMSO.

DOE 1973c. *Land availability for housing*. Circular 122/73. London: HMSO.

DOE 1974. *Land*. Cmnd 5730. London: HMSO.

DOE 1975a. *Sport and recreation*. Cmnd 6200. London: HMSO.

DOE 1975b. *Housing land availability in the South-East: a consultant's study*. London: HMSO.

DOE 1975c. *Review of development control: final report by George Dobry*. London: HMSO.

DOE 1976a. *British cities: urban population and employment trends*. Res. Rep. no. 10. London: DOE.

DOE 1976b. *Development involving agricultural land*. Circular 75/76. London: HMSO.

DOE 1977a. *General Development Order*. SI 289/77. London: HMSO.

DOE 1977b. *Local government and the industrial strategy*. Circular 71/77. London: HMSO.

DOE 1977c. *Memorandum on structure and local plans*. Circular 55/77. London: HMSO.

DOE 1977d. *Sutton Coldfield District Plan: inspector's report*. London: DOE.

DOE 1977e. *Hertfordshire Structure Plan – examination in public: report of the panel*. London: DOE.

DOE 1978a. *Strategic Plan for the South East review: government statement*. London: HMSO.

DOE 1978b. *Land availability: a study of land with residential planning permission*. London: The Economist Intelligence Unit.

DOE 1978c. *Buckinghamshire Structure Plan – examination in public: report of the panel*. London: DOE.

DOE 1978d. *Developed areas 1969: a survey of England and Wales from air photography*. London: DOE.

DOE 1978e. *Report of the advisory committee on aggregates*. Circular 50/78. London: HMSO.

DOE 1978f. *Production of aggregates in Great Britain*. Statistics Construction Division, DOE. London: HMSO.

DOE 1978g. *Report of the committee on planning control over mineral working*. Circular 58/78. London: HMSO.

DOE 1979a. *Buckinghamshire County Structure Plan – statement related to the secretary of state's proposed modifications*. London: DOE.

DOE 1979b. *Organic change*. Cmnd 7457. London: HMSO.

DOE 1979c. *Hertfordshire County Structure Plan – statement related to the secretary of state's proposed modifications*. London: DOE.

DOE 1979d. *Development control and agricultural land*. Press Notice 131, 21 March 1979.

DOE 1980a. Letter from the secretary of state to Standing Conference entitled *South East regional strategic guidance* 7 August. London: DOE.

DOE 1980b. *Development control – policy and practice*. Circular 22/80. London: HMSO.

DOE 1980c. *Local Government, Planning and Land Act*. London: HMSO.

DOE 1980d. *Surrey County Structure Plan – statement related to the secretary of state's proposed modifications*. London: DOE.

DOE 1980e. *Land for private housebuilding*. Circular 9/80. London: HMSO.

DOE 1980f. *Bedfordshire County Structure Plan – statement related to the secretary of state's proposed modifications*. London: DOE.

DOE 1980g. *Central Berkshire Structure Plan – statement related to the secretary of state's proposed modifications*. London: DOE.

DOE 1980h. *West Sussex County Structure Plan – statement related to the secretary of state's proposed modifications*. London: DOE.

DOE 1981a. *Local Government, Planning and Land Act 1980 (Town and Country Planning: Development Control Functions)*. Circular 2/81. London: HMSO.

DOE 1981b. *Essex County Structure Plan – statement related to the secretary of state's proposed modifications*. London: DOE.

DOE–DTp 1980. *Policy for roads: England 1980*. Cmnd 7908. London: HMSO.

DOE–DTp 1981. *The motorway between Swanley and Sevenoaks: decision of the secretary of state and the minister following the public inquiry.* London: DOE/DTp (South East Regional Office).

DOE, MAFF and SAGA (Sand and Gravel Association) 1977. *Joint agricultural land restoration experiments: a study of the technical requirements for the restoration of high quality agricultural land following sand and gravel extraction.* Progress Rep. No. 1. London: DOE.

Dolman, J. H. 1981. Agricultural permitted development – intensive livestock units. *J. Plann. Environ. Law*, November, 795–802.

Drewett, R. 1973. The developers' decision processes, and land values and the suburban land market. In *The containment of urban England*, P. Hall *et al.* (eds), vol. II, 163–245. London: George Allen & Unwin.

Dunsire, A. 1978. *Implementation in a bureaucracy: the execution process*, vol. I. Oxford: Martin Robertson.

Dunsire, A. 1981. Central control over local authorities: a cybernetic approach. *Publ. Admin.* **59**, 173–88.

Edwards, A. M. and G. P. Wibberley 1971. *An agricultural land budget for Britain 1965–2000.* Studs in Rural Land Use, no. 10. Ashford: Wye College.

Edwards, C. J. W. 1978. The effects of changing farm size upon levels of farm fragmentation: a Somerset case study. *J. Agric. Econ.* **29**, 143–54.

Elliott, H. 1979. The effects of urban development on agriculture. *Insight* **78,** 4–5. London: National Farmers' Union.

Elson, M. J. 1979a. *The urban fringe: open land policies and programmes in the metropolitan counties.* Work. Pap. no. 14. Cheltenham: The Commission.

Elson, M. J. (ed.) 1979b. *Perspectives on green belt local plans.* Work. Pap. no. 38. Oxford Polytechnic: Dept of Town Planning.

Elson, M. J. 1979c. Recreation, green belts and green belt local plans. In *Perspectives on green belt local plans*, M. J. Elson (ed.), 34–72. Work. Pap. no. 38. Oxford Polytechnic: Dept of Town Planning.

Elson, M. J. 1979d. *The leisure use of green belts and urban fringes.* SSRC/Sports Council, Joint Panel on Recreation and Leisure Research.

Elson, M. J. 1980. What future for the Green Belt? *Arch. J.*, May, 711–14.

Elson, M. J. 1981. Farmland loss and the erosion of planning. *Town and Country Planning* **50**, 20–1.

Elson, M. J., I. Gault and P. Healey 1979. *Seminar report: local needs in areas of restraint.* Oxford Work. Pap. no. 42. Oxford Polytechnic: Dept of Town Planning.

Elson, M. J., S. A. Terry and P. F. McNamara 1981. *Employment change in restraint areas.* Restraint Policies Project: Pap. no. 1. Oxford Polytechnic: Dept of Town Planning.

Essex County Council 1978. *Essex Structure Plan – draft written statement.* Chelmsford: Essex CC.

Eve, J. R. T. 1981. The Town and Country Planning (Minerals) Act 1981. *J. Plann. Environ. Law*, December, 857–63.

Feist, M. J. 1978. *A study of management agreements.* CCP 114. Cheltenham: The Commission.

Ferguson, M. J. 1979. A strategic choice approach to recreation site resource allocation. *Town Plann. Rev.* **50**, 325–45.

Ferguson, M. J. and R. J. C. Munton 1978. *Informal recreation in the urban fringe: the provision and management of sites in London's Green Belt.* Work. Pap. no. 2, Land for Informal Recreation. University College London: Dept of Geography.

Ferguson, M. J. and R. J. C. Munton 1979. Informal recreation sites in London's Green Belt. *Area* **11**, 196–205.

Ferguson, M. J., B. Sloane and A. Warren 1980. *Styles of site management in the South London Green Belt*. Work. Pap. no. 6, Land for Informal Recreation. University College London: Dept of Geography.

Fitton, M. 1976. The urban fringe and the less privileged. *Countryside Recreation Rev.* **1**, 25–34.

Fitton, M. J. 1979. Countryside recreation – the problems of opportunity. *Local Government Studs* **4**, 57–90.

Foley, D. L. 1963. *Controlling London's growth: planning in the Great Wen 1940–60*. Berkeley: University of California Press.

Frost, S., A. Lothian, I. Button and M. P. Thomas 1976. A survey on the impact of motorways on agriculture. *Int. J. Environ. Studs* **9**, 169–75.

Gasson, R. M. 1966. *The influence of urbanisation on farm ownership and practice*. Studs in Rural Land Use, no. 7. Ashford: Wye College.

Gasson, R. M. (ed.) 1977. *The place of part-time farming in rural and regional development*. Ashford: Wye College.

Gault, I. 1981. *Green belt policies in development plans*. Work. Pap. no. 41. Oxford Polytechnic: Dept of Town Planning.

Geddes, P. 1904. *City development: a study of parks, gardens and culture institutes*. Edinburgh: Geddes.

Gibbon, G. and R. W. Bell 1939. *History of the London County Council, 1889–1939*. London: Macmillan.

GLC (Greater London Council) 1969. *Greater London Development Plan: report of studies*. London: GLC.

GLC 1975–6. *Greater London recreation study*. Res. Rep. 19, parts 1–3. London: GLC.

GLC 1976. *Greater London Development Plan*. London: GLC.

GLRPC (Greater London Regional Planning Committee) 1929. *First report*. London: GLRPC.

GLRPC 1933. *Second report*. London: GLRPC.

Goodchild, R. N. 1978. The operation of the private land market. In *Land, planning and the market*, B. J. Pearce (ed.), 11–48. Occ. Pap. no. 9. University of Cambridge: Dept. of Land Economy.

Goode, D. 1981. The threat to wildlife habitats. *New Scientist* **89**, no. 1237, 219–23.

Green, B. 1981. *Countryside conservation*. London: George Allen & Unwin.

Gregory, D. G. 1970. *Green belts and development control: a case study in the West Midlands*. Occ. Pap. no. 12. University of Birmingham: Centre for Urban and Regional Studies.

Gregory, D. G. 1977. Green belt policy and the conurbation. In *Metropolitan development and change: the West Midlands: a policy review*, F. Joyce (ed.), 231–52.

Hall, P. and D. Hay 1980. *Growth centres in the European urban system*. London: Heinemann.

Hall, P., H. Gracey, R. Drewett and R. Thomas, 1973. *The containment of urban England*. Vol. I. London: George Allen & Unwin.

Hansen, D. E. and S. I. Schwartz 1975. Landowner behaviour at the urban–rural fringe in response to preferential property taxation. *Land Econ.* **51**, 341–54.

Harrison, A. 1975. *Farmers and farm businesses in England*. Misc. Stud. no. 62. University of Reading: Dept of Agricultural Economics and Management.

Harrison, C. M. 1980–1. Recovery of lowland grassland and heathland in southern England from disturbance by seasonal trampling. *Biol. Conserv.* **19**, 119–30.

Harrison, C. M. 1981a. A playground for whom? Informal recreation in London's Green Belt. *Area*, **13**, 109–14.

Harrison, C. M. 1981b. *Preliminary results of a survey of site use in the South London Green Belt*. Work. Pap. no. 9. University College London: Dept of Geography.

Harrison, M. L. 1972. Development control: the influence of political, legal and ideological factors. *Town Plann. Rev.* **43**, 254–74.

Hawke, J. N. 1981a. Planning agreements in practice: I. *J. Plann. Environ. Law*, January, 5–14.

Hawke, J. N. 1981b. Planning agreements in practice: II. *J. Plan. Environ. Law*, February, 86–97.

Healey, P. 1979. Central-local relations in green belt local plans. In *Perspectives on green belt local plans*, M. J. Elson (ed.), 3–33. Work. Pap. no. 38. Oxford Polytechnic: Dept of Town Planning.

Healey, P. 1980. Regional policy in the South East: how far can development and local needs be reconciled? *Town and Country Planning* **49**, 406–407.

Healey, P., S. Evans and S. Terry, 1980. *The implementation of selective restraint policy: approaches to land release for local needs in the South East*. Work. Pap. no. 45. Oxford Polytechnic: Dept of Town Planning.

Heap, D. 1961. Green belts and open spaces: the English scene today. *J. Plann. Property Law*, 16–24.

Heap, D. and A. J. Ward 1980. Planning bargaining – the pros and cons: or, how much can the system stand? *J. Plann. Environ. Law*, October, 631–7.

Hearne, A., M. Bell and D Van Rest 1977. The physical and economic impact of motorways on agriculture. *Int. J. Environ. Studs* **11**, 29–33.

Hebbert, M. 1979. Green belt policy and the farmer. In *Perspectives on green belt local plans*, M. J. Elson (ed.), 73–100. Work. Pap. no. 38. Oxford Polytechnic: Dept of Town Planning.

Hebbert, M. and I. Gault 1978. *Green belt issues in local plan preparation*. Work. Pap. no. 34. Oxford Polytechnic: Dept of Town Planning.

Hellard, D. A. 1976. Farmers and landowners – allies or protagonists. In *Recreation and the urban fringe*, A. S. Travis and A. J. Veal (eds), 44–56. University of Birmingham.

Hertfordshire County Council 1976. *Hertfordshire County Structure Plan: submitted written statement*. Hertford: Hertfordshire CC.

Hertfordshire County Council 1981. *Annual monitoring report*. Hertford: Hertfordshire CC.

Hillingdon LB 1973. *Open land and the Green Belt: an interim policy*. Uxbridge: Planning Department.

Hillingdon LB 1977. *Green belt policy review: 1977*. Uxbridge: Planning Department.

Hood, C. C. 1976. *The limits of administration*. Chichester: Wiley.

Hookway, R. J. S. 1977. Countryside management: the development of techniques. *Proc. Town and Country Planning Summer School*. London: RTPI.

House of Commons 1977. *Eighth report of the expenditure committee of the House of Commons: planning procedures*. Paper 395–1. London: HMSO.

House of Commons 1978. *Eleventh report of the expenditure committee of the House of Commons*. Paper 564. London: HMSO.

Howard, E. 1898. *Tomorrow: a peaceful path to real reform*. London: Swan Sonenschein. Republished under better known title of *Garden cities of tomorrow*, 1901.

Johnston, R. J. 1981. The political element in suburbia: a key influence on the urban geography of the United States. *Geography* **66**, 286–92.

Jones, G. E. and A. J. Simmons 1965. Towards an interpretation of change in farm structure: a Nottinghamshire case study. *Farm Economist* **10**, 332–44.

Jowell, J. 1977. Bargaining in development control. *J. Plann. Environ Law*, July, 414–33.

Jowell, J. and D. Noble 1981. Structure plans as instruments of social and economic policy . *J. Plann. Environ. Law*, July, 466–80.
JURUE (Joint Unit for Research into the Urban Environment) 1974. *Land availability and the residential land conversion process*. Birmingham: University of Aston.
JURUE 1977. *Planning and land availability*. Birmingham: University of Aston.

Kent County Council 1977. *Kent Structure Plan: written statement*. Maidstone: Kent CC.
Kent County Council Planning Department 1976. *The Green Belt*. Maidstone: Kent CC.

Law, S. and N. H. Perry 1971. Countryside recreation for Londoners – a preliminary research approach. *GLC Intelligence Unit Q. Bull.* **14**, 11–26.
Layton, R. L. 1978. The operational structure of the hobby farm. *Area* **10**, 242–6.
Leach, S. and N. Moore 1979. County/district relations in shire and metropolitan counties in the field of town and country planning: a comparison. *Policy and Politics* 7, 165–79.
Leung, H. L. 1979. *Redistribution of land values: a re-examination of the 1947 Scheme*. Occ. Pap. no. 11. University of Cambridge: Dept of Land Economy.
Lewis, J. and R. Flynn 1979. The implementation of urban and regional planning policies. *Policy and Politics* **7**, 123–42.
Lichfield, N. and H. Darin-Drabkin 1980. *Land policy in planning*. London: George Allen & Unwin.
Loughlin, M. 1978. Bargaining as a tool of development control: a case of all gain and no loss. *J. Plann. Environ. Law*, May, 290–5.
Low, N. 1973. Farming and the inner Green Belt. *Town Plann. Rev.* **44**, 103–16.
Lowe, P. and J. Goyder 1983. *Environmental groups in British politics*. London: George Allen & Unwin.
Lowe, P. *et al.* 1977. *Land-use conflicts in the urban fringe: a case study of aggregate extraction in the London Borough of Havering*. Town Planning Discussion Pap. no. 26. University College London.
Lund, P. J. and J. M. Slater 1978. *A study of agricultural landownership: report on the Wyre Forest survey*. Unpubl. paper presented to the Agricultural Economics Society, December 1978, London.
Lund, P. J. and J. M. Slater, 1979. Agricultural land: its ownership, price and rent – a guide to sources of statistical information. *Econ. Trends* **314**, 97–110.

Mabey, R. 1980. *The common ground*. London: Hutchinson/NCC.
McAuslan, P. 1981. Local government and resource allocation in England: changing ideology, unchanging law. *Urban Law and Policy* **4**, 215–68.
MacEwen, A. and M. MacEwen 1982. *National parks: conservation or cosmetics*. London: George Allen & Unwin.
McKay, D. M. and A. W. Cox 1979. *The politics of urban change*. London: Croom Helm.
McLoughlin, J. B. 1973. *Control and urban planning*. London: Faber & Faber.
MAFF (Ministry of Agriculture, Fisheries and Food) 1973. *Agriculture in the urban fringe: Slough/Hillingdon area*. ADAS Tech. Rep. no. 30. London: HMSO.
MAFF 1975. *Food from our own resources*. Cmnd 6020. London: HMSO.
MAFF 1976a. *Agriculture in the urban fringe: Metropolitan County of Tyne and Wear*. ADAS Tech. Rep. no. 30/1. London: HMSO.
MAFF 1976b. *Wildlife conservation in semi-natural habitats on farms: a survey of farmers' attitudes and intentions in England and Wales*. London: HMSO.
MAFF 1977a. *The changing structure of agriculture 1968–1975*. London: HMSO.
MAFF 1977b. *Farm classification in England and Wales, 1975*. London: HMSO.

MAFF 1979. *Farming and the nation*. Cmnd 7458. London: HMSO.

MAFF 1980. *Agricultural statistics: United Kingdom 1976–1977*. London: HMSO.

MAFF 1981a. *Agricultural statistics: England 1978/9*. London: HMSO.

MAFF 1981b. *Annual review of agriculture 1981*. Cmnd 8132. London: HMSO.

MAFF 1982. *Annual review of agriculture 1982*. Cmnd 8491. London: HMSO.

Mandelker, D. 1962. *Green belts and urban growth*. Madison: University of Wisconsin Press.

Manners, G. 1981. Regional policies and the national interest. *Geoforum* **12**, 281–99.

Massey, D. and A. Catalano 1978. *Capital and land: landownership by capital in Great Britain*. London: Edward Arnold.

Mellanby, K. 1975. *Can Britain feed itself?* London: Merlin Press.

Meller, H. 1981. Raymond Unwin 1863–1940. In *Pioneers in British planning*, G. Cherry (ed.), 72–102. London: Architectural Press.

MHLG (Ministry of Housing and Local Government) 1955. *Green belts*. Circular 42/55. London: HMSO.

MHLG 1957. *Green belts*. Circular 50/57. London: HMSO.

MHLG 1962. *The green belts*. London: HMSO.

MHLG 1963. *London – employment: housing: land*. Cmnd 1952. London: HMSO.

MHLG 1964. *The South-East study, 1961–1981*. London: HMSO.

MHLG 1965. *The future of development plans* (Report of the Planning Advisory Group). London: HMSO.

MHLG 1970. *Development plans: a manual on form and content*. London: HMSO.

Moran, W. 1978. Land value, distance and productivity on the Auckland urban periphery. *New Zealand Geographer* **34**, 85–96.

Moran, W. 1979. Spatial patterns of agriculture on the periphery: the Auckland case. *Tijds. Econ. Soc. Geog.* **70**, 164–76.

Morris, C. N. 1980. The Common Agricultural Policy. *Fiscal Studies* **1** (2), 17–35.

Moss, G. 1981. *Britain's wasting acres: land use in a changing society*. London: Architectural Press.

Munton, R. J. C. 1974. Farming on the urban fringe. In *Suburban growth: geographical processes at the edge of the Western city*, J. H. Johnson (ed.), 201–23. Chichester: Wiley.

Munton, R. J. C. 1979. *London's Green Belt: restraint and the management of agricultural land*. Unpubl. report. London: DOE.

Munton, R. J. C. 1981a. Management expenditure on informal recreation sites in the London Green Belt. *The Planner* **67**, 93–5.

Munton, R. J. C. 1981b. Agricultural land use in the London Green Belt. *Town and Country Planning* **49**, 17–9.

Nature Conservancy Council 1977. *Nature conservation and agriculture*. London: Nature Conservancy Council.

NEDO (National Economic Development Office) 1977. *Agriculture into the 1980s: land use*. London: NEDO.

Neuburger, H. L. I. and B. M. Nicol 1976. *The recent course of land and property prices and the factors underlying it*. DOE Res. Rep. no. 4. London: HMSO.

Neutze, G. M. 1973. *The price of land and land use planning: policy instruments in the urban land market*. Paris: OECD.

Newby, H., C. Bell and P. Saunders 1978. *Property, paternalism and power: class and control in rural England*, London: Hutchinson.

Newby, H., C. Bell, P. Saunders and D. Rose 1977. Farmers' attitudes to conservation. *Countryside Recreation Rev.* **2**, 23–30.

Northfield committee report 1979. *Committee of inquiry into the acquisition and occupancy of agricultural land*. Cmnd 7599. London: HMSO.

OECD (Organisation for Economic Co-operation and Development) 1979. *Agriculture in the planning and management of peri-urban areas*. Vol. I: *Synthesis*. Paris: OECD.

OPCS (Office of Population Censuses and Surveys) 1982. *Census 1981 – county monitor*. London: OPCS.

Pearce, B. J. 1980. Instruments for land policy: a classification. *Urban Law and Policy* **3**, 115–56.

Pepler, G. L. 1911. A green belt round London. *Garden Cities and Town Planning* NS **1**, 39–43; 64–8.

Porchester, Lord 1977. *A study of Exmoor*. MAFF/DOE. London: HMSO.

Purdom, C. B. (ed.) 1921. *Town theory and practice*. London: Benn.

Rettig, S. 1976. An investigation into the problems of urban fringe agriculture in a green belt situation. *Plann. Outlook* **19**, 50–73.

Rhodes, R. A. W. 1980. Some myths in central–local relations. *Town Plann. Rev.* **51**, 270–85.

Ritson, C. 1980. *Self-sufficiency and food security*. Pap. no. 8. University of Reading: Centre for Agricultural Strategy.

Roberts, N. A. 1976. *The reform of planning law*. London: Macmillan.

Rogers, A. (ed.) 1978. *Urban growth, farmland losses and planning*. On behalf of Rural Geography Study Grp. London: Institute of British Geographers.

Rose, D., H. Newby, P. Saunders, and C. Bell 1977. Land tenure and official statistics: a research note. *J. Agric. Econ.* **28**, 69–75.

Royal Commission on Environmental Pollution 1979. *Agriculture and pollution*. 7th Rep., Cmnd 7644. London: HMSO.

Rural Planning Services 1979. *The Oxford green belt*. Oxford: Rural Planning Services.

Scott committee report 1942. *Land utilisation in rural areas*. Cmd. 6378, Ministry of Works and Planning. London: HMSO.

SEJPT (South East Joint Planning Team) 1970. *Strategic Plan for the South East: report*. London: HMSO.

SEJPT 1971. *Strategic Plan for the South East: social and environmental aspects*. Studies vol. II. London: HMSO.

SEJPT 1976. *Strategy for the South East: 1976 review*. London: HMSO.

SEJPT (Land Group) 1976. *Strategy for the South East: 1976 review – report of the land group*. London: DOE.

Sharp, E. G. in preparation. *The acquisition of the London Green Belt estates: a study of inter-authority relations*. PhD Thesis. University of London.

Shoard, M. 1979. Metropolitan escape routes. *The London Journal* **5**, 87–112.

Shoard, M. 1980. *The theft of the countryside*. London: Temple Smith.

Shoard, M. 1981. Why landscapes are harder to protect than buildings. In *Our past before us: why do we save it?* D. Lowenthal and M. Binney (eds), 83–107. London: Temple Smith.

Simmie, J. M. and D. J. Hale 1978. The distributional effects of ownership and control of land use in Oxford. *Urban Studs* **15**, 9–21.

Sinclair, R. 1967. Von Thünen and urban sprawl. *Ann. Assoc. Am. Geogs* **57**, 72–87.

Skinner, D. N. 1976. *A situation report on green belts in Scotland*. Countryside Commission for Scotland, Occ. Pap. no. 8. Perth: The Commission.

Solesbury, W. 1981. Strategic planning: metaphor or method. *Policy and Politics* **9**, 419–37.

South East Economic Planning Council 1967. *The Strategy for the South East*. London: HMSO.

Standing Conference (Standing Conference on London and South East Regional Planning – SCLSERP) 1975. *Sand and gravel: scale and distribution of further workings in the South East*, SC 372. London: Standing Conference.

Standing Conference 1976. *The improvement of London's Green Belt*, SC 620. London: Standing Conference.

Standing Conference 1977a. *The improvement of London's Green Belt – a second report*, SC 860R. London: Standing Conference.

Standing Conference 1977b. *Strategy for the South East: 1976 review – a Conference response to government*, SC 700. London: Standing Conference.

Standing Conference 1977c. *Informal recreation in the South East*, SC 786R. London: Standing Conference.

Standing Conference 1978. *The improvement of London's Green Belt: a second report – views of member authorities*, SC 1030R. London: Standing Conference.

Standing Conference 1979a. *Policy guidelines to meet the South East Region's need for aggregates in the 1980s*, SC 1151R. London: Standing Conference.

Standing Conference 1979b. *Restoration of sand and gravel workings*, SC 1241R. London: Standing Conference.

Standing Conference 1979c. *Strategic Plan for the South East: government statement*, SC 1150, Rep. by Tech. Panel. London: Standing Conference.

Standing Conference 1979d. *Green Belt 2000 acres exercise – release and development of identified land*, SC 1122, Rep. by Secretariat. London: Standing Conference.

Standing Conference 1979e. *Policy towards the provision of recreation facilities in London's Green Belt*, SC 1111 revised. London: Standing Conference.

Standing Conference 1981a. *South East Regional Planning: the 1980s*, SC 1500. London: Standing Conference.

Standing Conference 1981b. *Housing land in South East England*, SC 1600. Joint Rep. with the House-Builders Federation. London: Standing Conference.

Standing Conference 1982. *The impact of the M25*, SC 1706. London: Standing Conference.

Stevens committee report 1976. *Planning control over mineral working*. London: HMSO.

Surrey County Council 1978. *Surrey Structure Plan: submitted written statement*. Kingston-upon-Thames: Surrey CC.

Surrey County Council 1981. *Annual monitoring report, 1980*. Kingston-upon-Thames: Surrey CC.

Sutcliffe, A. 1981. *British town planning: the formative years*. Leicester: Leicester University Press.

Sutherland, A. 1980. Capital transfer tax and farming. *Fiscal Studs* **1**(2), 51–65.

Teaford, J. C. 1979. *City and suburb*. Baltimore: Johns Hopkins Press.

Thomas, D. 1963. London's green belt – evolution of an idea. *Geogr. J.* **129**, 14–24.

Thomas, D. 1964. Components of London's green belt. *J. Town Plann. Inst.* **50**, 434–9.

Thomas, D. 1970. *London's Green Belt*. London: Faber & Faber.

Thomson, K. J. 1981. *Farming in the fringe*, CCP 142. Cheltenham: Countryside Commission.

Tucker, L. 1978. Planning agreements: the twilight zone of *Ultra Vires*. *J. Plann. Environ. Law*, December, 806–809.

Turner, D. M. 1977. *An approach to land values*. Berkhamsted: Geographical Publications.

Turrall-Clarke, R. T. F. 1981. Horses and planning: recent developments. *J. Plann. Environ. Law*, November, 792–4.

Underwood, J. 1981. Development control: a case study of discretion in action. In *Policy and action*, S. Barrett and C. Fudge (eds), 143–62. London: Methuen.

University of Reading 1975. *Milton Keynes 1975: farming in and out of the designated area.* Misc. Study no. 61. University of Reading: Dept of Agricultural Economics and Management.

Unwin, R. 1912. *Nothing gained by overcrowding.* London: Garden Cities and Town Planning Association.

Unwin, R. 1921. Some thoughts on the development of London. In *The future of London,* Sir Aston Webb (ed.), 177–92. London: Dutton.

Verney committee report 1976. *Aggregates: the way ahead.* Rep. Advisory Committee on Aggregates. London: HMSO.

Warren-Evans, J. R. 1974. The growth of urban areas. In *The future of the Green Belt.* Occ. Paps Estate Manage. no. 5, 19–24. University of Reading: College of Estate Management.

Webb, Sir Aston 1918. The London Society's map, with its proposals for the improvement of London. *Geogr. J.* **51**, 273–93.

Westmacott, R. and T. Worthington 1974. *New agricultural landscapes: a report.* Cheltenham: Countryside Commission.

Wibberley, G. P. 1959. *Agriculture and urban growth: a study of the competition for rural land.* London: Michael Joseph.

Wibberley, G. P. 1981. Permanent changes in land use and agricultural realities. *Town and Country Planning* **50**, 13–15.

Williams, H. M. 1979. *The management of publicly-owned land in the Hertfordshire/Barnet experiment area.* Work. Pap. no. 17. Cheltenham: Countryside Commission.

Wise, W. S. and E. Fell 1978. UK agricultural productivity and the land budget. *J. Agric. Econ.* **29**, 1–8.

Yorkshire and Humberside Regional Economic Planning Council 1974. *Joint green belt study.* London: HMSO.

Young, K. and P. L. Garside 1982. *Metropolitan London: politics and urban change 1837–1981.* London: Edward Arnold.

Young, K. and L. Mills 1980. *Public policy research: a review of qualitative methods.* London: Social Science Research Council.

Index

Numbers in italics refer to text figures.